Designing Emergency

This book looks at the then-nascent emergency management sector in China, specifically the 2003–2012 period, that arose from the 2003 Severe Acute Respiratory Syndrome (SARS) crisis and subsequently set the stage for its responses to the COVID-19 pandemic.

Covering not only the amended and new laws and regulations at the national level, the book also includes the rearrangement and creation of the organizational structures, as well as the response plans for individual emergencies that were either recrafted or created during this period. Beyond chronicling the milestones and products of this transformation, this book highlights the key ideas and ideals that guided the various stakeholders, from the governing elites to the policy experts during this process.

The book demonstrates how definitions of emergency management and emergency categories, as well as other ideational objects, were initially either absent or weakly developed, but were refined to the extent that they helped corral disparate actors into China's then-new organizational field of emergency management.

Wee-Kiat Lim is Associate Director, Centre for Management Practice at Singapore Management University. Since 2006, Wee-Kiat has been investigating how organizations make sense of, prepare for, and respond to sociotechnical disruptions. His research interests lie at the intersection of risk, disaster, and organization. Besides academic research, he has written and taught cases on organizations that are based in China, Indonesia, and Singapore, covering issues related to innovation, entrepreneurship, crisis management, and governance. Wee-Kiat holds a PhD in Sociology from University of Colorado Boulder, specializing in the sociology of disaster, and a Bachelor of Communication Studies (Hons.) from Nanyang Technological University, Singapore.

China Policy Series

Series Editor: Zheng Yongnian
The Chinese University of Hong Kong, Shenzhen

For more information about this series, please visit: www.routledge.com/China-Policy-Series/book-series/SECPS

Designing Emergency Management

China's Post-SARS Experience, 2003–2012

Wee-Kiat Lim

Routledge
Taylor & Francis Group

LONDON AND NEW YORK

First published 2021
by Routledge
2 Park Square, Milton Park, Abingdon, Oxon OX14 4RN

and by Routledge
52 Vanderbilt Avenue, New York, NY 10017

Routledge is an imprint of the Taylor & Francis Group, an informa business

© 2021 Wee-Kiat Lim

British Library Cataloguing-in-Publication Data
A catalogue record for this book is available from the British Library

Library of Congress Cataloging-in-Publication Data
A catalog record for this book has been requested

ISBN: 978-0-367-19697-4 (hbk)
ISBN: 978-0-429-24265-6 (ebk)

Typeset in Galliard
by Apex CoVantage, LLC

I dedicate this book to my late maternal grandmother, Geok Eng Teo, late maternal first uncle, Hock Miang Tan, my parents, Cheng Sun Lim and Gek Kheng Tan, my sisters, Cai Hui Lim and Cai Lin Lim, as well as my wife, Kerry Tan.

Contents

Tables

Figures

Parts of the monograph have been presented at or published in the following forums.

Book chapter

Lim, Wee-Kiat. (2020). Building emergency management in post-SARS China. In T. W. Lim and Carol Ma (Editors), *Leadership: Political-economic, Regional Business and Socio-Community Contexts*. Singapore: World Scientific. www.worldscientific.com/doi/10.1142/9789811213236_0006

Conference proceedings and presentations

Lim, Wee-Kiat. Designing through distress: Enacting emergency management in post-SARS China. Presented at *From the Management of Crisis to the Governance of Risk: Time for a Paradigm Shift?* Haikou, China, 2017.

Lim, Wee-Kiat. Fieldwork: Governmentalizing emergency management in China in the post-SARS Era. Presented at *Sun Yat-Sen University Business School Paper Development Workshop*, Guangzhou, China, 2016.

Lim, Wee-Kiat. Enacting risk governance in China after the 2003 SARS crisis. Presented at *Society on Risk Analysis (SRA) World Congress on Risk.* Singapore, 2015.

Lim, Wee-Kiat. Enacting disaster governance: Governmentalizing emergency management in China in the post-SARS Era. Presented at *Workshop on Decentralized Disaster Governance in Urbanising Asia*, Asia Research Institute, National University of Singapore, Singapore, 2015.

Acknowledgements

There are so many individuals to whom I extend my deepest gratitude. Without your guidance, encouragement, and support, I would not have completed my dissertation, let alone this book.

First and foremost, my advisor and mentor, Dr. Kathleen Tierney for your guidance and confidence in me.

Next, my family. Despite their modest resources, my parents gave me the freedom to pursue what I (thought I would) love to do, however impractical and "useless" my aspirations were. My gratitude to my sisters, Cai Hui and Cai Lin: Thank you so much for being there for me and taking care of our family when I was away.

Kerry, my wife, to whom I am obliged to include her title of "the bestest wifey in the whole wide world who ever walked on earth." Without her encouragement and understanding, I would not have completed the book.

My late maternal grandmother, Geok Eng, and late maternal first uncle, Hock Miang: It is my eternal regret that I can never share with you what I have achieved. I want you to be proud of me.

To my gatekeepers, informants, and members of China's disaster management academic communities: Without your generous and gracious support, I would have been much worse off in this project. Thank you so very much. You have been my mentor, my *laoshi* (teacher).

Finally, my gratitude for the financial support from the Sociology Department (Graduate Student Research Awards, 2012 and 2013) and the Graduate School (Center to Advance Research and Teaching in the Social Sciences [CARTSS] Graduate Fellowship, 2012; Summer Graduate Fellowship, 2013). I also want to acknowledge the partial but no less significant financial support for my Beijing fieldwork from the Ministry of Science and Technology, People's Republic of China (Grant No. 2012CB955404 and 2012DFG20710).

Prologue: designing through distress

Creating a new organizational field of emergency management in post-SARS China

With the world hit by another novel coronavirus crisis that first came to light in China, the beginning of 2020 looked a lot like 2003. The virus is a close cousin of the one that caused the Severe Acute Respiratory Syndrome (SARS) which sickened more than 8,000 people and killed close to 800 worldwide in 2003. Similar to the 2003 public health crisis, the Lunar New Year was around the corner and *chun yun* was already set in motion, when hundreds of millions of Chinese travelled to return to their hometowns for festive celebration. This time, however, China seemed better prepared with protocols – such as raising the severity level of the emergency at provincial and national levels, as well as taking a risk-based approach – that were put in place to detect, trace, and respond to the brewing crisis. The playbook for the protocols, not just for coping with public health crises but also a broad spectrum of emergencies, was written from their SARS experience.

The 2003 SARS crisis therefore was a landmark, what is called a "focusing event" (Birkland 1997) in social science research on disasters where the phenomenon was so disruptive that it created opportunities to modify the status quo. The epidemic sparked off more than just incremental improvements in protocols on infectious disease transmissions. In China, it triggered a revision in the Constitution, birthed new disaster laws and amended old ones, and its impact further spread to emergency response plans and administrative reorganization.

Five years after the SARS crisis, a massive earthquake struck Sichuan shortly after lunch, killing close to 70,000 people (Salazar et al. 2011; Zhang 2012), including over a thousand Beichuan Middle School pupils in their classrooms. While visiting Beichuan's temporary school compound, then-Premier Wen Jiabao, the de-facto national consoler-in-chief who had started his second term in office less than two months before, chalked four characters on a blackboard: *duo nan xing bang* (多难兴邦). Political scientist Zheng Wang (2012) translates the four-character phrase as "distresses rejuvenate a nation." Wang recounts the widely reported event in Chinese media:

> After his departure, teachers and students could not bear to erase his chalk inscription, which was covered in plastic until the Sichuan Cultural Relics Bureau could devise a method for permanently preserving Wen's

handwriting . . . .[The Chinese] believe that a nation can be successful only after experiencing some hardships and difficulties, as a disaster can also open new opportunities and bring new changes.

(p. 160)

The imagery of a nation invigorated by serial disasters has enjoyed a long and fecund history in China. It is an idea and an ideal often invoked by the governing elite during times of crises. Since 2003, several more conspicuous episodes of distress, such as the massive ice storm that struck the nation in 2008, have been assiduously harnessed by the Chinese party-state as opportunities to revisit and revise its national disaster management design. One result of such persistent administrative attention was the creation of the organizational field of emergency management. From 2003 to 2012, China created and reconfigured its ensemble of laws, regulations, plans, and organizational processes on disaster management. The nascent field of emergency management was its de facto "laboratory" for experimenting with and refining its ideas on disaster management – particularly about governing risks – as it went about designing policies and organizations related to this function. The genesis and early development of what I call China's organizational field of emergency management following the 2003 SARS crisis is the topic of this book.

By tracking the trajectory of China's emergency management field, I seek to understand three aspects of early organizational field formation. First, I study which ideas – both indigenously produced in China and imported from afar – provided the intellectual resources for the Chinese party-state to not only stitch together the new yet somewhat familiar emergency management organizational field from existing disaster management domains, but to also breathe legitimacy into it. The second aspect focuses on the organized actors who mobilized these ideas in creating the new organizational field. I invoke the term "establishment," following disaster sociologist Robert Stallings's (1995) account of how the entrepreneurial efforts of a network of actors – such as scientists, policy analysts, and government officials – contributed to earthquakes being framed as a social problem in the United States. In doing so, I draw attention to a specific kind of policy elites, the academic experts – scholars, scientists, and government advisors in China – who mobilized their intellectual hands to mold the conceptual models salient for the field's design and definition.[1] The involvement of academic experts becomes obvious when I trace the careers of ideas germane to the field's genesis and growth. For the third aspect, I take a process view to integrate the first two elements – the ideas that were used and diffused by the establishment, especially the academic experts – and show how various episodes of distress became conduits enabling the process to unfold. I examine the laws, plans, regulations, and academic works that are outcomes of the complex interactions between ideas and the establishment. In turn, these intellectual products become the basis that further shape the then-nascent emergency management field.

Although emergency management in China, according to its legal mandate, covers a wide spectrum of events including industrial accidents, demonstrations and protests, and health crises, this book focuses on natural disasters – a category of perennial concern even before China's imperial history.[2] An organizational field formation, particularly in its early manifestations, is not readily discernible. It typically takes a long time for an organizational field to coalesce and become obvious enough for researchers to build a retrospective account of its genesis. However, because China's attention to emergency management was not only persistent but also comparatively intensive and pervasive, we have a natural case of an organizational field with clear beginnings.

The rest of the book proceeds as follows. In Chapter 1, I assemble the theoretical toolkit that I use to analyze the genesis and growth of the Chinese emergency management field. I draw from sociological neoinstitutional theory (DiMaggio and Powell 1983; Powell and DiMaggio 1991; Scott 2014), the concept of governmentality (Foucault 1991), and the sociological basis of social science disaster research to build my initial analytic approach. Briefly, institutional theory focuses on how entities and activities become taken for granted, while governmentality explains which ones are viewed as more valuable in the first place. My research fills a knowledge gap that is a result of disaster and risk research's preoccupation with single events, such as floods, earthquakes, and landslides. Bringing neoinstitutional theory and governmentality together further contributes to a maturing stream of social constructionist research in disaster studies that highlights how an establishment or a network of organized actors (such as the state and academics) frame risks and disasters as problems that pose a putative threat to society (Stallings 1995; Stallings 1997; Tierney 2014).

Following Chapter 1 are two empirical segments. The first segment focuses on the administrative and legal changes, as well as the main events that define the emergency management organizational field. Comprising Chapters 2 and 3, it highlights the institutionalized organizations and processes in which the academic experts who participated in defining emergency management in the Chinese context were embedded. These two chapters speak directly to readers who are more interested in the meat and minutiae concerning the milestones and activities that constituted China's emergency management.

The second segment turns toward theory building efforts to understand early formation of China's emergency management. It closes in on what I consider to be the ideational centerpiece of the new organization field – the risk governance framework (Chapter 4) – and the legitimizing claims that the establishment mobilized to enact the framework and begin to institutionalize the field of emergency management (Chapter 5). The final empirical chapter (Chapter 6) traces how the risk governance framework became inscribed into the organizational field, specifically how it "governmentalized" notable institutional arrangements that were apparent in written text and organizational configurations. Here, I elaborate on ideas that had become entrenched in regulations, plans, laws, and organizations, as well as the distinct role academics played to insure success.

Finally, in Chapter 7, I return to my toolkit and elaborate on my findings. In view of the findings, I also clarify and highlight the contributions that this monograph adds to research and how its limitations could be addressed by future studies, especially with the COVID-19 pandemic still unfolding in June 2020. In my epilogue, I offer an early and (very) preliminary read of the impact of the coronavirus crisis on the (more) settled organizational field.

Last but not least, the appendix elaborates on the multi-method approach I used during fieldwork and data collection, including how I performed data analysis using the conceptual tools from Chapter 1. Specifically, I performed document review, in-depth interviews, and participant observation during my fieldwork. The appendix also offers a platform for me to recount and elaborate on the evolution of my research design and to touch on the issues that follow from my identity as a third-generation Chinese Singaporean conducting fieldwork in China.

Notes

1 I draw inspiration from the now-classic article by Hirsch, Michaels, and Friedman (1987) for the imagery of "intellectual hands."
2 In a related project (Lim 2015), I highlight how the "moral reading of disasters" (Janku 2009:232) while expressed in the Confucian vocabulary of piety and paternalistic care during the Qing dynasty – in which heaven-sent disasters (*tianzai*, 天灾) were tied to the legitimacy of the leaders, or their "mandate of heaven" (*tianming*, 天命) – not only preceded Confucianism, but was also deeply embedded in Chinese mythology.

References

Birkland, Thomas A. 1997. *After Disaster: Agenda Setting, Public Policy, and Focusing Events.* Washington, DC: Georgetown University Press.

DiMaggio, Paul J. and Walter W. Powell. 1983. "The Iron Cage Revisited: Institutional Isomorphism and Collective Rationality in Organizational Fields." *American Sociological Review* 48(2):147–60.

Foucault, Michel. 1991. "Governmentality." Pp. 87–104 in *The Foucault Effect: Studies in Governmentality*, edited by G. Burchell, C. Gordon and P. Miller. Hemel Hempstead: Harvester Wheatsheaf.

Hirsch, Paul, Stuart Michaels and Ray Friedman. 1987. "'Dirty Hands' Versus 'Clean Models': Is Sociology in Danger of Being Seduced by Economics?" *Theory and Society* 16(3):317–36.

Janku, Andrea. 2009. "'Heaven-Sent Disasters' in Late Imperial China: The Scope of the State and Beyond." Pp. 233–64 in *Natural Disasters, Cultural Response: Case Studies toward Global Environmental History*, edited by C. Mauch and C. Pfister. Landham, MD: Rowman & Littlefield.

Lim, Wee-Kiat. 2015. "Of Minds, Morals, and Methods: Combining Moral Meteorology and Disaster Relief in Historiography of China's Disaster Management." *Social Science Research Network.* https://dx.doi.org/10.2139/ssrn.3526648.

Powell, Walter W. and Paul J. DiMaggio, eds. 1991. *The New Institutionalism in Organizational Analysis.* Chicago, IL: University of Chicago Press.

Salazar, Miguel, Qibin Lu, Xiaojiang Hu, Xinsong Wang, Qiang Zhang, Ling Zhou and Zhang Xiulan. 2011. "The Impact of Natural Disaster on Social Protection System: Empirical Evidences from Wenchuan Earthquake." Vol. 11. *CSP Research*

Report. Brighton, UK: Centre for Social Protection, Institute of Development Studies, University of Sussex.

Scott, W. Richard. 2014. *Institutions and Organizations: Ideas, Interests, and Identities*. Los Angeles, CA: Sage Publications.

Stallings, Robert A. 1995. *Promoting Risk: Constructing the Earthquake Threat*. New York, NY: Aldine de Gruyter.

Stallings, Robert A. 1997. "Sociological Theories and Disaster Studies." *University of Delaware Disaster Research Center Preliminary Paper 249*. Retrieved from (https://udspace.udel.edu/bitstream/handle/19716/135/PP2?sequence=1).

Tierney, Kathleen J. 2014. *The Social Roots of Risk: Producing Disasters, Promoting Resilience*. Stanford, CA: Stanford University Press.

Wang, Zheng. 2012. *Never Forget National Humiliation: Historical Memory in Chinese Politics*. New York, NY: Columbia University Press.

Zhang, Haibo. 2012. "What Has China Learnt from Disasters? Evolution of the Emergency Management System after Sars, Southern Snowstorm, and Wenchuan Earthquake." *Journal of Comparative Policy Analysis: Research and Practice* 14(3):234–44.

1 Assembling the theoretical toolkit

Conceptualizing the field and its formation

How did the 2003 SARS epidemic turn out to be such a catalyzing event? Based on any objective criteria of losses, the crisis did not kill or injure nearly as many people as several more prominent disasters in China, such as the 1976 Tangshan earthquake (at least 240,000 versus 349 during SARS), which never triggered institutional reforms in disaster management. The outbreak was also different from natural disasters, protests, or industrial accidents, categories of emergencies the governing elites were able to recognize and manage. Unlike natural disasters, SARS did not announce its arrival with rapid death and mayhem. Unlike public security emergencies, there were no physical sites of protests where the government could direct its security forces. Unlike industrial accidents, no sophisticated technologies and heroic efforts could be mounted, for example to access flooded mines. SARS came silently and namelessly, not even recognized as a distinctive virus when it struck its first victims in southern China.

This chapter assembles the theoretical tools that will enable me to show how I have analyzed the genesis of China's emergency management following the 2003 SARS crisis, especially the ideational basis that led to its genesis and early development. The organizational field drawn from sociological institutional theory is the centerpiece construct from my toolkit as it arranges the newly formed emergency management into an intelligible entity. As I will explain and discuss further in this chapter, apart from institutional theory, Foucauldian studies of governmentality and sociological disaster research are the other two broad theoretical bases from which I assemble my toolkit. When used together, the toolkit allows me to perform a social autopsy of this phenomenon (Klinenberg 2002), highlighting the network of organized actors, as well as the ideas and arguments they draw upon to build emergency management as a new and discernible entity to respond to crises swiftly and conspicuously.

This chapter proceeds as follows. First, I provide a brief overview of institutional theory, especially the premises and contributions that I find useful for my project. Besides the concept of organizational field, I also highlight the role of ideas and the processes invoked in institutional theory (e.g., institutional vocabulary and theorization), as well as the importance of legitimacy to such organizing efforts.

Next, I introduce Foucault's concept of governmentality as a means to fill in institutional theory's relative silence on power relations. By taking into account power relations as espoused in Foucault's idea of governmentality, institutional theory can better explain the ideational genesis and growth of an organizational field, especially by governing elites. Following that, I discuss social science disaster studies, particularly from sociological research, and highlighting social constructionism as the shared ontological root with institutional theory. In the same section, I elaborate on Stallings's concept of establishment, which I reference on several occasions because it is a central concept in my theoretical toolkit. I also tie Foucauldian studies and institutional theory to disaster research in my discussion.

Simply put, the concepts of organizational field, legitimacy, institutional vocabulary, and theorization in institutional theory expand and deepen the understanding of how the institutional context in which disasters are constructed and managed. In turn, the concepts of establishment, claims-making, and putative problems from disaster studies clarify the role of organized actors and institutional processes associated with field-building. Finally, by bringing in Foucault's concept of governmentality, I offer a corrective to the neglect of power relations in institutional theory, showing how institutionalization can be read as governmentalization when we account for the exercise of power.

Sociological institutional theory

I draw several critical pieces of my conceptual tools from institutional (also neo-institutional) theory, so it makes sense to briefly introduce the theoretical base. It is one of the most significant research programs in contemporary sociology, especially in organizational studies (Jepperson 2002). The theory began as a project that deliberately shifted away from the atomistic and realist philosophical commitments that were entrenched in the intellectual culture of American sociology in past decades. This intellectual movement recognizes that collective action is not simply the sum of individual actions and inter-relationships among social collectivities, and thus reinstates society as a distinct and meaningful level of analysis (Friedland and Alford 1991).

This perspective is also a refutation of the *tabula rasa* claim in which social aggregates not only exist but function in a vacuum (Jepperson and Meyer 1991; Perrow 1986). Instead, the social aggregates are conceived as entities well-embedded in their cultural environments (Meyer 2008; Powell and DiMaggio 1991); consequently, their conduct is organized by the scripts and schemas that are available to them in those environments. In particular, organizations sharing the same organizational field (e.g., the U.S. radio industry in Leblebici et al. 1991) become institutionalized and look increasingly similar in response to three environmental pressures: (1) political or regulatory pressures (coercive isomorphism), (2) an uncertain or ambiguous environment (mimetic isomorphism), and (3) professionalization efforts (normative isomorphism) (DiMaggio and Powell 1983). Research has also shown that organizations exhibit various degrees of institutional isomorphism; they are hardly "imitative dopes" that are uniformly incapable of resisting and therefore readily succumb to isomorphic pressures (Lounsbury 2008; Oliver 1991; Scott 2008; Suddaby 2010).

The ontological core of institutional theory is social constructionist, meaning that it emphasizes the shared knowledge and meanings that emerge through social interactions (Berger and Luckmann [1966] 1991). It takes social collectivities – communities, organizations, and nations alike – seriously as interpretive systems (Daft and Weick 1984), noting how they purposefully tap into wider worlds of meaning and leverage their power (Mohr and Friedland 2008; Oliver 1991; Scott 2014). This perspective emphasizes the cultural-cognitive elements of the institutional order, the most deeply rooted conceptions of social reality that have become taken for granted (Scott 2014). In other words, cultural-cognitive elements formulate the meaning, rationality, and the categories and classification systems of the scripts and schemas available in the institutional environments. Scott (1991) provides a lucid description of how organized actors import and improvise such scripts and schemas from their environments, rather than reinvent the wheel from within: "All of us to some degree design or tailor our worlds, but we never do this from raw cloth; indeed, for the most part we get our worlds ready to wear" (p. 170).

It is this "ready-to-wear" quality in organized action that is useful as a first principle and thus the utility of institutional theory in assembling my conceptual toolkit. Organized actors strive to configure their structures and practices, and develop products that demonstrate alignment with the goals espoused and values expected of them within their institutional environment, such as the need to be efficient or productive in their performance (DiMaggio and Powell 1983; Meyer and Rowan 1977). Consequently, actors that appropriately adapt to these expectations gain social acceptance from other actors sharing the same institutional environment. In other words, the means as expressed through such necessary adaptations (e.g., appearing to be compliant or efficient) serve the ultimate ends of attaining legitimacy within the field.

Organizational field: "mutual awareness of common enterprise"

An organizational field is a collection of "sets of institutions and networks of organizations that together constitute a recognizable area of life" (DiMaggio and Powell 1983:148). As a foundational conception of an organizational field that remains highly influential even today (Scott 2014), this definition can also be more concretely expressed using a plethora of organizational types: from other organizations that produce identical products and services (in which the effects of isomorphic pressures are likely most salient), to key suppliers, to resource and product consumers, as well as to regulatory bodies. In terms of properties or characteristics, a field is seen to manifest itself when it demonstrates an increase in the interaction and information load among a set of organizations to the extent that "interorganizational structures of domination and patterns of coalition" become obvious and "mutual awareness of a common enterprise" emerges among participants in that organization set (DiMaggio and Powell 1983:148).

While an organizational field can also be established a priori according to readily available administrative categories (e.g., Standard Industrial Classifications, or

SIC codes), commonly recognizable organization populations (such as banks), well-defined geopolitical boundaries, or function, I use a more recent definition that corrals a field according to issues. This maneuver not only returns to and emphasizes the "common enterprise" undertaken by entities in the same field, as in earlier foundational definitions (see for example, DiMaggio and Powell 1983), but also introduces a more deliberative and dynamic quality to what an organizational field entails and engenders in institutional terms: the persistent quest for legitimacy. An issue-centered organizational field also offers a more sophisticated reading of the varying degrees of influence each constituent exerts and a more dynamic view of field membership (Wooten and Hoffman 2017). It also carries theoretical significance in this study for two reasons. First, this definition conspicuously references the power inequality of constituents embedded in organizational fields, a rare observation that is either absent or at best implied in other definitions. As I highlighted earlier, the issue of power relations in institutional theory is an area I seek to address in my research. Second, in addition to emphasizing the processes of field formation and evolution, an issue-based conceptualization of an organizational field also necessitates a closer examination of how ideas (and their appending arguments) are implicated in shaping field-level debates around the central issue, especially during the genesis of the field.

The emerging or formative phase of China's emergency management organizational field provides an occasion to generate insights on the dynamics of early field formation, a knowledge gap that has been recently acknowledged and highlighted (Wooten and Hoffman 2017). Until a few years ago, most institutional analyses focused on organizational fields that were already well-established or mature (Greenwood and Suddaby 2006). More recently, however, a growing number of studies have examined early field formation or emerging fields (Lawrence and Phillips 2004; Maguire, Hardy and Lawrence 2004; Purdy and Gray 2009).

However, apart from studies that attend to founding institutional or structural conditions, to date few studies on emerging fields or founding conditions in institutional contexts contribute to a better understanding of the ideational basis and legitimacy issues associated with that specific phase of field formation; this is perhaps not surprising given that there is broad tacit acknowledgement in the literature that institutional change comes partially through ideas, albeit embedded in logics, discourses, and structures (Czarniawska and Joerges 1996; Meyer et al. 2009; Zilber 2008). Nonetheless, this literature gap is puzzling, because the genesis of any organizational field should logically be regarded as an intensive, and, therefore, a productive period for opportunistic incursions and institutional entrepreneurship by organized actors (DiMaggio 1988; Hardy and Maguire 2017). In the next section, I elaborate on the tools from institutional theory that allow closer examination of the role of ideas in early field formation.

The role of ideas in institutional theory

Working with and on ideas is a vexing task, given their often elusive and amorphous character. To illustrate, the web version of the *Oxford English Dictionary*

(OED) shows that there are 13 definitions of the word "idea." I highlight the one that seems most germane to my study: "Any product of mental apprehension or activity, existing in the mind as an object of knowledge or thought; an item of knowledge or belief; a thought, *a theory, a way of thinking*" (italics mine).[1] Linking to institutional theory, I see ideas as sites to understand how organized actors attribute meaning and rationality (i.e., legitimization or de-legitimization) to some events, activities, and objectives, but not others (Suddaby 2010; Zilber 2008).

The emphasis on ideas in institutional studies dwindled when researchers turned to intermediate and more observable objects such as actions, practices, and structures (Christensen et al. 1997; Suddaby 2010; Zilber 2008). As Zilber (2008) notes, the focus on practices and structures, while attending to their institutionalization process, suffers the following pitfall: "Researchers studied structural and practical dimensions of institutions, assuming – rather than directly studying – their symbolic, meaningful character" (p. 154).

One notable stream of work on ideas in institutional studies focuses on the "travel of ideas," a notion that is well anchored in the social constructionist tradition. The "travel of ideas" connotes how ideas as images diffuse through organizations across time and space (Czarniawska and Joerges 1996). Ideas are circulated through waves of fashion, and are translated into objects and actions. Occasionally they survive succeeding waves and condense into institutions in the form of public administrative reforms, developmental models, and best practices. Seen this way, ideas can also be expressed in more tangible and material forms, from artifacts that are conceptual and provisional such as designs and prototypes, to those that offer concrete, itemized checklists and prescriptions, such as standards and guidelines, and then finally to those that have become more ideal-typical, obdurate, and taken for granted, such as archetypes and templates (Czarniawska and Joerges 1996; Greenwood and Hinings 1993; Greenwood and Hinings 1996; Purdy and Gray 2009; Wedlin and Sahlin 2017). Ideas also morph into ideologies when they are reified by authority (Czarniawska and Joerges 1996). As ideological products (Meyer et al. 2009), they are further rendered as "meaning deployed in the service of power" (Thompson 1996:7). The usefulness of the above notions will become more obvious in Chapter 4, when I discuss the development of the risk governance framework, which the Chinese establishment assembled using ideas that originated in China and elsewhere.

With ideas increasingly becoming an important topic of study, the literature has highlighted how ideas in their travels are used by organized actors in institutional settings to legitimize change. Attempts at achieving legitimacy involve organized actors mobilizing institutional vocabularies, which are "clusters of repetitive words, attributes, and referential texts linked to distinct conceptions" associated with specific ideas, for instance articulating the archetypical qualities of professionalism (Suddaby and Greenwood 2005:43). However, mobilizing institutional vocabularies alone is not sufficient. "Theorizing" or the theorization of change is also an integral part of the ensemble of tools that organized actors deploy to legitimize change (Greenwood, Suddaby and Hinings 2002; Strang and Meyer 1993;

Suddaby and Greenwood 2001). By theorizing, I refer to purposeful actions and accounts that assemble, develop, and specify abstract categories, and articulate their patterned relationships; for example, in the forms cause-and-effect where activity A leads to activity B, which in turn brings about outcome C (Greenwood, Suddaby and Hinings 2002; Strang and Meyer 1993; Zilber 2008).

Theorizations are also typically conducted and promoted vigorously by communities of "culturally legitimated theorists" which occupy prestigious and influential positions within their institutional environments (Strang and Meyer 1993). These intellectual communities include scientists, policy analysts, and professionals. Such bodies are considered "the bona fide producers" of specialized knowledge (Ainsworth and Hardy 2012:1703).

Other organized actors in organizational fields are also implicated in how ideas travel in organizational space, even though relative to intellectual communities they are usually not the originators of ideas or models. Instead, they contribute by reproducing the shared meanings and understandings within the field (Ruef and Scott 1998). This is especially true for regulatory agencies, which also adjudicate and push for negotiations among competing claims. Regulatory agencies include nation-state and government bodies but are not limited to them. Non-governmental organizations such as professional bodies also serve similar purposes. Interestingly, as researchers using institutional theory in the organizational domain move away from studying the state and its associated bodies, one starts to see calls to reclaim the state as an organized actor in organizational fields and to pay closer attention to, for example, state-corporate dynamics (Barley 2010; Greenwood 2008). My study is one such attempt, in that it illustrates and discusses the dominance of the state in creating an organizational field and its implications for institutional theory.

Legitimacy in institutional theory

Compared to disaster sociological research and Foucauldian studies, legitimacy in institutional theory has been more fleshed out theoretically. Therefore, it makes sense to draw upon institutional theory to inform the former two research bases.

Legitimacy in institutional theory focuses on the processes through which organizations attain "social fitness" with (Oliver 1991; Scott 1991) and gain "cultural support" from other actors in the institutional environment (Meyer and Scott 1983:201). The institutionalization process itself is a main source of legitimacy (Suchman 1995). Said in another way, the attainment of legitimacy and the process of institutionalization constitute each other with the effect that what appears to be natural and meaningful has to be acceptable at the same time. Seen this way, my study is one that investigates the institutionalization processes that were unfolding during the nascent emergency management organizational field in China, and the extent to which the new risk governance framework is becoming legitimized.

Legitimacy can also be "short-circuited" when the institutionalization process leverages existing ideas and practices that are already legitimate. Akin to bouts of infection, the "contagion of legitimacy" (Zucker 1988:38) is capable of "infecting" new roles, actions, structures – even new expert knowledge – with acceptance and support because highly institutionalized elements are simultaneously legitimate and sources of legitimization (Zucker 1987). In fact, these elements tend to persist over time with minimal justification or elaboration once institutionalized and rendered legitimate, to the extent that more effective or productive alternatives available in the environment may be ignored (Zucker 1977).

Not surprisingly, institutional literature also considers legitimacy as arising from endorsements by sources both within and outside of organizational fields (Jepperson 2002; Suchman 1995). However, literature has been focusing on external sources, such as investors and mass media (Deephouse et al. 2017). While necessary, this attention to the public sphere neglects questions on how internal "legitimacy projects" are conducted within organizational fields to foster a "common enterprise" outlook and commitment (Goodstein, Blair-Loy and Wharton 2009; Suchman 1995). By looking at interactions within the emerging organizational field of China's emergency management, my research attempts to fill this deficiency by focusing "inward" on the organized actors that occupy the field. Focusing on legitimacy from an internal audience perspective is also particularly intriguing in an emerging organizational field because organized actors – especially the institutional entrepreneurs (Hardy and Maguire 2017) and critical stakeholders – need to contend with the double challenge of forming membership in the face of still-ambiguous boundaries with existing fields and domains, and at the same time, solidifying their positions as the authoritative "custodians" of the nascent field.

There are various typologies of legitimacy in the institutional literature (see, for example, Deephouse 1996; Fiol and Aldrich 1994; Vergne 2011). The dominant conceptualization of legitimacy follows Suchman's (1995) typology of pragmatic, moral, and cognitive legitimacy. Pragmatic legitimacy refers to exchange-based "self-interested calculations of an organization's most immediate audiences" (Suchman 1995:578). The exchange could be material (e.g., money and resources) or something more abstract, such as commitment and even co-optation. Moral legitimacy reflects normative judgment on a collective and its associated activities, especially whether the latter are deemed to follow "the right thing to do." As explained by Suchman (1995:579), such judgment is based on "beliefs about whether the activity effectively promotes societal welfare, as defined by the audience's socially constructed value system." For moral legitimacy, Suchman (1995) also offers the forms in which they can be observed: (a) evaluations of outputs and consequences; (b) evaluations of procedures and techniques (in which results are accomplished; (c) the organizing structures in which (a) and (b) take place; and (d) evaluations of the individuals (e.g., leaders and managers) involved in the respective organizations and activities. Finally, stakeholders confer cognitive legitimacy on other organizations and their associated activities by basing their judgment on meaningful and intelligible cultural accounts. This can either be actively achieved when organized actors purposefully make sense of environmental chaos or ambiguity, or passively accepted in situations where alternatives are not even thinkable or conceivable to them.

Introducing Foucauldian governmentality

Students of institutional theory have striven in and struggled with explaining change adequately (DiMaggio 1988; Hirsch and Lounsbury 1997; Scott 2008; Suddaby 2010). One reason stems from institutional theory's blind spot on power. By paying scant attention to power, especially positions that organized actors occupy and the contentious interactions among them, institutional theorists miss out on opportunities to highlight power relations that help or hinder change (DiMaggio 1988; Scott 2008). Yet, while power relations have seldom been an explicit topic of inquiry in institutional studies, it is also a stretch to claim that institutional theorists dismiss it as unimportant (Meyer et al. 2009). On some occasions, power is tacitly acknowledged to engender institutional change, even while it is not directly examined (see, for example, Greenwood and Suddaby 2006). In other instances, power is also tempered in a language that smooths out its inherent privileged and conflictual nature, such as when it is expressed as "parochial interests" (DiMaggio 1988). In fact, there have been efforts to render institutional theory more sensitive to inquiries related to power, albeit distilled to the more prosaic notions of agency and interests (see most notably DiMaggio 1988).

Foucault's idea of governmentality introduces a corrective for this relative silence on the exercise of power because it treats institutionalization as attempts at naturalization, as a "social alchemy" of sorts that transforms what is institutionalized to what is simultaneously considered a logical and unproblematic progression that is self-evident from an earlier stage of development. The emphasis on categories, classifications, scripts, and schemas in institutional theory also provides a natural entry point to introduce Foucauldian conceptions about the deep coupling between power and knowledge (Power 2011).

Foucault coined the term "governmentality" to refer to the array of institutions, forms of knowledge, and techniques that enable the exercise of power over some target population. In other words, when Foucault says a state has been governmentalized, he is saying that it has assumed a particular form and style of managing its subjects. Foucault (1991) arrives at this conclusion through his historical analysis of how Machiavellian ideas around the sovereignty of the state no longer constituted the only form of power in society from the eighteenth century on, and thus was further complemented by other forms of power – discipline and government.[2] Foucault uses the term "government" in a more esoteric way, to gesture toward forms of power and processes of subjectification. While it can be as broad as governing the self and others, "government" is best read as the "conduct of conduct" (Dean 2010; Vallentin and Murillo 2009:14).

Governmentality can be read in two different but related ways. First, as an analytic of government, it attempts to shed light on our taken-for-granted ways of doing things, revealing how we think about and question (or fail to question) these ways (Dean 2010; Lemke 2002). Second, as a problematic of government (Foucault 1991), governmentality also shows how an issue is constructed as a problem that offers opportunities for solution (Rose and Miller 1992). For example, in the early twentieth century, the UK population was constructed under welfarism as vulnerable to "social ills," thereby requiring the state to provide security, housing, healthcare, and education (Rose and Miller 1992). This provides another convergence point, as it relates to and gels with acts of theorization highlighted in institutional theory (Strang and Meyer 1993), and furthers it by showing how a solution can be purposively reverse engineered onto an issue.

The analytic and problematic of government are both germane to my research on China's emergency management. By extending them to emergency management, we see that occurrences such as natural disasters have the potential to be rendered governable by the complex of technologies of governmentality, such as plans and regulatory practices (Gordon 1991; Rose and Miller 1992). For example, they can be turned into categories of risk that could be redistributed through insurance (Ewald 1991).

Even though Foucault originally discounted the importance of states and state sovereignty, more recent governmentality studies find that state power has not declined.[3] In addition, new actors such as nongovernmental bodies (e.g., emerging new professions) are gaining importance and reconfiguring the nature of relations between the state and civil society (Deuchars 2010; Lemke 2002; Rose 1999). This corresponds to the "hollowing out of the state" thesis (Rhodes 2007; Roberts 2010), which refers to the trend of transferring services and functions from governments to private firms. In other words, the advent of governance as a form of control intimates that the ability of the state to act unilaterally has weakened and continues to diminish. In essence, it can no longer rely on a "command operating code" and has to rely on "diplomacy," which refers to management through negotiation (see Rhodes 2007:1248).

How governmentality connects to institutional theory

The process of governmentalization in Foucauldian studies can be equated with institutionalization in institutional theory. Both highlight the process through which particular rationalities are embedded and become taken for granted. However, by using the term governmentality, I specifically highlight how the process is less benign than it is portrayed in institutionalist accounts; it embeds not only the interests of those organized actors, but also the specific rationalities they espouse – the ideas, especially the categories and classification systems, they mobilize to cast events and practices as problems that necessitate their intervention in the first place. By doing so, I make obvious the powerful organized actors and how they create and infuse a new organizational field.

Because Foucault pays close attention to ideational aspects of institutional life such as "archaeologies of knowledge, genealogies of micro-technologies, accounts of epistemic breaks, and regimes of truth" (Mohr and Neely 2009:237), his conceptions of power can be particularly productive for institutional theory and could be even understood as an implicit theory of institutional power. To offer a concrete point of connection between the Foucauldian conceptualization of power and institutional theory, DiMaggio and Powell (1991) argue that technologies of governmentality correspond well to the influence the institutional environment exerts on organizations (see Power 2011:50):

> Environments . . . are more subtle in their influence: rather than being co-opted by organizations, they penetrate the organization, creating the lenses through which actors view the world and the very categories of structure, action, and thought.

Seen this way, ideas central to the creators of China's emergency management establishment are "lenses" through which actors gain their "categories of structure, action, and thought." These ideas also form the basis for the technologies of governmentality to take shape.

Connecting institutional theory and Foucauldian studies to social science disaster research

Social science disaster research, particularly of sociological roots, has departed from a functionalist conception of natural disasters as purely obdurate, physical events that are "out there," disrupting society. The social constructionist tradition in disaster research asserts that extreme events – despite their resultant human injuries and deaths as well as economic costs – are not disasters in and of themselves, but they accomplish that status only when refracted through social interpretation and action. For example, heat waves are usually not treated as disasters, even though they kill more people than floods and hurricanes combined in the United States in some years (Klinenberg 2002).

Foucauldian connections

The focus on knowledge differentials and vested interests provides a bridge to connect Foucauldian studies to disaster studies. Foucault's concept of governmentality contributes to a maturing stream of social constructionist research not only by continuing its emphasis of treating the problematization of risks and natural disasters as contested products of social definition over time (Tierney 2007), but also by highlighting the fact that the particular styles and forms they assume are contingent upon the institutional context. Seen this way, Foucauldian governmentality also helps to flesh out the deeply cultural arguments embedded in the emerging risk governance framework in the Chinese case, making it possible to see how the emergency management establishment infuses its actions with meaning. In addition, it problematizes existing frameworks that are predominantly prescriptive and practice-oriented, such as the putative "integrated risk governance" framework (Renn 2008) which often accepts the risk definitions and problem framings promoted by established actors at face value. I will elaborate on the "integrated risk governance" framework later in my empirical chapters.

Dombrowsky's (1995) elaboration of the tautological relationship between the definition and the definers (i.e., organized actors) of disasters is particularly illuminating. Referring to the German government's definitions of disasters, Dombrowsky (1995:242) points out how the self-referential claim is enshrined into legislation:

> The German law . . . defines "disaster" . . . by saying it involves "such severe interference of the public order and safety that an intervention of the centralized, coordinated disaster protection units is necessary" (Seeck 1980). . . . Even more tautological is the definition by law: A disaster is what the intervention of disaster relief units make necessary. . . . For the state, the breakdown of public order and safety is the key, not the phenomena [i.e., storm, flood etc.] . . .

As I will demonstrate in the empirical chapters where the emergence of the "risk governance" which justifies interventions by the establishment, such definitions are self-serving and hide why the tautological definitions of disasters are highly problematic in the first place (Tierney 1999).

Institutional connections

Social science disaster researchers have examined the production and reproduction of disasters by the state and other institutionalized organizations. The state and organizations are legitimate actors in society that select and define what counts as risks and disasters, and what does not (Clarke 1988; Stallings 1995). Whether the reading of those events is "distorted" through the prism of cognitive biases or mental heuristics becomes moot because the broader institutional arrangements have already "decided" what should constitute disaster risks for the public and which parties should bear them. In other words, the state and organizations have become the "true assessors for society" in terms of disasters and risks (Clarke 1988:30).

More salient to my research and institutional theory is the insight that disasters are shaped and produced by ensembles of institutions, institutionalized organizations, and social facts. This insight from constructionist disaster studies is also often explicit in its reference to power dimensions and the political domain, which involves the state and its apparatuses. For example, U.S. presidential declarations of disaster are often invoked with an eye for political mileage, especially during election years, and do not necessarily satisfy needs-based criteria (c.f. Tierney 2007).

While the disaster literature does focus on institutionalized organizations, institutional theory has not been a prominent theoretical perspective in disaster research. When terms such as institutions and legitimacy are deployed in disaster research, they are seldom if ever anchored in institutional theory. Formal use of institutional theory, in part or in whole, is infrequent (Aguirre et al. 2005; Eden 2004 are exceptions). In fact, these terms are seldom formally defined, such as O'Neill et al.'s (2007) study of the miscommunication in the 2001 anthrax attacks and Baldi's (1995) account of the transformation of the U.S. Nuclear

Regulatory Commission after the Three Mile Island nuclear accident. Otherwise, institutions are reduced to linguistic shorthand to reference established government functions and institutionalized organizations, such as the military and U.S. Federal Emergency Management Agency (FEMA) (e.g., Perrow 2011; Short and Clarke 1992; Tierney and Bevc 2007).

This gap is unfortunate because there are broad ontological and specific theoretical points of convergence between institutional theory and sociological disaster research in the social constructionist stream of work. Ontologically speaking, both agree that social definitions and the processes through which they come about are consequential in social life. The merits of using an institutional perspective become more apparent when I argue how it also fills a knowledge gap in social construction studies on disasters.

Both sets of literature agree on the significance and impact of events that are perceived as exogenous and catalysts for transformational change, which is evidenced by the plethora of terms in their vocabulary, such as "focusing events" (Birkland 1996; Birkland 1997; Birkland 2007), "critical junctures" (Collier and Collier 1991; Olson and Gawbronski 2003) from social science disaster research; "jolts" (Meyer 1982), "shocks" (Fligstein 1990; Fligstein and McAdam 2012), "field events" (Edelman 1992; Schneiberg and Clemens 2006), and "punctuated events" (Tilcsik and Marquis 2013) from institutional studies. In addition, both recognize that the selection and presentation of organizational problems and their solutions are not independent of the specialized knowledge that organized actors, particularly experts, bring to bear on the issues (Knowles 2011). This is germane to the ideational aspects of my research and institutional theory.

Based on what I have highlighted in the preceding paragraphs, the affinity between institutional theory and social science disaster research allows me to use the social constructionist stream of work on disasters as a theoretical resource. Here, I highlight "establishment," which emerged from the social constructionist literature on disasters.

Coining the term "establishment," disaster sociologist Robert Stallings (1995) calls attention to a loose but stable network of U.S. technocrats and bureaucrats that professes and promotes the threat of earthquake as a problem to be managed, particularly with government support. Just as important, the process of claims-making is restricted to the establishment because its members are the ones who are deemed to possess the requisite research, managerial, and policy skills to address the putative problem. These members are connected through interlocking webs of elite and specialized knowledge production entities, and social facts, such as universities, research programs, government policies, and mission-oriented operational agencies. The network that formed from these webs receives and accumulates resources that allow them to finance projects and training, and build technical standards. In addition, earthquakes offer "teachable moments" (Stallings 1986; Stallings 1995) that can also be capitalized on not only for public awareness but also to garner funds and political influence. Through this concerted effort by organized actors in problem selection, and their subsequent definitions and solutions, the expert class and their espoused ideas made inroads into policies and policymaking (Stallings 1995). This general insight of establishment influence is well-documented in the organizational analyses of disaster, albeit limited to single disaster triggers or events (e.g., Chen 2012), and seldom applied at the organizational field level to natural disasters in general.

The term "establishment" is useful in my conceptual toolkit because it emphasizes the entrenched positions expert networks occupy at the national level, the extent to which their roles have been institutionalized, and, in the emergency management case, their role in shaping disaster policies. This also ties in to treating China's emergency management as an issue-based organizational field in institutional theory, as it highlights the "relational space" in which organized actors, through the process of referencing one another, bring a field into existence (Wooten and Hoffman 2017). It also lends definition to the specific elites that are not only invested with agency and interest, but who also enjoy access to the resources and positions to create specialized knowledge and weave together the intellectual building blocks to form a new organizational field. In addition, by referencing "establishment," I tie my case of China's emergency management organizational field to disaster studies and institutional theory. Using institutional theory also responds to disaster sociologist Quarantelli's (2005) call to integrate disaster research with core sociological concerns and within broader theoretical frameworks, and moves sociological disaster studies beyond the inertia and comfort of the parochial set of theoretical perspectives endemic in the subfield today (Tierney 2007).

To link disaster studies forward to institutional theory, I highlight the construct of legitimacy. Legitimacy is not anchored in institutional theory when used in disaster research. For example, the processes and products of formal risk assessments often represent claims by organizations that their decisions are not only rational but comprehensive. As a result, they serve more as "tools of legitimation" than tools of decision making (Clarke 1988:30). Although the construct represents a degree of social appropriateness and acceptability that is similar to institutional theory, it is not explicitly spelled out that way in disaster research.

Conclusion

Up to this point, I have set up my toolkit by carefully selecting concepts from institutional theory, Foucauldian studies on governmentality, and sociological research on disasters. By applying a mainly institutional perspective, I show that what is observed empirically – the creation of emergency management as a governmental function – can be read theoretically as an internal legitimacy project that built an organizational field. This is in part because the establishment's strategy to render emergency management as viable and distinctive from established policy domains cannot be treated naively as simply an instrument, just a means to an end. The means *and* the ends that emerged within the Chinese context did not come about *de novo*. Putting it more plainly, the choice of creating emergency management as a governmental function was a solution that was readily available and acceptable to the establishment within China's political and cultural contexts. Just as important, the ideas and ideals that were gaining traction at that time were also highly consequential to the genesis and growth of the emergency management organizational field.

Like a restaurant menu, the institutional environment promises plentiful choices, but its content has been pretty much narrowed down to specific cuisines and even more defined templates of ingredients, condiments, and cooking techniques. The means and ends that the emergency management establishment should and could be preoccupied with in the wake of the SARS crisis, and the repertoire of ideas that were available to it, were already somewhat constrained, if not fully determined. Still, the choices were challenging.

Thankfully, a legitimacy project of this scale and speed inevitably leaves clues of the choices the establishment had made.

Notes

1 All 13 definitions on OED can be found at www.oed.com/view/Entry/90954?rskey= MGBoao&result=1&isAdvanced=false#eid. The definition I highlight is the twelfth.
2 Foucault attaches specific meanings to sovereignty and discipline. By sovereignty, he refers to the theory and practice of royal administrative rule under feudal monarchy, depending solely on the formal, juridical, and the executive arm of the state (Dean 2010). Discipline refers to practices that are based in the military, monasteries, schools, and even prisons (Foucault 1991, [1977] 1995).
3 This seems to be *modus operandi* for governmentality research. It refuses to reify any particular social entity, even prominent and established ones such as the state. For example, the state is conceived as a nominal entity with no essential function or necessity (see Gordon 1991; Rose and Miller 1992).

References

Aguirre, B. E., Russell R. Dynes, James Kendra and Rory Connell. 2005. "Institutional Resilience and Disaster Planning for New Hazards: Insights from Hospitals." *Journal of Homeland Security and Emergency Management* 2(2):1–17.

Ainsworth, Susan and Cynthia Hardy. 2012. "Subjects of Inquiry: Statistics, Stories, and the Production of Knowledge." *Organization Studies* 33(12):1693–714. doi: 10.1177/0170840612457616.

Baldi, Brunetta. 1995. "Institutional Change Versus Institutional Persistence? The Transformation of the U.S. Nuclear Regulatory Commission since Three Mile Island." *University of Delaware Disaster Research Center Preliminary Paper 236.* Retrieved from (https://udspace.udel.edu/bitstream/handle/19716/644/PP236. pdf?sequence=1&isAllowed=y).

Barley, Stephen R. 2010. "Building an Institutional Field to Corral a Government: A Case to Set an Agenda for Organization Studies." *Organization Studies* 31(6):777–805.

Berger, Peter L. and Thomas Luckmann. [1966] 1991. *The Social Construction of Reality: A Treatise in the Sociology of Knowledge.* New York, NY: Penguin Books.

Birkland, Thomas A. 1996. "Natural Disasters as Focusing Events: Policy Communities and Political Responses." *International Journal of Mass Emergencies and Disasters* 14(2):221–43.

Birkland, Thomas A. 1997. *After Disaster: Agenda Setting, Public Policy, and Focusing Events.* Washington, DC: Georgetown University Press.

Birkland, Thomas A. 2007. *Lessons of Disaster: Policy Change after Catastrophic Events.* Washington, DC: Georgetown University Press.

Chen, Gang. 2012. "China's Management of Natural Disasters: Organizations and Norms." Pp. 130–48 in *China's Crisis Management,* edited by J. H. Chung. Abindon, Oxon: Routledge.

Christensen, Søren, Peter Karnøe, Jesper Strandgaard Pedersen and Frank Dobbin. 1997. "Actors and Institutions." *American Behavioral Scientist* 40(4):392–96.

Clarke, Lee. 1988. "Explaining Choices among Technological Risks." *Social Problems* 35(1):22–35.

Collier, Ruth Berins and David Collier. 1991. *Shaping the Political Arena: Critical Junctures, the Labor Movement, and Regime Dynamics in Latin America.* Princeton, NJ: Princeton University Press.

Czarniawska, Barbara and Bernward Joerges. 1996. "Travels of Ideas." Pp. 13–48 in *Translating Organizational Change,* edited by B. Czarniawska and G. Sevón. Berlin; New York, NY: Walter de Gruyter.

Daft, Richard L. and Karl E. Weick. 1984. "Toward a Model of Organizations as Interpretation Systems." *Academy of Management Review* 9(2):284–95.

Dean, Mitchell. 2010. *Governmentality: Power and Rule in Modern Society.* Thousand Oaks, CA: Sage Publications.

Deephouse, David L. 1996. "Does Isomorphism Legitimate?" *Academy of Management Journal* 39(4):1024–39.

Deephouse, David L., Jonathan Bundy, Leigh Plunkett and Mark Suchman. 2017. "Organizational Legitimacy: Six Questions." Pp. 27–54 in *The Sage Handbook of Organizational Institutionalism,* edited by R. Greenwood, C. Oliver, T. B. Lawrence and R. E. Meyer. Thousand Oaks, CA: Sage Publications.

Deuchars, Robert. 2010. "Towards the Global Social: Sociological Reflections on Governance and Risk in the Context of the Current Financial Crisis." *Cambridge Review of International Affairs* 23(1):107–25.

DiMaggio, Paul J. 1988. "Interest and Agency in Institutional Theory." Pp. 3–21 in *Institutional Patterns and Organizations: Culture and Environment,* edited by L. G. Zucker. Cambridge, MA: Ballinger Publishing Company.

DiMaggio, Paul J. and Walter W. Powell. 1983. "The Iron Cage Revisited: Institutional Isomorphism and Collective Rationality in Organizational Fields." *American Sociological Review* 48(2):147–60.

DiMaggio, Paul J. and Walter W. Powell. 1991. "Introduction." Pp. 1–38 in *The New Institutionalism in Organizational Analysis,* edited by Walter W. Powell and Paul J. DiMaggio. Chicago, IL: University of Chicago Press.

Dombrowsky, Wolf R. 1995. "Again and Again: Is a Disaster What We Call a 'Disaster'? Some Conceptual Notes on Conceptualizing the Object of Disaster Sociology." *International Journal of Mass Emergencies and Disasters* 13(3):241–54.

Edelman, Lauren. 1992. "Legal Ambiguity and Symbolic Structures: Organizational Mediation of Civil Rights Law." *American Journal of Sociology* 97(6):1531–76.

Eden, Lynn. 2004. *Whole World on Fire: Organizations, Knowledge, and Nuclear Weapons Devastation.* Ithaca, NY: Cornell University Press.

Ewald, François. 1991. "Insurance and Risk." Pp. 197–210 in *The Foucault Effect: Studies in Governmentality,* edited by G. Burchell, C. Gordon and P. Miller. Chicago, IL: University of Chicago Press.

Fiol, C. Marlene and Howard E. Aldrich. 1994. "Fools Rush In? The Institutional Context of Industry Creation." *Academy of Management Review* 19(4):645–70.

Fligstein, Neil. 1990. *The Transformation of Corporate Control.* Cambridge, MA: Harvard University Press.

Fligstein, Neil and Doug McAdam. 2012. *A Theory of Fields.* New York, NY: Oxford University Press.

Foucault, Michel. 1991. "Governmentality." Pp. 87–104 in *The Foucault Effect: Studies in Governmentality*, edited by G. Burchell, C. Gordon and P. Miller. Hemel Hempstead: Harvester Wheatsheaf.

Foucault, Michel. [1977] 1995. *Discipline and Punish.* Translated by A. Sheridan. New York, NY: Vintage Books.

Friedland, Roger and Robert R. Alford. 1991. "Bringing Society Back in: Symbols, Practices, and Institutional Contradictions." Pp. 232–63 in *The New Institutionalism in Organizational Analysis*, edited by W. W. Powell and P. J. DiMaggio. Chicago, IL: University of Chicago Press.

Goodstein, Jerry, Mary Blair-Loy and Army S. Wharton. 2009. "Organization-Based Legitimacy: Core Ideologies and Moral Action." Pp. 44–62 in *Meaning and Method: The Cultural Approach to Sociology*, edited by I. Reed and J. C. Alexander. Boulder, CO: Paradigm Publishers.

Gordon, Colin. 1991. "Governmental Rationality: An Introduction." Pp. 1–51 in *The Foucault Effect: Studies in Governmentality*, edited by G. Burchell, C. Gordon and P. Miller. Chicago, IL: University of Chicago Press.

Greenwood, Royston. 2008. "Focusing the Asteroid Belt of Organizations." *Journal of Management Inquiry* 17(3):152–6.

Greenwood, Royston and C. R. Hinings. 1993. "Understanding Strategic Change: The Contribution of Archetypes." *Academy of Management Journal* 36(5):1052–81.

Greenwood, Royston and C. R. Hinings. 1996. "Understanding Radical Organizational Change: Bringing Together the Old and the New Institutionalism." *Academy of Management Journal* 21(4):1022–54.

Greenwood, Royston and Roy Suddaby. 2006. "Institutional Entrepreneurship in Mature Fields: The Big Five Accounting Firms." *Academy of Management Journal* 49(1):27–48.

Greenwood, Royston, Roy Suddaby and C. R. Hinings. 2002. "Theorizing Change: The Role of Professional Associations in the Transformation of Institutionalized Fields." *Academy of Management Journal* 45(1):58–80.

Hardy, Cynthia and Steve Maguire. 2017. "Institutional Entrepreneurship and Change in Fields." Pp. 261–80 in *The Sage Handbook of Organizational Institutionalism*, edited by R. Greenwood, C. Oliver, T. B. Lawrence and R. E. Meyer. Thousand Oaks, CA: Sage Publications.

Hirsch, Paul M. and Michael Lounsbury. 1997. "Ending the Family Quarrel: Toward a Reconciliation of 'Old' and 'New' Institutionalism." *American Behavioral Scientist* 40(4):406–18.

Jepperson, Ronald L. 2002. "The Development and Application of Sociological Neo-institutionalism." Pp. 229–66 in *New Directions in Contemporary Sociological Theory*, edited by J. Berger and M. Zelditch, Jr. Lanham, MD: Rowman & Littlefield Publishers, Inc.

Jepperson, Ronald L. and John W. Meyer. 1991. "The Public Order and the Construction of Formal Organizations." Pp. 204–31 in *The New Institutionalism in Organizational Analysis*, edited by W. W. Powell and P. J. DiMaggio. Chicago, IL: University of Chicago Press.

Klinenberg, Eric. 2002. *Heat Wave: A Social Autopsy of Disaster in Chicago*. Chicago, IL: University of Chicago Press.

Knowles, Scott Gabriel. 2011. *The Disaster Experts: Monitoring Risk in Modern America*. Philadelphia, PA: University of Pennsylvania Press.

Lawrence, Thomas B. and Nelson Phillips. 2004. "From Moby Dick to Free Willy: Macro-Cultural Discourse and Institutional Entrepreneurship in Emerging Institutional Fields." *Organization* 11(5):689–711.

Leblebici, Huseyin, Gerald R. Salancik, Anne Copay and Tom King. 1991. "Institutional Change and the Transformation of Interorganizational Fields: An Organizational History of the U.S. Radio Broadcasting Industry." *Administrative Science Quarterly* 36(3):333–63.

Lemke, Thomas. 2002. "Foucault, Governmentality, and Critique." *Remaking Marxism* 14(3):49–64.

Lounsbury, Michael. 2008. "Institutional Rationality and Practice Variation: New Directions in the Institutional Analysis of Practice." *Accounting, Organizations and Society* 33(4–5):349–61. http://dx.doi.org/10.1016/j.aos.2007.04.001.

Maguire, Steve, Cynthia Hardy and Thomas B. Lawrence. 2004. "Institutional Entrepreneurship in Emerging Fields: Hiv/Aids Treatment Advocacy in Canada." *Academy of Management Journal* 47(5):657–79.

Meyer, Alan D. 1982. "Adapting to Environmental Jolts." *Administrative Science Quarterly* 27(4):515–37.

Meyer, John W. 2008. "Reflections on Institutional Theories of Organizations." Pp. 790–812 in *The Sage Handbook of Organizational Institutionalism*, edited by R. Greenwood, C. Oliver, K. Sahlin and R. Suddaby. Thousand Oaks, CA: Sage Publications.

Meyer, John W. and Brian Rowan. 1977. "Institutionalized Organizations: Formal Structure as Myth and Ceremony." *American Journal of Sociology* 83(2):340–63.

Meyer, John W. and W. Richard Scott, eds. 1983. *Organizational Environments: Ritual and Rationality*. Beverly Hills, CA: Sage.

Meyer, Renate E., Kerstin Sahlin, Marc J. Ventresca and Peter Walgenbach. 2009. "Ideology and Institutions: Introduction." Pp. 1–15 in *Institutions and Ideology*, Vol. 27, *Research in the Socology of Organizations*, edited by R. E. Meyer, K. Sahlin, M. J. Ventresca and P. Walgenbach. Bingley, UK: Emerald Group Publishing.

Mohr, John W. and Roger Friedland. 2008. "Theorizing the Institution: Foundation, Duality, and Data." *Theory and Society* 37:421–6.

Mohr, John W. and Brooke Neely. 2009. "Modeling Foucault: Dualities of Power in Institutional Fields." Pp. 203–55 in *Institutions and Ideology*, Vol. 27, *Research in the Socology of Organizations*, edited by R. E. Meyer, K. Sahlin, M. J. Ventresca and P. Walgenbach. Bingley, UK: Emerald Group Publishing.

Oliver, Christine. 1991. "Strategic Responses to Institutional Processes." *Academy of Management Review* 16(1):145–79.

Olson, Richard Stuart and Vincent T. Gawbronski. 2003. "Disasters as Critical Junctures? Managua, Nicaragua 1972 and Mexico City 1985." *International Journal of Mass Emergencies and Disasters* 21(1):5–36.

O'Neill, Karen M., Jeffrey M. Calia, Caron Chess and Lee Clarke. 2007. "Miscommunication during the Anthrax Attacks: How Events Reveal Organizational Failures." *Human Ecology Review* 14(2):119–29.

Perrow, Charles. 1986. *Complex Organizations: A Critical Essay*. New York, NY: Newbery Award Records.

Perrow, Charles. 2011. *The Next Catastrophe: Reducing Our Vulnerabilities to Natural, Industrial, and Terrorist Attacks*. Princeton: NJ: Princeton University Press.

Powell, Walter W. and Paul J. DiMaggio, eds. 1991. *The New Institutionalism in Organizational Analysis*. Chicago, IL: University of Chicago Press.

Power, Michael. 2011. "Foucault and Sociology." *Annual Review of Sociology* 37:35–56.

Purdy, Jill M. and Barbara Gray. 2009. "Conflicting Logics, Mechanisms of Diffusion, and Multilevel Dynamics in Emerging Institutional Fields." *Academy of Management Journal* 52(2):355–80.

Quarantelli, Enrico Louis. 2005. "A Social Science Research Agenda for the Disasters of the 21st Century: Theoretical, Methodological and Empirical Issues and Their Professional Implementation." Pp. 325–96 in *What Is a Disaster?: New Answers to Old Questions*, edited by R. W. Perry and E. L. Quarantelli. Philadelphia, PA: Xlibris.

Renn, Ortwin. 2008. *Risk Governance: Coping with Uncertainty in a Complex World*. London: Earthscan.

Rhodes, R. A. W. 2007. "Understanding Governance: Ten Years On." *Organization Studies* 28(8):1243–64.

Roberts, Patrick S. 2010. "Private Choices, Public Harms: The Evolution of National Disaster Organizations in the United States." Pp. 42–69 in *Disaster and the Politics of Intervention: The Privatization of Risk*, edited by A. Lakoff. New York, NY: Columbia University Press.

Rose, Nikolas. 1999. *Governing the Soul: The Shaping of the Private Self*. London: Free Association Books.

Rose, Nikolas and Peter Miller. 1992. "Political Power beyond the State: Problematics of Government." *British Journal of Sociology* 43(2):173–205.

Ruef, Martin and W. Richard Scott. 1998. "A Multidimensional Model of Organizational Legitimacy: Hospital Survival in Changing Institutional Enginronments." *Administrative Science Quarterly* 43(4):877–904.

Schneiberg, Marc and Elisabeth S. Clemens. 2006. "The Typical Tools for the Job: Research Strategies in Institutional Analysis." *Sociological Theory* 24(3):195–227.

Scott, W. Richard. 1991. "Unpacking Institutional Arrangements." Pp. 164–82 in *The New Institutionalism in Organizational Analysis*, edited by W. W. Powell and P. J. DiMaggio. Chicago, IL: University of Chicago Press.

Scott, W. Richard. 2008. "Approaching Adulthood: The Maturing of Institutional Theory." *Theory and Society* 37:427–42.

Scott, W. Richard. 2014. *Institutions and Organizations: Ideas, Interests, and Identities*. Los Angeles, CA: Sage Publications.

Seeck, Erich. 1980. *Gesetz über den Katastrophenschutz in Schleswig-Holstein (LkatSG) vom 9 Dezember 1974*. Wiesbaden, Germany: Kommunal und Schul-Verlag A.Heinig (in German).

Short, James F., Jr. and Lee Clarke, eds. 1992. *Organizations, Uncertainties, and Risk*. Boulder, CO: Westview Press.

Stallings, Robert A. 1986. "Reaching the Ethnic Minorities: Earthquake Public Education in the Aftermath of Foreign Disasters." *Spectra* 2(4):695–702.

Stallings, Robert A. 1995. *Promoting Risk: Constructing the Earthquake Threat*. New York, NY: Aldine de Gruyter.

Strang, David and John W. Meyer. 1993. "Institutional Conditions for Diffusion." *Theory and Society* 22(4):487–511.

Suchman, Mark. 1995. "Managing Legitimacy: Strategic and Institutional Approaches." *Academy of Management Review* 20(3):571–610.

Suddaby, Roy. 2010. "Challenges for Institutional Theory." *Journal of Management Inquiry* 19(1):14–20.

Suddaby, Roy and Royston Greenwood. 2001. "Colonizing Knowledge: Commodification as a Dynamic of Jurisdictional Expansion in Professional Service Firms." *Human Relations* 54(7):933–53.

Suddaby, Roy and Royston Greenwood. 2005. "Rhetorical Strategies of Legitimacy." *Administrative Science Quarterly* 50:35–67.

Thompson, John B. 1996. *Ideology and Modern Culture Critical Social Theory in the Era of Mass Communication*. Oxford, UK: Polity Press.

Tierney, Kathleen J. 1999. "Towards a Critical Sociology of Risk." *Sociological Forum* 14(2):215–42.

Tierney, Kathleen J. 2007. "From the Margins to the Mainstream? Disaster Research at the Crossroads." *Annual Review of Sociology* 33:503–25.

Tierney, Kathleen J. and Christine Bevc. 2007. "Disaster as War: Militarism and the Social Construction of Disaster in New Orleans." Pp. 35–50 in *The Sociology of Katrina: Perspectives on a Modern Catastrophe*, edited by D. L. Brunsma, D. Overfelt and J. S. Picou. Maryland: Rowman & Littlefield Publishers, Inc.

Tilcsik, András and Christopher Marquis. 2013. "Punctuated Generosity: How Mega-Events and Natural Disasters Affect Corporate Philanthropy in U.S. Communities." *Administrative Science Quarterly* 58(1):111–48.

Vallentin, Steen and David Murillo. 2009. "C.S.R. as Governmentality." *CSR & Business in Society Working Paper 04-2009*. Retrieved November 3, 2013, from (http://openarchive.cbs.dk/bitstream/handle/10398/7908/wp%20cbscsr%202009-4.pdf).

Vergne, Jean-Philippe. 2011. "Toward a New Measure of Organizational Legitimacy: Method, Validation, and Illustration." *Organizational Research Methods* 14(3):484–502.

Wedlin, Linda and Kerstin Sahlin. 2017. "The Imitation and Translation of Management Ideas." Pp. 102–27 in *The Sage Handbook of Organizational Institutionalism*, edited by R. Greenwood, C. Oliver, T. B. Lawrence and R. E. Meyer. Thousand Oaks, CA: Sage Publications.

Wooten, Melissa and Andrew J. Hoffman. 2017. "Organizational Fields: Past, Present and Future." Pp. 55–74 in *The Sage Handbook of Organizational Institutionalism*, edited by R. Greenwood, C. Oliver, T. B. Lawrence and R. E. Meyer. Thousand Oaks, CA: Sage Publications.

Zilber, Tammar B. 2008. "The Work of Meanings in Institutional Processes and Thinking." Pp. 151–69 in *The Sage Handbook of Organizational Institutionalism*, edited by R. Greenwood, C. Oliver, K. Sahlin and R. Suddaby. Thousand Oaks, CA: Sage Publications.

Zucker, Lynne G. 1977. "The Role of Institutionalization in Cultural Persistence." *American Sociological Review* 42(5):726–43.

Zucker, Lynne G. 1987. "Institutional Theories of Organization." *Annual Review of Sociology* 13:443–64.

Zucker, Lynne G., ed. 1988. *Institutional Patterns and Organizations: Culture and Environment*. Cambridge, MA: Ballinger Publishing Company.

2 Intensive institutionalization (2002–2007)

> SARS is a societal phenomenon. It's about transmission between individuals. Because of that, even if we had mobilized the masses (to deal with the crisis), and tried to resolutely defend ourselves (from the epidemic), without (putting in place) a system, without a way to organize everyone based on some strategy, we basically cannot resist it. . . . It's . . . something related to what you have called social structure. It's a reality of China at that point in time, our *danwei* system (单位制) had collapsed, and we had not formed new mechanisms to defend and prevent (such crises).[1]
>
> – Zhuang, a policy researcher[2]

During our interview, Zhuang pressed me to appreciate why the SARS outbreak could have been the cataclysmic event that brought China to its knees, in light of the various institutional dislocations brought about by the various rapid transitions following the post-1978 "reform and opening up" period. The crisis was seeded way before the virus struck China and many Chinese academics saw the need to be prepared. Understood this way, SARS was more of the catalyst, not the cause.

Since the 1990s, there were already calls for creating a more integrated disaster management system to consolidate disparate resources across government bodies and unify the multiple disaster-specific laws.[3] In fact, suggestions to elevate crisis management to a core governmental function in view of the 9/11 terrorist attacks were also raised on the eve of the SARS outbreak.[4] However, such discussions did not feature visibly in the priorities of Chinese governing elites. Even before the SARS outbreak, even though China had already witnessed multiple major calamities, including the catastrophic 1976 Tangshan earthquake and the Yangtze River flood of 1998, none triggered significant rethinking on national emergency management.[5]

Not surprisingly, there was no issue-based organizational field to speak of prior to the SARS outbreak. Existent laws and administrative regulations were drawn parochially according to specific disaster agents, such as earthquakes or floods. An overarching legal framework to govern natural disasters was absent, let alone a law that incorporated other types of emergency, such as epidemics or large-scale industrial accidents. For example, the 1995 Administrative Regulation on Emergency Response for Destructive Earthquakes reflected this fragmentation. It pertained only to one disaster agent and its processes were generally idiosyncratic to the earthquake management domain.[6]

This trend of fragmentation was also obvious in organizational terms. Disaster management in China was traditionally organized according to governmental units that provided specific surveillance and response functions toward one disaster agent. For instance, the State Council's now-defunct China Earthquake Administration (CEA) was created specifically to manage that natural extreme event. CEA in turn had corresponding organizations replicated at provincial and prefectural levels of government. This functional arrangement strengthened hierarchical control at the expense of horizontal coordination. This intense fragmentation has been a perennial feature of China's government and considered a hindrance to effective disaster management. In fact, academics have long highlighted the importance of research to reform the fragmented legal landscape pertaining to natural disasters.[7]

Before the organizational field emerged and developed, there was no consistent or equivalent phrase in Chinese for the term "emergency management." Initially, terms specifically referenced emergency response (e.g., *yingji* 应急) and not emergency management. Over time, the *yingji* term also became widely accepted by constituents of the organizational field and expanded to include other aspects of emergency management such as mitigation and recovery activities when it was coupled with the Chinese term for management (*guanli* 管理) to form *yingji guanli*.

Just as important, there was also no consistent term for "emergency" in Chinese before the SARS crisis. An emergency is defined as a sudden and unexpected incident, expressed in the Chinese term *tufa shijian* (突发事件). The other definition for emergency is most salient in the term "state of emergency," which is *jinji zhuangtai* (紧急状态) in Chinese. This definitional distinction between emergency as an incident and a state of declaration plays out in this chapter and Chapter 3 when one reads how the State of Emergency Bill (*Jinji Zhuangtai Fa* 紧急状态法) that was originally proposed as law to the national legislature evolved to become the National Emergency Response Law (*Tufa Shijian Yingdui Fa* 突发事件应对法) that was passed in 2007.

For the rest of this chapter, I recount the initial period through which emergency management came to form a nascent field.

2002–2003: SARS, the crisis that catalyzed emergency management

Emergency management was not a priority on the eve of the final leadership transition at the National People's Congress (NPC) in spring 2003.[8] Hu Jintao, Wen Jiabao, and other party cadres who formed the Politburo Standing Committee (PSC) of the Central Committee of the Communist Party of China (CPC) were waiting to assume their government appointments at the NPC. They were elected to the PSC, the highest decision-making authority in the party, at the 16th party national congress in late 2002.[9] When outgoing premier Zhu Rongji gave his final government report at the NPC in March 2003, the focus was on the economic achievements of the past five years and the continuation of sustainable economic development and governmental reforms, particularly in fighting corruption. With regard to emergency management, the government's preoccupation was to contain civil unrest and arrest the rising crime rate.[10]

Meanwhile, by the end of March 2003 the SARS virus had spread beyond its original Guangdong since late 2002. The virus – diagnosed by the Guangdong provincial government and the Ministry of Health as atypical pneumonia with non-vital consequences (Xue and Zhong 2010) – had claimed five lives and infected more than 300 individuals. However, the incident was not mentioned at the NPC, as if the outbreak had never happened. In fact, then-Minister for Health Zhang Wenkang at a press conference on April 3 insisted SARS was not only controllable, it would not pose a threat to Chinese citizens and tourists. On April 8, four months after the first incidence and five days after Zhang's pronouncement, SARS was finally officially recognized as a statutory contagious disease that required state intervention. Soon it was revealed that the actual number of people infected was 10 times what had been reported. By then, SARS had spread internationally and led to the World Health Organization (WHO) issuing two global alerts successively within three days in mid-March.[11] Facing tremendous international pressure and criticism, China finally acceded to WHO's request, allowing its epidemiologists to assess the situation in Guangdong.[12] As the SARS crisis unfolded, it was clear that the competency and political standing of the new regime, both domestically and internationally, was at stake.

The PSC,[13] the pinnacle of the CPC decision-making apparatus, convened on April 17 specifically to discuss the SARS crisis for the first time. Swift action ensued. Health Minister Zhang and Beijing mayor Meng Xue-nong were removed from office by the end of April. Around the same time, the State Council SARS Prevention and Control Headquarters – the highest level of authority to strategize and coordinate the crisis response – was also established. Vice-Premier Wu Yi was appointed the "commander" and Hua Jianmin, a state councilor and Secretary General of the State Council, became second-in-charge.[14] In late April, the fourth collective study session of the 16th CPC central committee (which had come into office only five months previously) focused on how science could combat SARS.

When the State Council convened its regular executive meeting in late April, there were already murmurs of moves to formalize emergency management as a governmental function based on principles that were later enshrined in the emergency response law, such as central command under one authority.[15] At the same time, the Ministry of Health and the Legislative Affairs Office of the State Council (LAO-SC) began to draft a new administrative regulation on public health emergencies.[16] The draft was ready for comments as early as April 24. In another two weeks, the State Council passed the regulation (*tufa gonggong weisheng shijian yingji tiaoli* 突发公共卫生事件应急条例).[17] In retrospect, this regulation marked the first administrative move in building the organizational field of emergency management.

The administrative regulation on public health emergencies stated that the State Council would establish the highest unified authority in crisis response for public health emergencies. The criteria to establish the authority were anticipatory rather than reactive: as long as there was a potential for severity and contagion in such sudden health incidents, even when the disease had not yet been identified, the protocol would be to set up a temporary headquarters at the State Council as soon as possible. The regulation also stipulated prompt information disclosure on health emergencies by government agencies, with failure to disclosure punishable according to law. This stipulation was a direct response to multiple instances when authorities did not update the central government in a timely manner regarding the critical nature of the SARS outbreak during the earlier stages of the crisis.

Two months later, Premier Wen presided over a special expert conference, exhorting attendees on the need to improve national emergency response and strengthen legislation. Similar rallying calls were made at the state SARS work conference in July. By then, the SARS outbreak had mostly been contained, albeit with significant human and economic costs. The epidemic killed 349 individuals out of 5,327 who were infected in China (World Health Organization 2004).

The state SARS work conference received high political signature, given that both Hu and Wen spoke at the event. They highlighted how the virus exploited the "misalignment" between national economic and social development, and between rural and urban regions. According to them, China succeeded in controlling SARS because of the close collaboration between the state and the public and the swift response according to rule of law. They announced that the government would devote the next three years to improving the national health crisis response system, especially in rural areas.

Steps to build an emergency management organizational field became more obvious during the latter part of 2003. At a State Council executive meeting in September, Premier Wen revealed the plan to improve and build a better health emergency response system. The Ministry of Health and the powerful National Development and Reform Commission (NDRC) were tasked to design the strategy. In November, a working group was created in the State Council to draft emergency response plans, supplemented by an advisory team of over 20 experts.[18] During the third plenum of the 16th Central Committee of the CPC in late 2003, Hu Jintao mentioned "emergency response" seven times, highlighting that the need for developing emergency management was gaining attention on policy and party agendas. In contrast, emergency response was not mentioned at all in the third plenum of the 15th committee.[19]

2004: the "one 'case' three mechanisms" framework

By July 2004, the strategy that turned the SARS crisis around and created the organizational field of emergency management was known as the "one 'case' and three mechanisms" (*yi'an san zhi* 一案三制) framework.[20] The "case" refers to the creation of emergency response plans across different levels of government, from the central to the local. It also includes the creation of emergency response plans within state and government-linked enterprises. The groundwork for that initiative had already begun: emergency response plans and planning processes would become the centerpiece of the framework that was used to build the organizational field of emergency management. The three "mechanisms" refer to the setting up of the emergency management offices, promulgating standard operating procedures (e.g., activation and mobilization of resources according to the severity of the emergencies), and enacting the umbrella legislation, the National Emergency Response Law. The workings and outcomes from the "case" become more apparent in 2005 and 2006, while those associated with the "three mechanisms" component of the framework become more obvious in 2006 and 2007 of the intense institutionalization period.

The pithy four-character phrase *yi'an san zhi* was purportedly coined by State Councilor Hua Jianmin[21] at a meeting on amending the draft State Master Plan for Emergency Response, which was attended by both government officials and academic experts.[22] As it becomes clearer later, the establishment could not have formed the field in such a short time if not for the close participation from the academic experts who advised the government officials and suggested ideas that later became entrenched as regulations, laws, and training frameworks.

2004 was also the year when the reforms on national emergency management started to move beyond agent-specific disaster planning, especially when the state was preoccupied with responding to the public health crises emanating from SARS. The most significant legislative event was the amendment of the Constitution of the People's Republic of China. There were several significant amendments, but perhaps the most important in terms of emergency management was the replacement of the term "martial law" (*jie-yan* 戒严) with the broader term "state of emergency" (*jinji zhuangtai* 紧急状态).[23] By expanding the coverage of scenarios that could threaten the Chinese state, this amendment paved the way for the National Emergency Response Law that would be enacted three years later. In May, the State Council issued guidance for two distinct target audiences on writing emergency response plans. One guiding document was directed at its subordinate bodies (e.g., the China Earthquake Administration), and the second was directed at provincial-level governments, including municipalities (e.g., Beijing) and autonomous regions (e.g., Tibet).

On the organizational front, entities were created to support the training, research, and advisory requirements of the still-forming emergency management field, which are also elements that build and provide the ideational resources needed for field development. The Ministry of Civil Affairs and the China National School of Administration jointly conducted a seven-day course for provincial-level officials in May 2004.[24] This was the first emergency management training session organized for such high-level officials. Efforts to develop the research capability to support emergency management were also initiated. In September 2004, the Beijing municipal government established the Center for Crisis Management Research (CCMR) in the School of Public Policy and Management of Tsinghua University.[25] The newly established crisis management research center offered academic research and training, as well as consulting in crisis management to the government.[26] The choice of Tsinghua University was not accidental: it is one of the first and most highly ranked tertiary education centers in China to establish public administration as a discipline.[27]

2005: releasing the state master plan for emergency response

Stories on emergency management were played up in the media, especially in terms of events at which academic experts played key advocacy and outreach roles. For example, the China Association for Disaster Prevention (CADP) organized *A Century of China's Disaster Prevention*, an event that was promoted by academic experts. In July, Premier Wen attended the first annual Emergency Management Conference, underscoring the four principles of governance that would be enshrined in the emergency response law, which was still in draft form at that point. Wen emphasized the importance of mitigation and preparedness using the Chinese proverb, *ju' an si wei* (居安思危), meaning one should still ponder about danger even when living in peace. The use of proverbs such as this one was not accidental: this was how the governing elites were tapping into a deep and intuitive resource that was available to them and other educated Chinese, including the academic experts, to present foreign ideas in culturally familiar terms so that these ideas could gain acceptance more rapidly. In Chapter 5, I will show how academic experts mobilized indigenous cultural knowledge as a conceptual heuristic to introduce new ideas that concerned risk and governance within academia and to the emergency management establishment.

In terms of administrative advancement, in 2005 the State Council passed the State Master Plan for Emergency Response (*Guojia Tufa Gonggong Shijian Zongti Yu'an* 国家突发公共事件总体预案). The state master plan was a key document for several reasons. Even though it was neither a law nor an administrative regulation, it was the first policy document to elaborate how China would conduct emergency management and what governments *should* do as part of their obligation to economic development and societal stability. The master plan could be seen as the base document that provided the content for the creation of the emergency response law passed two years later.

During his annual government report to the NPC in March 2005, Premier Wen emphasized industrial accidents – a sub-category that was considered an emergency in the state master plan – as a key focus and revealed that more than a hundred specialized emergency response plans were being drafted. The State Council and the State Central Military Commission jointly issued a new administrative regulation regarding the People Liberation Army's participation in disaster response and relief. The 1991 Flood Control administrative regulation was also revised in July, most significantly adding an article stating clearly the process for cross-administrative boundary approval for flood control plans for rivers that cross multiple administrative units. In October, the 11th Five-year Plan – a standing feature of centralized planning in communist states – was passed, and emergency management was highlighted. The Chinese state's 11th Five-year Plan (*Shiyi Wu Guihua* 十一五规划) covered a series of socioeconomic development and administrative reform initiatives by the Chinese state from 2006 to 2010, a highly visible government document that elaborated key policy agenda and their associated goals.[28]

On the organizational front, the State Council renamed the China International Committee for Disaster Reduction (CICDR) to the State Commission for Disaster Reduction (SCDR). This newly renamed unit carried a significant legacy. CICDR was originally the China International Decade for Natural Disaster Reduction Committee (CIDNDRC). Created in 1989, the CIDNDRC was part of the United Nation International Decade for Natural Disaster Reduction (UN IDNDR) initiative to establish national-level committees to implement its disaster reduction strategy.[29] When the UN IDNDR initiative was superseded by the International Strategy for Disaster Reduction (ISDR) in 2000, the CIDNDRC became the CICDR and emphasized drafting its own national disaster reduction strategy. Being an originally UN-led initiative, it was a landmark in the history of disaster management, especially in gathering attention from the Chinese governing elites.

Beyond its legacy, the SCDR's expanded political and administrative responsibilities also warrant attention: with the help of an expert committee, it would become the coordinating body for natural disaster management in the State Council. The SCDR was also granted power to strategize and coordinate efforts across different ministries and government units on matters concerning natural disaster, including international collaboration.[30]

2006: emergency management office established at the state council

The year was marked by a series of administrative and organizational advancements in emergency management. The Chinese state launched its online government portal on New Year's Day, with emergency management having its own conspicuous sidebar that announced it as a governmental function and an integral part of the mission to build "a harmonious society based on a scientific outlook," the most prominent political ideology of the Hu-Wen administration.[31]

Administratively, the State Council released the Master Plan for Emergency Response Plans (*Guojia Tufa Gonggong Shijian Zongti Yu'an* 国家突发公共事件总体预案) to the public via the online government portal on January 8. It was the authoritative document that directed all levels of government and administrative departments to create emergency response plans, but was also a foundational document because it contained the key ideas and language that would subsequently be reflected, almost verbatim, in the emergency response law. Over the next few months, the State Council successively released 14 emergency response plans covering forest fires, nuclear emergencies, earthquakes, floods, and environment disasters. The State Council Work Plan for the year highlighted emergency management as a priority, and the State Council was identified as the entity that would lead the government-wide effort to build it.

Two other significant administrative events took place in 2006. First, a collective study session for the PSC conducted in March chose to focus on industrial safety. Two prominent academic experts in emergency management were the lecturers for the session.[32] Such collective study sessions are not merely educational forums. A legacy of Mao's cadre study programs, the latter-day study sessions are venues used by the top political leadership to promote its ideologies and policies. The lecturers, typically academic experts, provide the theoretical basis to buttress specific perspectives that argue for the policies and strategies advocated by CPC leadership.

The next event was the second annual National Emergency Management conference, which was convened in July 2006 and emphasized the need to push forward reforms in emergency management, echoing a recent directive released by the State Council.[33] The plan to improve and build national emergency management capability during the 11th Five-year Plan period (2006–2010) was released by the State Council at the end of the year. The new plan released by the State Council included forest fires, sandstorms, and, more importantly, acknowledged lessons learned from the SARS crisis by specifying emergency response toward epidemics originating in terrestrial wildlife.

On the organizational front, two events were important in 2006. First, a new emergency management office (EMO-SC) in the General Office of the State Council was approved in April. Because the premier is the highest ranking official and the State Council is the ranking organization in the government in terms of both function and hierarchy, EMO-SC had the power to overcome the fragmentation issues that prevented swifter and more coordinated response in disasters. By law, the State Council had to be involved in emergencies that were escalated beyond a certain grade of severity, and it also controlled the state master plan for emergency response, which was the framework that all governmental and government-related organizations had to consult to make such plans.

Next, an expert committee attached to the emergency management office at State Council was officially announced at year's end. The committee, composed of 40 experts across several domains, most prominently included those who would be enshrined in the emergency response law come the following year: natural disasters, industrial accidents, public health emergencies, and public security emergencies. With the formation of this committee, the "systems" mechanism of the "one 'case' three mechanisms" framework was put in place.

Organizationally, in addition to the CCRM in Tsinghua University, another new research center on emergency management was established in one of the longstanding powerhouses in disaster management research. The Academy of Disaster Reduction and Emergency Management (ADREM) was inaugurated at Beijing Normal University (BNU) in late 2006. The ADREM can be seen as a conspicuous effort by the establishment to provide national level research support in emergency management: it was created with the authorization of the

Ministries of Civil Affairs and Education, and in accordance with various plans, included the National Disaster Reduction Plan put forth by the SCDR.

2007: enacting the national emergency response law

The year 2007 was an important landmark for the legislative component of the organizational field of emergency management. The umbrella law for emergency management, the Emergency Response Law, was passed in August by the NPC. Given its importance, I will describe it in detail.

Comprising seven chapters and 70 articles, the law took an "all-hazards approach" toward emergency management. It was all-encompassing, legally acknowledging what the United States and other Western countries consider the four phases in the disaster or hazard cycle: *mitigation* and *preparedness* prior to an emergency, and *response* and *recovery* after the onset of the event. Most important, the law also stated principles of governance based on unified leadership under the State Council, with it being the highest authority to integrate and coordinate inter-agency operations based on the category of emergency and its assessed grade of severity, while allowing the local government or the appropriate specialized agency to lead the emergency operations. Specifically, there are four grades of severity: Grade I (Severe), II (Serious), III (Major), and IV (Ordinary).[34]

The new law also highlighted the role of insurance, not only within the emergency management sector, but also for all work units (*danwei* 单位) and individual citizens. To implement this provision of the law, the state was to develop a national insurance industry, with a special emphasis on establishing a national insurance system to manage catastrophes. The law also meant that the state would need to establish an integrated risk assessment system at the national level and raise awareness of the risks posed by four officially recognized categories of emergencies:[35] natural disasters, accident-disasters,[36] public health emergencies, and public security emergencies.[37] Additionally, the law specified that the disaster plans had to be based on risk identification and assessments.[38]

The drafting of the law began in earnest in May 2003, only weeks after the SARS outbreak was recognized as a national crisis. Led by the State Council and involving Renmin and Tsinghua Universities (the two premier universities in public administration) as well as the Shanghai's municipal government, the law was developed over a four-year period. The draft went through several rounds of revision, taking into account advice from experts, local governments, and legislative committees at the NPC.[39]

On the administrative front, the State Council passed a new regulation in April requiring all levels of governments and their respective departments to improve information disclosure, including making emergency response plans and updates on early disaster warning publicly available. While the regulation did not directly regulate emergency management, it signified a significant change in the government mindset. In May, the State Councilor Hua Jianmin emphasized that emergency management needed to be closer to grassroots organizations. Soon after, the State Council issued a directive suggesting that its subordinate organizations and local governments needed to improve emergency management at the grass-roots level. In August, the same month the emergency response law was passed, the State Council also issued the new integrated disaster management plan based on the 11th Five-year Plan. In November, when the emergency response law officially came into effect, the State Council took another step to issue a reminder to its subordinate agencies and lower levels of governments that they had to take the implementation of the law seriously.

Organizationally, the State Council founded the journal *China Emergency Management* (*Zhongguo Yingji Guanli* "中国应急管理") in January. According to the press release issued by the State Council in February, the journal would promote theoretical research and practice-based interaction and exchange and disseminate information on and enhance awareness of emergency management. The banal press release announcing the journal's launch belied the significant ideational role *China Emergency Management* played in the development of the organizational field. This journal could be seen as the flagship journal of the field, as it disseminated all party-state messages and served as the platform from which members of the field could observe what was highlighted by the establishment. It also encouraged government officials from local governments, especially those who helmed the emergency management function, to contribute articles. Jun, an engineering expert in emergency planning and editorial team member of the journal, pointed out that government officials were enthusiastic to write for *China Emergency Management*.[40] Their articles gave them an avenue to showcase their achievements, which would hopefully gain the attention of their superiors, especially in Beijing. However, because the journal was less scholarly driven, academic experts were less enthusiastic about contributing articles. Not surprisingly, because it was not indexed as a research publication, academics were also reluctant to contribute new unpublished scholarly work to *China Emergency Management*. That said, many senior academic experts periodically contribute to the journal. As a clue to which discipline held stronger sway over its content, the Chinese Public Administration Society handled the day-to-day management of the journal, even though the publication was under the EMO-SC. This disciplinary emphasis will become clearer in Chapter 5 when I elaborate on the increasing acceptance of governance as an approach to government.

By the end of 2007, when the emergency response law came into effect, the government proclaimed that various initiatives to build the government's capability in emergency management had reaped benefits. For example, State Councilor Hua Jianmin highlighted in a news editorial that the death toll from natural disasters, accident-disasters, and public health emergencies was declining steadily.[41]

Conclusion

The new Hu-Wen regime learned to frame SARS not merely as an epidemic, but also as a revelation of the risks that attend a society in transition. One such "misalignments" cited as a source of SARS was the dissolution of the traditionally more collective and static society in favor of a more individualistic and mobile society that was slipping beyond the grip of party-government control, as pointed out by Zhuang in a quote I highlighted at the beginning of the chapter.

The SARS epidemic triggered a legitimacy crisis also because accounts of this event were highly contested and some directly challenged the legitimacy of the party-state during its sensitive period of political leadership transition. It directed intense domestic attention on issues concerning accountability that were also spawning adverse international publicity. The confluence of both domestic and international scrutiny drove institutional transformation (Hoffman and Ocasio 2001).

With the SARS crisis, the party-state seized the opportunity to review comprehensively its established organizational model and practices and to move toward "a risk-based, all-hazards integrated national system" (Xue and Zhong 2010:190). The government launched initiatives to centralize and standardize planning and operations and strengthen interagency coordination. Some analyses even hold that China's "modern" emergency management system only began after the SARS crisis (e.g., Bai 2009).

The organizational field of emergency management coalesced and developed rapidly immediately after the 2003 SARS outbreak. As a period of intense institutionalization, the establishment acted with a clear idea of how to develop emergency management as quickly as possible. The outcome was that critical legal, administrative, and organizational components of the organizational field were in place by the end of 2007. To illustrate, one of the key administrative components, the State Master Plan for Emergency Response, was passed in early 2005. By early April 2006, the first emergency management office was approved at the national level within the State Council. By the time the most important legislative component, the Emergency Response Law, was enacted in 2007, nationwide emergency planning was already implemented, and a national authority to coordinate and strategize emergency management was also being established.

Thus, as a focusing event (Birkland 2007), the SARS outbreak significantly modified the former fragmented patterns spread across disparate legislative, regulatory, and organizational spaces. As the organizational field developed, subsequent laws, administrative regulations, and organizational arrangements established substantial workarounds to fragmentation challenges. Over time, ideas that helped form these workarounds achieved a level of familiarity among members of the newly formed emergency management organizational field. In fact, the ideas that had guided the dramatic turnaround in 2003 were considered canonized as received wisdom by 2012.

Creating and establishing critical components of an organizational field is a necessary but insufficient condition for field formation. To ensure that the initial successes do not fade away, efforts are needed to further "harden" and consolidate them. In the next chapter, I discuss how the establishment, along with academic experts, further established the organizational field of emergency management.

Notes

1 *Danwei* can be translated as a work unit and refers to one's place of employment when China embraced more Soviet-style planning. Work units were part of the Communist Party of China (CPC) infrastructure. Each *danwei* was responsible for almost all basic services and infrastructure, from housing, child care, and schools, to clinics, shops, and post offices. The influence of work units on the lives of their members was pervasive. For example, members needed permission from their work units to travel, marry, and even have children. In many ways, the *danwei* system became a social institution in post-1949 China.

   However, with economic reform and the subsequent restructuring of the *danwei* vis-à-vis the rise and expansion of private enterprises, the system gradually lost its grip on the everyday lives of Chinese. Adapted from *Wikipedia*'s entry on work units: http://en.wikipedia.org/wiki/Work_unit. See also Chapter 7, specifically pp. 194–5, in Saich (2015).

2 Interview with Zhuang. Unless specified, names of my informants are pseudonyms. For details about fieldwork and my research methodology, please refer to the Appendix.

3 See for example Yang, Huating. 1992. "Guanyu woguo jianzai fangzhen he guanli tizhi de taolun (Discussion on the natural disaster reduction policy and management system in China)." *Ziran Zaihai Xuebao (Journal of Natural Disasters)* 1(1):19–27 and Jin, Lei. 1993. "Dui Zhongguo jianzai guanli gongzuo de sikao he jianyi (A reflection and suggestions for China's disaster reduction management work)." *Zaihai Xue (Journal of Catastrophology)* 8(4):94–6.

4 See Xue, Lan, Qiang Zhang and Kaibin Zhong. 2003. *Weiji Guanli: Zhuangxingqi Zhongguo Mianlin De Tiaozhan (Crisis Management in China: The Challenge of Transition)*. Beijing, China: Qinghua Daxue Chuban She.

5 The death toll for the 1976 Tangshan earthquake (Mw 7.8) is estimated to be between 240,000 and 655,000, more than four times that of the 2008 Wenchuan earthquake. The 1998 Yangtze River flood was one of the worst in recent Chinese history, resulting in about 3,000 dead, 15 million homeless, and direct economic loss amounting to about US$20 billion. See Reliefweb's. *Final Report on 1998 Floods in the People's Republic of China*. Retrieved from https://reliefweb.int/report/china/final-report-1998-floods-peoples-republic-china.

6 The administrative regulation in Chinese: 破坏性地震应急条例 (*Pohuaixing Dizhen Yingji Tiaoli*). The State Council passed the regulation on February 11, 1995.

7 See for example Yang, Huating. 1992. "Guanyu woguo jianzai fangzhen he guanli tizhi de taolun (Discussion on the natural disaster reduction policy and management system in China)." *Ziran Zaihai Xuebao (Journal of Natural Disasters)* 1(1):19–27, especially pp. 25–6.

8 The NPC is China's national legislature.

9 See Chapter 4 in Saich (2015), pp. 85–115, for the organization of the CPC.

10 For 2003 State Council's Government Report, see www.gov.cn/test/2006-02/16/content_201173.htm.

11 For details, see Fleck, Fiona. 2003. "How SARS changed the world in less than six months." *Bulletin of the World Health Organization* 81(8):625–6.

12 Ibid.

13 The Chinese term is *Zhongyang Zhengzhiju Changwu Weiyuanhui* (中央政治局常务委员会).

14 I retain the somewhat awkward translation to reflect the original militaristic flavor in its Chinese name: *Guowuyuan Fangzhi Feidianxing Feiyan Zhihuibu* (国务院防治非典型肺炎指挥部).

15 The State Council is China's de facto cabinet. The State Council is headed by the premier.

16 The now-defunct LAO-SC (*fazhiban* 法制办) assisted the premier by providing legal advice and drafting laws and administrative regulations that governed governmental departments (e.g., ministries). In this context, it was organizing the drafting of the administrative regulation on public health.

17 Administrative regulations are passed by the State Council and their legal power is weaker than that of laws passed by the NPC, China's national legislature. The regulations in theory reference the Constitution of the People's Republic of China and the corresponding laws that invest in them the legal power to direct and regulate the conduct of governmental units, including lower levels of governments (e.g., provincial and prefectural governments) and subordinate units under the State Council (e.g., ministries and commissions).

18 See for example Zhong, Kaibin. 2009. "Huigu yu qianzhan: Zhongguo yingji tixi jianshe (Constructing China's emergency management system: A review and its prospects)." *Zhengzhi Xue Yanjiu (CASS Journal of Political Science)* 1:78–88 and Shan, Chun Chang. 2011. *Yingji Guanli: Zhongguo Tese De Yunxing Moshi Yu Shijian (Emergency Management: The Operation Model and Practice with Chinese Characteristics)*. Beijing, China: Beijing Normal University Publishing Group.

19 The Hu-Wen regime formed the 16th and 17th CPC Central Committees from 2002 to 2012. The third plenum has over time been institutionalized as the meeting for key declarations in new policies or shifts in current policies by the new regime. This could be traced to the third plenum of the 11th Central Committee in which Deng Xiaoping proposed economic and social reforms that have reshaped China's political economy since the early 1980s. For details, see Saich (2015).

20 The phrase *yi'an san zhi* seemed to be first used at an expert conference *Disasters and Societal Management* organized by the China Democratic League (*Zhongguo Minzhu Tongmeng* 中国民主同盟) on July 3, 2004. It was also attended by CPC party cadres and the State Council working group on emergency response plans. Retrieved from www.dem-league.org.cn/mmyw/10174.aspx.

21 He was second-in-command at the temporary State Council SARS Prevention and Control Headquarters. As a senior government official, Hua was a key figure who played an instrumental role in advocating for and building the emergency management organizational field. In part he implemented several of the changes necessary for emergency management training because he was also the principal of the Chinese Academy of Governance (CAG), the national training center for middle- to senior-level government officials. The new National Institute of Emergency Management (NIEM) was established in the CAG in 2010. The CAG subsequently merged with CPC Central Party School in 2018.

22 Interview with Yin. Yin was a senior policy researcher-official in industrial safety.

23 However, media attention on inclusion of the acknowledgement and protection of human rights and citizens' right to private property into the constitution eclipsed that of the martial-law/state of emergency amendment.

24 The China National School of Administration was renamed the Chinese Academy of Governance in 2010. Interestingly, its Chinese name (*Guojia Xingzheng Xueyuan* 国家行政学院) was not changed.

25 Specifically, the CCMR in Tsinghua University was established with the support of the Beijing Planning Office of Philosophy and Social Science.

26 While its English name says crisis management, its Chinese name refers to emergency management: *Yingji Guanli Yanjiu Jidi* (应急管理研究基地), or literally Emergency Management Research Base in English.

27 As you will see later in this chapter and succeeding chapters, the university also played a critical role in the field development of emergency management.

28 The other five-year plan that was released during the Hu-Wen regime was the 12th Five-year Plan (*Shi'er Wu Guihua* 十二五规划) and it covered initiatives from 2011 to 2015. While the meaning of *guihua* (规划) gestures toward broader programmatic initiatives, and is closer to guidelines than to plans (*jihua* 计划), in essence the documents, especially the targets embedded in them, still remain more of the plans than either programs or guidelines. The Chinese state has adopted the phrase since the 11th Plan to signify its transition from rigid Soviet-style planning to guidelines that emphasize flexibility and its fledgling "socialist market economy." I acknowledge Saich (2011:105) for in addition to seeing them as guidelines, five-year plans can also be interpreted as programs.

29 For membership of the inaugural CIDNDRC, see p. 1 of issue 3, volume 3 of *Zaihai Xue (Journal of Catastrophology)*. The 1989 issue also contains speeches by the then-vice premier Tian Jiyun and minister for civil affairs Cui Naifu who were the chairman and vice-chairman of the committee respectively. See pp. 2–6. For historical development of the UN disaster reduction strategy, see www.undrr.org/about-undrr/history.

30 Several of my informants are either members of or are closely associated with the expert committee of the SCDR.

31 I elaborate on the scientific view on development in Chapter 5 as it is related to how academic experts mobilize this political ideology to build the organizational field of emergency management.

32 For details on collective study sessions, see for example Tsai, Wen-Hsuan and Nicola Dean. 2013. "The CCP's (Chinese communist party's) learning system: Through unification and regime adaptation." *The China Journal* 69:87–107.

33 The directive, *Suggestions on Comprehensively Strengthening Emergency Management Work* (*Guanyu quanmian jiaqiang yingji guanli gongzuo de yijian* 《关于全面加强应急管理工作的意见》), was released on June 15, 2006.

34 The actual terms in Chinese from Article 3 of the National Emergency Response Law are: *te-bie zhong-da* (特别重大), *zhong-da* (重大), *jiao-da* (较大), and *yi-ban* (一般). Their literal translation respectively is: Especially and Seriously Big (*da* literally means big), Seriously Big, Relatively Big, and Ordinary. There is no standardized English translation for the four grades. For example, Xue and Zhong (2010) translate them as Most Serious, Serious, Relatively Serious, and Ordinary. In another instance, the emergency management office of the Guangdong provincial government used Highest, Ultra High, Very High, and Normal. I follow the terminology in Chen and Tiehan (2008).

35 See National Emergency Response Law, Articles 5, 6, 20, 27, and 35.

36 The Chinese law included transport accidents on the road, in the air, and at sea in this category, therefore making such accidents the category with the highest number of casualties in any given year, notwithstanding the occurrence of catastrophic disasters, most likely from natural hazards (e.g., 2008 Wenchuan earthquake).

37 Some Chinese texts translate the fourth category *shehui anquan shijian* (社会安全事件) as social safety or social security emergencies, or as public security crises. This category of emergency covers terrorist attacks and what the Chinese euphemistically termed "mass incidents" (*quntixing shijian* 群体性事件), which refer to episodes of civil unrest and demonstrations, such as labor and environmental protests.

38 See Article 20 in National Emergency Response Law.

39 For example, in the third NPC review, advocates argued that ecological emergencies should be an independent fifth category. However, the suggestion was not adopted because ecological emergencies, as some argued, contained both

natural and man-made components, and allowing it to be a separate category would thereby conflate with the existing categories natural disasters and accident-disasters. See pp. 32–3 in Mo, Yu Chuan, ed. 2007. *Zhonghua Renmin Gonghe Guo Tufa Shijian Yingdui Fa Shiyi (Interpretation of People's Republic of China Emergency Response Law)*. Beijing, China: China Legal Publishing House.

40   Interview with Jun.

41   Hua, Jianmin. 2007, December 27. "Woguo yingji guanli gongzuo de jige wenti (Some issues concerning the efforts on national emergency management)." *People's Daily*, p. 6. Hua's article with amendments was also carried in the December 2007 issue of the *China Emergency Management* journal. It is a common practice in China that speeches, editorials, and articles by key government officials and political figures are published in multiple venues, with or without revision.

References

Bai, Victor. 2009. "Emergency Management in China." *Comparative Emergency Management: Understanding Disaster Policies, Organizations, and Initiatives from Around the World*. Retrieved from (http://training.fema.gov/EMIWeb/edu/Comparative%20 EM%20Book%20-%20Chapter%20-%20Emergency%20Management%20in%20 China.doc).

Birkland, Thomas A. 2007. *Lessons of Disaster: Policy Change after Catastrophic Events*. Washington, DC: Georgetown University Press.

Hoffman, Andrew J. and William Ocasio. 2001. "Not All Events Are Attended Equally: Toward a Middle-Range Theory of Industry Attention to External Events." *Organization Science* 12(4):414–34.

Saich, Tony. 2011. *Governance and Politics of China*. New York, NY: Palgrave Macmillan.

Saich, Tony. 2015. *Governance and Politics of China*. New York, NY: Palgrave Macmillan.

World Health Organization. 2004, "Summary of Probable Sars Cases with Onset of Illness from 1 November 2002 to 31 July 2003." Retrieved July 23, 2013, from (www.who.int/csr/sars/country/table2004_04_21/en/).

Xue, Lan and Kaibin Zhong. 2010. "Turning Danger (危) to Opportunities (机): Reconstructing China's National System for Emergency Management after 2003." Pp. 190–210 in *Learning from Catastrophes: Strategies for Reactions and Response*, edited by H. Kunreuther and M. Useem. Upper Saddle River, NJ: Pearson Education/Prentice Hall.

3   Consolidation and stabilization (2008–2012)

> The national emergency management system has basically been built.
> – Premier Wen Jiabao, 2008 Government Work Report[1]

2008–2009: momentum and consolidation

The year 2008 marked the beginning of the second five-year term of the Hu-Wen regime, a moment when most of the administration were either re-elected or re-appointed to the respective national party and legislative congresses. Riding on the momentum from its first term, the Hu-Wen regime continued to implement legislative, administrative, and organizational initiatives in emergency management. This series of achievements cemented the basic components of the organizational field, most significantly a national emergency management authority. On the ideational front, with the creation of a China chapter of an international professional emergency management association, efforts to formalize emergency management as an expert body of knowledge were becoming apparent.

2008: annus horribilis

Two prominent natural disasters in the first half of 2008 resulted in two of the worst calamities seen in recent years: the southern China winter storms and the Wenchuan earthquake. In between both disasters, the Hu-Wen regime began its second term in March, with one eye watching over the ongoing unrest in Tibet and the other looking toward the Olympic Games, which were slated for August.

The first major natural disaster was a series of winter storms in late January and early February; while the death toll was not large – about 110 people were killed – the storms were exceptionally disruptive because they coincided with "Spring Travel" (*chun yun*) for the Lunar New Year, which fell on February 7. The storms occurred when about 180 million Chinese were rushing to their hometowns to celebrate the most important traditional festival on its traditions calendar. To give an idea of the scale of this vast population movement: if the number of people who traveled for the Lunar New Year were a nation, it would have ranked as the sixth most populous country in the world. The snowstorms afflicted 20 of 34 provincial-level administrative units, resulting in direct economic losses of 150 billion yuan (about US$21 billion). The heavy snowfall hit provinces in southern China worse than those in the north because the former, having a warmer climate, were ill-prepared for cold or snow conditions. Some regions, like Jiangsu and Anhui, received their highest amount of snowfall in the past 50 years. Millions also lost heat and water. While most emergency processes were in place, there were still pressing issues. For example, while emergency response plans had already been created at the local level, they were not well integrated, due to the practice of developing specific plans for different kinds of disasters. This deficiency became most apparent when the snowstorms cascaded into widespread power failures, public transport paralysis, and price instability owing to agricultural product loss and logistical breakdowns.

The May 12 Wenchuan earthquake, which killed an estimated 70,000 people, was the other major disaster to occur that year. In addition to massive injuries and loss of life, the earthquake displaced more than 15 million people and affected three provinces, resulting in direct economic losses of approximately US$192 billion (Daniell 2013), making it one of the costliest earthquakes in recorded history.[2] The disaster also created the most significant administrative event in 2008. The State Council issued a new regulation on the recovery and reconstruction of Wenchuan County on June 8, less than a month after the earthquake. It was one of the fastest regulations to be proposed, discussed, and passed.

Despite criticisms regarding how the government managed the winter storm disasters and how the two extreme events had tested the nascent emergency management system, the establishment was sufficiently satisfied and confident of what the organizational field had achieved. In fact, as highlighted above, the newly re-appointed Premier Wen declared in his annual State Council report in March 2008 that the basic overall architecture for national emergency management had been established. The government, in other words, was claiming victory that the critical building blocks of the organizational field of emergency management had been laid, and emergency management should be regarded as an entity in its own right.

On the legislative front, the government passed in December 2008 the 1997 Law on Protecting Against and Mitigating Earthquake (*Fangzhen Jianzai Fa* 防 震减灾法), the revision of one of the legal cornerstones of earthquake disaster management. It was the only emergency management-related law that saw major revision during the formative years of the organizational field. The process to revise the law began in 2004, and its draft was already on the NPC agenda before the earthquake struck Wenchuan. However, as a consequence of the Wenchuan earthquake, the draft underwent further scrutiny and stimulated more consultation with more stakeholders across more levels, including the Ministry of Civil Affairs (which was responsible for post-disaster relief and recovery) and local governments. The law was finally submitted to the NPC in October.

On the organizational front, the State Council elaborated on the organizational structure of its general office, an administrative unit that assists its management in day-to-day operations, in July 2008, three months after the Hu-Wen leadership assumed its second term in office. In the same announcement, the State Council revealed it had formally established an emergency management office within its general office, two years after it announced the approval of this new organizational entity within its structure. The Emergency Management Office of the State Council (EMO-SC) would serve as the government's highest coordinating and decision-making authority on emergency management. It would also serve as the 24-hour duty office, which was initially staffed under another department in the general office. The State Council announcement also revealed that the staff strength of the general office had reached 519, more than doubling since the 1998 reforms.

2009

While the Chinese state did not pass new laws related to emergency management, the State Council issued its first white paper on China's disaster reduction strategy on May 11, the eve of the first anniversary of the Wenchuan earthquake. The white paper declared May 12 as the annual "National Disaster Prevention and Reduction Day" (*Guojia Fangzai Jianzai Ri* 国家防灾减灾日) not only to commemorate the devastating earthquake and recount past successes in disaster prevention and reduction, but also to publicize the ongoing strategy to improve national disaster management capability. In essence, the strategy references recent efforts, particularly under the "unified leadership" of the State Council, to enact plans, processes, and legislation pertaining to emergency management. The white paper was also a proclamation in which disaster management – including established arrangements in earthquake management and flood control since the pre-SARS era – was folded into the recently articulated national emergency management strategy.

With the basic infrastructure in place as proclaimed by Premier Wen in 2008, the government started to pay closer attention to specific aspects of emergency management, such as training and the capacities of subordinate levels of government. This shift in governmental focus can be seen on the administrative front with the EMO-SC-issued guidance on exercises and training released in September 2009. The announcement was performed by the EMO-SC – not the State Council, which the emergency management office belongs to as per previous announcements – also demonstrating the status of the new organizational entity as the authoritative national government body to strategize, direct, and coordinate the emergency management organizational field. In quick fashion, the State Council further released a directive to reiterate the importance of an integrated response and the building of emergency rescue teams at lower levels of government, especially townships, neighborhoods, and work units (*danwei*).

There was also a flurry of activities on the organizational front. The country's very first department to offer tertiary emergency management education was established at Jinan University of Guangdong province in April. Guangdong, being one of the leading provinces in economic reform, experienced more than its fair share of crises since the 1980s, especially during SARS outbreak, as well as industrial accidents and labor conflicts. The International Emergency Management Society (TIEMS) established its Chinese chapter in July 2009. The national committee for TIEMS China was comprised of a "who's who" in emergency management, including members of the EMO-SC expert committee. It was announced that China's first emergency management training base would be established in the Chinese Academy of Governance (CAG), a subordinate organization under the State Council, reporting specifically to EMO-SC.[3] The training base was established owing to two initiatives: it was an implementation of the 11th Five-year Plan to develop emergency management, and it was also part of a collaborative project on disaster risk management between the German government's Agency for Technical Cooperation (Deutsche Gesellschaft für Technische Zusammenarbeit GmbH, or GTZ) and the CAG.[4]

By the end of 2009, the establishment had made efforts to consolidate the emergency management organizational field by paying closer attention to issues that it could not have attended to during the intense development period. An existing earthquake law was amended with the new emergency response law in mind. A white paper was released to elaborate on the national disaster reduction strategy vis-à-vis emergency management strategy. Furthermore, ideational resources centering on emergency management were being codified and transmitted through new training programs and new organizational bodies that promoted emergency management practices as a recognized body of knowledge. These events and activities helped further consolidate the new organizational field. In the next section, I discuss how between 2010 and 2012 the establishment capitalized on achievements attained in the earlier years to stabilize the organizational field.

2010–2012: provisional stabilization

By 2012, the initiatives that turned the SARS crisis around and created the organizational field of emergency management known as the "one 'case' and three mechanisms" (*yi'an san zhi* 一案三制) framework, were widely accepted as the reason why the governmental function of emergency management could be created and consolidated so quickly. By 2012, the EMO-SC, one of the "three mechanisms," was also widely recognized and accepted as the highest national authority to determine and coordinate emergency management within government.

Going by the relative proportion of local governments that had started emergency planning and the absolute number of response plans compiled by that point in time, the various achievements bordered on the fantastical. According to Xue and Zhong (2010), all provincial governments, 98 percent of prefecture-level governments, and 93 percent of county-level governments had drafted their plans by March 2009. This is in addition to the plans created by 138 major state-owned enterprises and corporations concerned with mining and chemical operations. Moreover, 25 emergency-specific and 80 sector-specific plans were already in place at the state level by 2010.

In fact, no major law pertaining to emergency management was passed between 2010 and 2012. There were new administrative regulations on disaster relief but they applied mainly to governmental units. Even though two major disasters – the 2010 Yushu earthquake and the Zhouqu mudslide – tested the new organizational field, they did not lead to significant change because the appropriate emergency processes were by then operational, albeit with both major and minor problems during actual implementation. For example, because the 2010 Yushu earthquake occurred at an elevation about 3.7 km (12,000 feet) above sea level, some disaster rescue teams had to leave the disaster area prematurely, sometimes even immediately upon arrival, due to high altitude sickness.[5]

On the ideational front, however, the field witnessed a continual accumulation of a body of knowledge around emergency management and was marked by the formation of quasi-professional associations that formalized the relationship between experts and the government, especially at lower levels of government. The "quasi" qualification is important because even with associations, there is currently neither an emergency manager profession nor a distinctive, formalized emergency management career route of advancement that Chinese officials can follow. Emergency management as a profession is at best nominal in China's context.

2010

Two prominent natural disasters marked the year. An earthquake struck Yushu county in Qinghai province on April 14, killing close to 2,700 people and injuring more than 12,000.[6] About four months later, a mudslide killed more than 1,700 in Zhouqu county, Gansu province. Notwithstanding these events, the Chinese by 2010 had gained significant familiarity in activating various emergency response plans and working with the EMO-SC following established activation, mobilization, and reporting protocols. To illustrate, the Qinghai provincial government activated emergency plans for a Grade I emergency less than two hours after the April 14 earthquake, with the State Council establishing the national level coordinating headquarters four hours later. The preliminary assessment of the severity of the disaster, coupled with the political sensitivities around Yushu, a region populated mostly by ethnic Tibetans, resulted in a swift and conspicuous response from the central government.

While no legislative change took place in 2010, on the administrative front the State Council issued new administrative regulations on natural disaster relief, laying out principles and guidelines to standardize and regulate disaster relief work at all levels of government. It seems that, as the organizational field became more stabilized, there was less legislative and administrative activity but more effort devoted by the establishment to the organizational development of the field, particularly in training. On the organizational front, the first national training base at the CAG hosted 50 directors of emergency management and provincial-level academies of governance for a 24-day course in May 2010, emphasizing practice-based instruction. For the May course, instructors included officials who participated in the rescue operations following a Shanxi coal mine accident two months earlier. The training base was expected to be officially inaugurated only at the end of the year as the National Institute of Emergency Management (NIEM). It was designed to train 2,000 middle- and senior-level government officials annually.[7]

A day after the announcement of the training base, China hosted its first conference of The International Emergency Management Society (TIEMS). In addition to domestic participants, the conference was also attended by officials from several international organizations, such as the World Bank, United Nations Development Programme (UNDP), and the Asian Disaster Reduction Center. The conference was organized by the China Earthquake Administration, an organization under the direct charge of the State Council. In July, the first Chinese emergency management association was established in Guangdong by the emergency management office of the provincial government. Its inauguration ceremony was held at a conference on Chinese emergency management legislation in Guangzhou, the provincial capital of Guangdong.

In addition to Jinan University, Henan Polytechnic University and the University of Electronic Science and Technology of China also began to offer tertiary specialization in emergency management. This brought the total number of universities offering emergency management studies from one to three in a year.

2011

In June, the EMO-SC issued a directive to provincial-level governments,[8] subordinate units of the State Council, and the general offices of administrative units. This directive requested that they not only provide better support for experts in their research, especially on critical challenge in emergency management, but also utilize experts more proactively in decision making in that domain.[9] Another significant administrative event was the revision of the emergency response plan for disaster relief, which was released in November 2011. It referenced and adopted operational requirements stipulated in the 2007 emergency response law, such as the four severity grades for emergencies. The State Council also released the National Integrated Disaster Prevention and Reduction Strategy (2011–2015) as an update following the 12th Five-year Plan. The strategy highlighted climate change and rapid urbanization as some key considerations, and proposed efforts to strengthen emergency management in urban and rural areas, for example through developing disaster early warning systems, risk management methods, and training of rescue teams.[10] In addition, markets related to emergency management were highlighted as areas to be promoted and developed. The products and services on offer cover the entire gamut, from risk appraisal consultancies, to earthquake insurance, post-disaster psychological counseling, and emergency kits and other emergency management-related supplies and equipment.[11]

Organizationally, the newly formed NIEM's initial efforts to identify "best practices" from other emergency management systems around the world began in earnest in 2011.[12] For example, the NIEM sent representatives in May to the U.S. International Accreditation Service, an organization that also certifies fire prevention. The Chinese delegates were interested in best practices, procedures, and technology in the United States, which they saw as helping China improve its standards for emergency management.[13] In June, the Disaster Resilience Leadership Academy at Tulane University also hosted a delegation from NIEM. These foreign visits constituted the efforts by the emergency management establishments to be exposed to and borrow ideas and ideals from afar.

2012: the year of decadal political leadership transition

The most significant political event of the year was in November at the start of the once-in-a-decade leadership transition from the Hu (Jintao)-Wen (Jiabao) to the Xi (Jinping)-Li (Keqiang) regime. Perhaps as an indication that emergency management may have achieved a level of maturity such that it did not warrant continual public exhortation, the new leader Xi made no mention of emergency management while the outgoing party general secretary Hu Jintao emphasized the continual strengthening of emergency management during the CPC National Congress.[14] Similar to the political transition in 2002, Xi and Li had yet to assume formally the highest executive office of the country in 2012. In due time, they would be elected president and premier respectively when the NPC convened in Spring 2013.

On the whole, the emergency management organizational field did not see prominent shifts in 2012. On the legislative front, the National Emergency Response Law, the umbrella law for emergency management, which had been passed in 2007, had been under review for some time.[15] On the administrative front, the most significant event was the release on Christmas Day of the revised emergency response plan for forest fires. The revised forest fire emergency response plan, first published in early 2006, now conspicuously referenced the National Emergency Response Law, taking into account its principles and stipulations, and using the law as its template.

On the organizational front, Shaanxi province established the second emergency management association in China in April, about two years after Guangdong province. Similar to the Guangdong emergency management association, the Shaanxi association was identified as the forum for both academic experts and practitioners of emergency management to collaborate and improve the quality of emergency management in the province. In June 2012, the NIEM, which had been officially established in 2010, was also inaugurated as the Sino-EU emergency management training institute, with the goal of transferring best practices in disaster management from Europe to China.[16] In December, the campus and accommodation facilities for the NIEM at the CAG were officially opened. Covering slightly over 252,000 square feet,[17] it included state-of-the-art simulation facilities for an emergency operations center. NIEM would not only prepare provincial officials and mayors for the practice of emergency management, but also train emergency management instructors who would staff similar institutes of emergency management at provincial academies of governance.

Conclusion

Under efforts to consolidate and stabilize the organizational field of emergency management, there were no significant changes to the legislative, administrative, and organizational components of or tectonic shifts by the end of 2012. The umbrella National Emergency Response Law was passed five years earlier and already considered by the establishment to be due for revision or amendment. Older laws and existing regulations and plans related to emergency management were being updated and new ones were being created, using the emergency response law as the template. This produced a homogenizing effect, standard-izing the fundamental principles, categories of emergencies, and types and phases of activities that constitute emergency management.

By 2012, the EMO-SC had been operational for close to six years, with similar offices established at provincial and municipal seats of government. A plethora of organizational types – suppliers, regulatory bodies, consultants, schools – have come to define "a recognizable area of life" that is described as emer-gency management (DiMaggio and Powell 1983; Scott 2014). In addition to emerging markets focusing on emergency management, there were also expert committees, training centers, and a specialized journal, as well as national and provincial quasi-professional organizations designed to create and consolidate a body of knowledge on emergency management. The research and training centers not only infused new and old members with "value beyond the technical requirements of the task at hand" (Selznick 1996:271), but these knowledge-based organizations were the sites of theorizing for borrowing, creating, and disseminating ideas that would further entrench the field. Figure 3.1 provides a visual sense of the profile and intensity of the institutional change on an annual basis. Tables 3.1 to 3.3 capture the main changes in the legislative, administra-tive, and organizational elements of the new organizational field, with a focus on natural disasters.[18]

An organizational field of emergency management had been created from longstanding disaster-related policy and organizational domains. As an example, the "one 'case' three mechanisms" (*yi'an san zhi*) framework was by 2012 rec-ognized as the strategy that, in addition to building the organizational field leg-islatively, administratively, and organizationally, importantly forged a common identity around a domain called "emergency management." As Yin, the veteran researcher-official, explained to me during a conference break: "As we raised this concept (*yi'an san zhi*) at the beginning, slowly over time it became something that we can fundamentally identify with the emergency management system."[19] In other words, *yi'an san zhi* was creating a "mutual awareness of a common enterprise" that was emerging among field members (DiMaggio and Powell 1983:148), another marker of an organizational field.

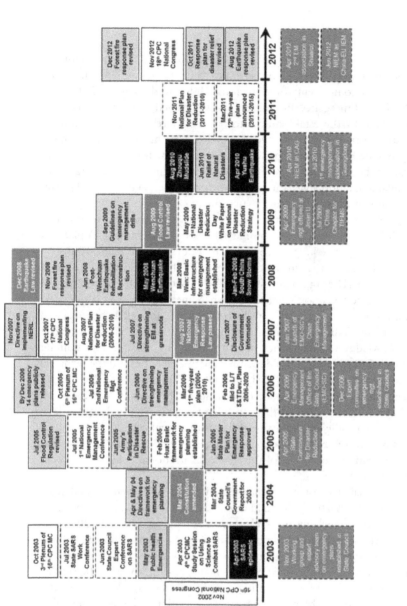

Figure 3.1 Main Events of the Emergency Management Field, 2003–2012

Note: Black text in black bordered boxes represent party events; white text in black boxes represent extreme events; black text in dotted boxes represent governmental events; white text in dark grey boxes stand for laws passed, revised, or amended; black text in light grey, bordered boxes stand for administrative events, such as regulations; white text in grey boxes with dotted lines represent organizational development, such as the creation of expert committees. EM is short for emergency management. (Organizational development was represented below the x-axis simply for visual simplicity.)

Table 3.1 Significant Change in Legislative Elements of the Emergency Management Organizational Field (Natural Disasters)

	2003	2007	2009	2012
Legislative (new laws in bold)	Water Law (2002)	**Constitution of the PRC (amended 2004)**	**Flood Control Law (revised 2009)**	Constitution of the PRC (amended 2004)
	Law on Desert Prevention and Transformation (2001)	**Emergency Response Law (2007)**	**Law on Protecting Against and Mitigating Earthquake Disasters (revised 2008)**	Emergency Response Law (2007)
	Interim Measures for Compensation for Utilization of Flood Detention Areas (2000)	Water Law (2002)	Constitution of the PRC (amended 2004)	Flood Control Law (revised 2009)
	Meteorology Law (1999)	Law on Desert Prevention and Transformation (2001)	Emergency Response Law (2007)	Law on Protecting Against and Mitigating Earthquake Disasters (revised 2008)
	Law on Donations for Public Welfare (1999)	Interim Measures for Compensation for Utilization of Flood Detention Areas (2000)	Water Law (2002)	Water Law (2002)
	The Forest Law (Amended 1998)	Meteorology Law (1999)	Law on Desert Prevention and Transformation (2001)	Law on Desert Prevention and Transformation (2001)
	Flood Control Law (1997)	Law on Donations for Public Welfare (1999)	Interim Measures for Compensation for Utilization of Flood Detention Areas (2000)	Interim Measures for Compensation for Utilization of Flood Detention Areas (2000)
	Law on Protecting Against and Mitigating Earthquake Disasters (1997)	The Forest Law (Amended 1998)	Meteorology Law (1999)	Meteorology Law (1999)
			Law on Donations for Public Welfare (1999)	Law on Donations for Public Welfare (1999)
			The Forest Law (Amended 1998)	The Forest Law (Amended 1998)

Table 3.2 Significant Change in Administrative Elements of the Emergency Management Organizational Field (Natural Disasters)

	2003	2007	2009	2012
Administrative (new regulation or plan in bold)	**Regulations** **Regulation on the Prevention and Control of Geologic Disasters (2003)** **Regulation on Public Health Emergency (2003)** Earthquake Rehabilitation and Reconstruction (1997) Regulation on Emergency Response for Destructive Earthquakes (1995) Regulation on Forest Pest Control (1989) Flood Control Regulation (1991) Regulations on Forest Fire Prevention (1988) **Plans*** NIL	**Regulations** **Regulation on the Disclosure of Government Information (2007)** **Flood Control Regulation (revised 2005)** **Regulation on the Army's Participation in Disaster Rescue (2005)** **Regulation on the Disclosure of Government Information (2007)** **Flood Control Regulation (revised 2005)** Regulation on the Prevention and Control of Geologic Disasters (2003) Regulation on Public Health Emergencies (2003) Earthquake Rehabilitation and Reconstruction (1997) Regulation on Emergency Response for Destructive Earthquakes (1995) Regulation on Forest Pest Control (1989)	**Regulations** **Regulations on Post-Wenchuan Earthquake Rehabilitation and Reconstruction (2008)** **Regulations on Forest Fire Prevention (revised 2008)** Regulation on the Disclosure of Government Information (2007) Flood Control Regulation (revised 2005) Regulation on the Army's Participation in Disaster Rescue (2005) Regulation on the Prevention and Control of Geologic Disasters (2003) Regulation on Public Health Emergencies (2003)	**Regulations** **Regulation on the Relief of Natural Disasters (2010)** Regulations on Post-Wenchuan Earthquake Rehabilitation and Reconstruction (2008) Regulations on Forest Fire Prevention (revised 2008) Regulation on the Disclosure of Government Information (2007) Flood Control Regulation (revised 2005) Regulation on the Army's Participation in Disaster Rescue (2005) Regulation on the Prevention and Control of Geologic Disasters (2003) Regulation on Public Health Emergencies (2003) Regulation on Emergency Response for Destructive Earthquakes (1995) Regulation on Forest Pest Control (1989)

Regulations on Forest Fire Prevention (1988)	Regulation on Emergency Response for Destructive Earthquakes (1995)	**Plans**
Plans	Regulation on Forest Pest Control (1989)	**National Earthquake Emergency Response Plan (revised 2012)**
State Master Plan for Emergency Response (2005)	**Plans**	**National Forest Fire Disaster Response Plan (revised 2012)**
National Flood Control and Drought Protection Plan (2006)	State Master Plan for Emergency Response (2005)	**National Emergency Response Plan for Disaster Relief (revised 2011)**
National Geologic Disasters Plans (2006)	National Flood Control and Drought Protection Emergency Response Plan (2006)	State Master Plan for Emergency Response (2005)
National Earthquake Plan (2006)	National Geologic Disasters Emergency Response Plans (2006)	National Flood Control and Drought Protection Emergency Response Plan (2006)
National Plan for Disaster Relief (2006)	National Earthquake Emergency Response Plan (2006)	National Geologic Disasters Emergency Response Plans (2006)
National Forest Fire Disaster (2006)	National Emergency Response Plan for Disaster Relief (2006)	
	National Forest Fire Disaster Response Plan (2006)	

Note: Translation was done mainly using www.lawinfochina.com. When its formal translation was not available, I translated the laws and regulations myself.

*There were some emergency response plans prior to 2003 (e.g., for earthquakes and floods) but they were fragmented and not available in the public domain. Several also did not further go by the title "emergency response plans".

Table 3.3 Significant Change in Organizational Elements of the Emergency Management Organizational Field (Natural Disasters)

	2003	2007	2009	2012
Organizational (New permanent organization in bold)	State Council working group on emergency response plans, supplemented by an expert advisory team (2003)	**China Emergency Management Journal (2007)** **State Council Expert Committee on Emergency Management (2006)** Joint Ministry of Civil Affairs and the China National School of Administration emergency management course for provincial-level officials (2004)	**School of Emergency Management (in School of Management), Jinan University (2009)** China Chapter for The International Emergency Management Society (2009) **Emergency Management Office of the State Council (2008)** *China Emergency Management Journal* (2007) State Council Expert Committee on Emergency Management (2006)	**Shaanxi Emergency Management Association (2012)** **National Institute of Emergency Management (2010)** **Guangdong Emergency Management Association (2010)** School of Emergency Management (in School of Management), Jinan University (2009) China Chapter for The International Emergency Management Society (2009) **Emergency Management Office of the State Council (2008)** *China Emergency Management Journal* (2007) State Council Expert Committee on Emergency Management (2006)

The emergency management establishment comprised selective members of the governing elites and academic experts who were invested in raising the profile of and entrenching emergency management in the national policy agenda. These efforts did not come about de novo, but relied upon established organized actors and individuals who were already advocates of, associated with, or exposed to crisis or disaster management. To give an example of a prominent official with such prior exposure, then-Premier Wen Jiabao who oversaw the State Council was no stranger to disaster management. A geologist by training, Wen held senior administrative and party positions concerning geological matters in provincial and state apparatuses before he assumed key appointments in the CPC and central government. As a first-term vice-premier, Wen helmed the disaster response efforts for the Yangtze River flood of 1998, and his leadership was severely tested during this event.[20]

Academic experts and their associated institutes (e.g., Tsinghua University) were also by no means fringe or peripheral actors marginalized by the state. Instead, on the eve of the SARS outbreak, they were already occupying niches requiring specialized knowledge in disaster and crisis management that could wield decisive influence over the governmental responses to the crisis. Seen this way, academic experts are "establishment intellectuals" (Hamrin and Cheek 1986): specialists with advanced training in both physical and social sciences who operate within "the governing institutions of the People's Republic (of China)" (p. 3). Even for new organizational entities, as long as they could boast a legacy in crisis or disaster management, they could also be networked into the establishment. What comes to mind is the newly renamed State Disaster Reduction Commission (SDRC) and its expert committees, with its organizational "imprints" (Stinchcombe 1965) that date back to the 1980s; not to mention the quasi-professional emergency management associations that were recently established regionally and had close ties with local emergency management offices and academic experts.

From the literature, recipes for organizational field formation include a combination of three critical actors in addition to "field events" (Edelman 1992; Schneiberg and Clemens 2006) or "critical junctures" (Collier and Collier 1991; Olson and Gawbronski 2003) that open windows for change. "Incumbents" are actors who exert disproportionate influence in a field. "Challengers" are occupants of less privileged niches in the field who can exert influence at opportune moments and "internal governance units" are charged with overseeing compliance within a field (Fligstein and McAdam 2012). The creation of Chinese emergency management therefore can be treated as an extreme case in which an organizational field was almost single-handedly created by incumbents in the broad institutional environment, who were embedded in (e.g., State Council) and also held the power to create internal governance units (e.g., EMO-SC), with no substantial challenge to their policy entrepreneurship.

The privileged positions occupied by members of the emergency management establishment in no way diminish the remarkable headway they made in forming the organizational field of emergency management. Indicative of this development is the establishment's bureaucratic achievements in laws and regulations: a total of 37 laws and 69 administrative regulations pertaining to emergency management were enacted by 2012.[21] This impressive legislative arsenal, which includes amendments to the Constitution itself, along with the creation of an all-encompassing umbrella law for emergency management, have to be put into the political and administrative context of Chinese reforms since the mid-1990s. The continual push toward instituting governance through the rule of law in the Chinese state suggests that both using laws and employing the legislative route to address issues defined as significant were by 2003 a readily available and legitimate solution to begin the task of creating the new emergency management organizational field. That said, "readily available" does not imply that the changes were implemented swiftly or smoothly. For example, the emergency response law, while passed in a relatively short time frame of four years, still underwent three reviews at the NPC and saw substantive rethinking and revisions that departed significantly from its original draft.

The State Council, playing multiple critical roles as the regulatory agency (Greenwood, Suddaby and Hinings 2002), peak organization (Barley 2010), and command post (Zald and Lounsbury 2010) in constructing the emergency management field, experimented with ideas underlying strategic principles that create and organize the field, its legal and administrative wording, its organizational constituents, and other elements of emergency management policy within the context of the security afforded by its legal power. To elaborate, by forming the EMO-SC, working groups, and expert committees, as well as using administrative regulations to produce emergency management-related directives and guidance documents, the State Council avoided the NPC, a higher authority, and protracted legislative processes that often accompanied the policy process in China. These moves by the State Council catalyzed field formation, which is probably why the field formed so quickly.

However, the situation of an organizational field being constituted administratively (i.e., through the State Master Plan and its component plans, directives, planning guidance, and expert committees) before the legislative components were in place – especially its signature emergency response law – created a specific challenge for the establishment. Because both the emergency response law and the revision of the law on earthquakes referenced or were adapted heavily from administrative documents, this prompted criticisms that the administrative elements of the field were moving ahead of the legislative function, contradicting the spirit of rule by law, which had been a prevailing ideological thrust since the 1990s.[22]

Five to six years after the SARS crisis, and with the organizational field entering some provisional form of consolidation and stability from 2009, there seemed to be a move toward canonizing the body of knowledge as "expert" and "professional" knowledge, further entrenching the field. What specific ideas were being canonized and what strategies were employed by the establishment to legitimize them? These questions are critical, because for emergency management to be accepted as a distinctive governmental function, the establishment needed to go beyond claims based on pragmatic legitimacy (the needs the new field served) and draw upon moral and cognitive legitimization schema (i.e., what is right, valued, and meaningful). I will explain how this was accomplished in the next part of this book.

Notes

1 People's Republic of China. 2008, March 5. *Government Work Report*. Retrieved from www.gov.cn/test/2009-03/16/content_1260198.htm.

2 To offer some comparison, the world's costliest earthquake is the Great Tohuku (Japan) earthquake in March 2011. Direct economic losses from the event total an estimated US$244 billion, slightly more than the entire GDP of Israel in 2012.

3 The CAG (*Guojia Xingzheng Xueyuan* 国家行政学院), located in the Chinese capital Beijing, is the national training center for middle- to senior-level government officials. It merged with the CPC Central Party School in 2018.

4 See, for example, www.giz.de/en/downloads/cn-Katastrophenrisikomanagement. pdf. Retrieved October 8, 2013.

5 See for example, the 2012 report by the Qinghai Provincial Academy of Governance: *Yushu Dizhen: Yingji Chuzhi yu Jiuyuan Jieduan Gongzuo Pinggu Baogao (Yushu Earthquake: Assessment Report of Emergency Response and Recovery Work)*. Xining: Qinghai People's Publishing House.

6 The earthquake registered a magnitude of 6.9 Mw (U.S. Geological Survey) or 7.1 Ms (China Earthquake Administration).

7 Retrieved September 6, 2013, from www.nsa.gov.cn/web/a/yingjiguanliz hongxin/20120906/894.html.

8 Provincial-level governments include not only governments of provinces, but also those of municipalities and autonomous regions.

9 国务院应急管理办公室, 应急办函(2011)14号,关于印发《应急管理专家组2011 年工作要点》的通知 (EMO-SC, EMO Letter [2011] No. 14, Notice on the Distribution of *Main Points for 2011 Emergency Management Expert Teams*).

10 For details, see the document released by the State Council on November 26, 2011. Retrieved December 20, 2013, from www.gov.cn/ zwgk/2011-12/08/content_ 2015178.html.

11 The prospects of promoting and developing products and services concerning emergency management were widely publicized. See for example Shan, Chun Chang. 2011. "Dali fazhan yingji chanye (Vigorously promoting emergency management industries)." *Zhongguo Yingji Guanli (China Emergency Management)* 3:17; Online interview with Gao Xiaoping on emergency management conducted on September 26, 2012. The transcript is available at http://news.sina.com. cn/c/2012-09-26/132625257663.shtml. Gao was the chief editor for *China Emergency Management*, Executive Vice-Chairman cum Secretary-General of the Chinese Public Administration Society, and also Vice-Chairman of the Chinese Political Science Society.

12 Another similar initiative is funded through the United States Agency for International Development's Office of U.S. Foreign Disaster Assistance (USAID/ OFDA). Project activities include curriculum development; training programs for senior government officials and operational officials involved in disaster management; carrying out research; and providing policy recommendations. For details, see http://asiafoundation.org/news/2010/07/asia-foundation-and-chinese-academy-of-governance-sign-agreement-to-cooperate-on-disaster-leadership-management-and-coordination-project/.

13 About the visit to the International Accreditation Service funded by the U.S. Trade and Development Agency (USTDA), see: www.iasonline.org/More/2011/ ChineseDelegation.html. Retrieved October 14, 2011.

14 At the third plenum of the new 18th Central Committee in November 2013, there was also no mention of emergency management or emergency response, resembling the pre-SARS status quo. Emergency management was no longer a conspicuous item on the policy agenda. Interviews and correspondence with informants, such as Yin and Tian support this observation.

15 This observation was initially based on my interviews with Yang and Guan separately. However, it is not clear from the interviews whether the review was in the consultation phase with experts or that it had been proposed at the National People's Congress. Subsequently, I found out that as early as late May 2008 and less than a month after the Wenchuan earthquake, Wu Bang-guo, Chairman of the NPC Standing Committee (who was ranked second after the General Secretary, Hu Jintao, in the Politburo Standing Committee of the CPC Central Committee) raised the idea of revising the emergency response law. Immediately following the March 2011 Tohuku earthquake, the idea of revising the emergency response law to improve natural disaster response was raised again at a seminar organized by the Legislative Affairs Commission of the NPC Standing Committee (not to be confused with the similarly named group within the State Council) in the same month. An EMO-SC directive that was publicly released on June 16, 2011 gave more conclusive evidence that reviewing the emergency response law was either formally explored or in process.

16 It is a common feature in the Chinese context for the same body of personnel to assume two organizational titles. For example, the State Archives Administration is also the CPC Archives Administration. The fusing of the political, administrative, and executive is even more conspicuous at the highest level of government. For example, the CPC Central Military Commission is also the State Military Commission. The NIEM/Sino-EU emergency management institute scenario, however, is uncommon, as it is not a coupling between governmental and CPC (party) organizations.

17 To provide some context on its size, the campus and residential area combined are slightly bigger than four American football fields.

18 Adapted from Chinese Emergency Management microsite at www.gov.cn, Shan (2011), and Shan et al. (2012).

19 Interview with Yin.

20 Interview with Gui. I checked Wen's official biography and searched for related news articles on his involvement during the 1998 Yangtze River flood. These documents seemed to corroborate Gui's account of Wen's trials and tribulations during the 1998 Yangtze River flood. See for example http://news.sina.com. cn/c/2013-11-01/095328592555.shtml.

21 See pp. 369–71 in Shan et al. (2012).

22 Guan, a public administration researcher, made the same observation, but argued that the circumstances then compelled expediency to be the most important consideration so that operational units (e.g., local governments, hospitals) could respond swiftly to the emerging SARS crisis. From interview with Guan.

References

Barley, Stephen R. 2010. "Building an Institutional Field to Corral a Government: A Case to Set an Agenda for Organization Studies." *Organization Studies* 31(6):777–805.

Chen, Fujin and Tiehan Tang. 2008. *Public Crisis Management in China*. Beijing, China: Foreign Languages Press.

Collier, Ruth Berins and David Collier. 1991. *Shaping the Political Arena: Critical Junctures, the Labor Movement, and Regime Dynamics in Latin America.* Princeton, NJ: Princeton University Press.

Daniell, James. 2013. "Sichuan 2008: A Disaster on an Immense Scale." Retrieved from (http://www.bbc.co.uk/news/science-environment-22398684).

DiMaggio, Paul J. and Walter W. Powell. 1983. "The Iron Cage Revisited: Institutional Isomorphism and Collective Rationality in Organizational Fields." *American Sociological Review* 48(2):147–60.

Edelman, Lauren. 1992. "Legal Ambiguity and Symbolic Structures: Organizational Mediation of Civil Rights Law." *American Journal of Sociology* 97(6):1531–76.

Fligstein, Neil and Doug McAdam. 2012. *A Theory of Fields.* New York, NY: Oxford University Press.

Greenwood, Royston, Roy Suddaby and C. R. Hinings. 2002. "Theorizing Change: The Role of Professional Associations in the Transformation of Institutionalized Fields." *Academy of Management Journal* 45(1):58–80.

Hamrin, Carol Lee and Timothy Cheek, eds. 1986. *China's Establishment Intellectuals.* Armonk, NY: M. E. Sharpe.

Olson, Richard Stuart and Vincent T. Gawbronski. 2003. "Disasters as Critical Junctures? Managua, Nicaragua 1972 and Mexico City 1985." *International Journal of Mass Emergencies and Disasters* 21(1):5–36.

Schneiberg, Marc and Elisabeth S. Clemens. 2006. "The Typical Tools for the Job: Research Strategies in Institutional Analysis." *Sociological Theory* 24(3):195–227.

Scott, W. Richard. 2014. *Institutions and Organizations: Ideas, Interests, and Identities.* Los Angeles, CA: Sage Publications.

Selznick, Philip. 1996. "Institutionalism: 'Old' and 'New'." *Administrative Science Quarterly* 41(2):270–7.

Shan, Chun Chang. 2011. *Yingji Guanli: Zhongguo Tese De Yunxing Moshi Yu Shijian (Emergency Management: The Operation Model and Practice with Chinese Characteristics).* Beijing, China: Beijing Normal University Publishing Group.

Shan, Chun Chang, Lan Xue, Xiu Lan Zhang and Hui Ding, eds. 2012. *Zhongguo Yingji Guanli Dashi Ji (2003–2007) (Memorabilia of China's Emergency Management).* Beijing, China: Shehui Wenxian Kexue Chuban She.

Stinchcombe, Arthur L. 1965. "Social Structure and Organizations." Pp. 142–93 in *Handbook of Organizations,* edited by James G. March. Chicago, IL: Rand McNally.

Xue, Lan and Kaibin Zhong. 2010. "Turning Danger (危) to Opportunities (机): Reconstructing China's National System for Emergency Management after 2003." Pp. 190–210 in *Learning from Catastrophes: Strategies for Reactions and Response,* edited by H. Kunreuther and M. Useem. Upper Saddle River, NJ: Pearson Education/Prentice Hall.

Zald, Mayer N. and Michael Lounsbury. 2010. "The Wizards of Oz: Towards an Institutional Approach to Elites, Expertise and Command Posts." *Organization Studies* 31(7):963–96.

4 Risk governance as a framework for emergency management

This chapter discusses the risk governance framework that academic experts created in the wake of the 2003 SARS crisis that provided the main ideational resources enabling the establishment to build the new organizational field. "Risk governance framework" is a term that I derived inductively from analysis to organize the ideas associated with risk and governance that were consequential to the creation of the emergency management field.

This chapter proceeds as follows. First, I will discuss the development of the risk governance framework, detailing the domestic and imported scholarly bodies of knowledge that academic experts from the establishment relied upon to construct the notion of risk governance. I highlight the growing preoccupation by Chinese governing elites with the notions of governance and risks put forth by the academic experts to preface my discussion on the popularity of risk governance as a concept. Next, I highlight the emergence of an indigenous risk governance framework that emphasized emergency management. By placing emergency management at the heart of the indigenized risk governance framework, the establishment created the ideational basis to insert and entrench emergency management in the national policy agenda.

The development of risk governance as a framework

Within the context of natural disasters, the risk governance framework is informed by three main bodies of knowledge. The first body of knowledge refers to risk as a theoretical concept to characterize the likelihood of disasters. Treating disasters as reflections of risks is an outgrowth of the disaster risk reduction movement advocated by the United Nations from the late 1990s and is also influenced by sociologist Ulrich Beck's concept of the "risk society," which has reached Chinese shores from Germany.

The second body of knowledge relates to governance and reflects a growing emphasis on governance – particularly the notion of "good governance" (*shan zhi* 善治) – by the Chinese research community focusing on government and public administration. The rising concern with governance coincides with China's entry into the World Trade Organization in 2001, when the Chinese state-driven economy became increasingly subject to international laws and market-oriented regulations, and also with the growing acceptance of corporate governance among Chinese state-owned enterprises.

The third body of knowledge concerns the concept of "risk governance," which originated in European-based risk research circles and gained traction among the Chinese academic community around 2005. The European "risk governance" model provided an opportune and much-welcome theoretical basis and the moral legitimacy conferred by a region of the world that is perceived by the Chinese as more "scientific" and advanced in research.

Without the prior introduction of concepts such as disaster risk reduction and risk society, along with rising concerns about governance since the late 1990s, as well as focusing events (Birkland 1998) such as the 9/11 terrorist attacks and the 2003 SARS outbreak, Chinese academic experts might not have felt the requisite urgency and impetus to build their own risk governance framework that in retrospect provided the ideational basis for the emergency management field.

The rise of the concept of risk and "risk society"

Chinese academic experts, especially those in natural disaster research, did not intuitively view the occurrence of natural disasters in terms of risks. To see natural disasters as risks is an acquired mentality, with the socialization beginning in the late 1990s, when the idea of "disaster risk reduction" was introduced into China at the advent of the United Nations' International Strategy for Disaster Reduction (UNISDR). The key Chinese organization that introduced this idea to natural disaster academic experts was the China International Committee for Disaster Reduction (CICDR),[1] which was established in 2000.[2] The diffusion of the UN disaster risk reduction concept also relied upon the advocacy of the China Association for Disaster Prevention (CADP, see Chapter 2) and disaster research publications such as *Ziran Zaihai Xuebao*(《自然灾害学报》 *Journal of Natural Disasters*) and *Zhongguo Jianzai*(《中国减灾》 *Disaster Reduction in China*). An environment that championed a disaster risk approach encouraged Chinese natural disaster researchers to graduate from a disaster reduction to a disaster *risk* reduction perspective.[3]

The trajectory of the ideational and organizational genesis of the emergency management field closely resembled the developments of the CADP and disaster-related publications, in which specialized associations (e.g., TIEMS China chapter) and publications (e.g., *China Emergency Management*) played key roles in knowledge production and dissemination. By the late 2000s, official strategies on managing natural disasters included clear risk reduction language. As an example, the 2009 White Paper on Disaster Prevention and Reduction shows that the influence of risk and the international imprint of the IDNDR were palpable:[4]

> As natural disasters pose a common challenge to mankind, disaster reduction is a global effort. China will continue to work unremittingly to reduce the risks and damage posed by natural disasters together with the rest of the world for the development and progress of human society.

> (p. 16)

The focus on risks and disaster risk reduction in China during the late 1990s also led Chinese academic experts to take interest in and accept German sociologist Ulrich Beck's notion of risk society. A concept popularized in the 1990s, "risk society" is an attempt to characterize the emergence, production, and predominance of risks that threaten society (Beck 1999; Luhmann 2005). It emphasizes the perils that are outgrowths of societal progress driven by advancements in science and technology. These perils turn societies into natural laboratories of dangerous experiments, which then lack the means to limit the destructive consequences of science and technology. The iconic disasters that led Beck to construct a society of risks were the mad cow disease scare and the Chernobyl nuclear plant disaster. These were occurrences that featured predominantly in the European continent. Not surprising, natural disasters that were less prevalent within that geography – such as earthquakes and typhoons in the Chinese context – were absent in the risk society narrative. However, such absence did not seem to deter or diminish Chinese interests in the risk society view. In fact, Beck's conceptualization of a risk society was not just accommodated but enthusiastically embraced by the Chinese research communities across several domains, from social sciences to natural disasters and public administration. Beck visited China and conducted substantial dialogue with Chinese scholars which resulted in expositions on the relevance of risk society to China.[5] In a prominent annual risk management report, the risk society concept was hailed to be "the most appropriate technical term to describe the characteristics of modern society".[6] And in another emergency management article, Chinese academics also regarded risk society to be not only at the cutting edge, but also one of the best explanatory terms in Western social science research on disasters and hazards.[7] Chi, a disaster social scientist, explained how risk society is applicable to China, particularly in the wake of the SARS crisis:

> At least to me, it's the first time I realized that China most likely is beginning to confront the challenges of modern risks. And China is also most likely already caught up in the waves of risks associated with globalization, as risk societies are being spread around the world. The research organization I work in began to be aware that risks are something worth researching. Why? This is especially because of what Beck mentioned in [his book] *Risk Society*, that the emergence of a risk society is closely associated with technological development. It is a reflexive risk. . . . During and after SARS, we realized that several risks in modern society emanated from science and technology themselves. In the process of resolving risks, they also produced them in great quantity. And such risks are endogenous. . . . And we feel the need to emphasize this nature of risk in the context of technological development, and we need to bring this perspective to decision makers, so as to offer them a means, another concept to think about (technological development).[8]

As Chi explained, Beck's "risk society" concept gained traction because it gave the Chinese the vocabulary to discuss and reflect upon the threats that come with development, especially the dangers associated with modernization and technological progress. China's entry into the WTO in 2001 and its increasing integration with the global political economy also made the Chinese particularly sensitive toward the risks emanating from modernization and progress. The initial confusion around the SARS outbreak, especially the government's inability to identify the virus and respond effectively to the contagion, further threw into even sharper relief the perils of a Chinese society that was experiencing drastic and dramatic transition. It is against this backdrop that the Europe-based integrated risk governance framework found an audience in China that was already primed and readied to accept the framework as a solution to an increasingly menacing risk society. At the same time, while Chinese academics familiarized themselves with the concepts of disaster risk reduction and risk society, the notion of governance was also gaining their attention.

The rise of the concept of governance

The transition toward a governance-centric ideational frame can be understood broadly as a global shift which began in the early 1990s from activities undertaken *by government* to more comprehensive activities *of governance* (see for example Hutter 2006). Governance, as opposed to governmental action, entails collective decision-making structures and processes of interaction among government and non-government actors (Nye and Donahue 2000). In developed countries such as the United States, governance has evolved toward increased participation by non-governmental and market actors; for example, we see this trend in the environmental sector (Cashore 2002), in the evolution of emergency management (Roberts 2010; Sylves 2008), and in the privatization of risk through insurance (Calhoun 2006).

The emergence of governance as an umbrella term was also animated by a need to aptly describe the attempts at regulation and control by both state and non-state actors (e.g., nonprofit organizations and for-profit corporations). As a result, scholars observe a deliberate maneuver of vocabulary to reflect the shift from specific acts *by the government* (i.e., the state) to a more strategically ambivalent term which reflects acts *of governance* (Hutter 2006). While governance as a form of control refers to decision-making structures and processes shared by state and non-state actors (Nye and Donahue 2000), the shift of power has moved precipitously toward the latter, particularly the private or business sector. Research also seems to corroborate the "hollowing out of the state" thesis (Roberts 2010), in which the provision of public services is transferred from governments to private firms. The main arguments for "hollowing out of the state" concern efficiency and effectiveness: private firms are argued to be more nimble and cost-effective than government agencies in providing services to the public (Rhodes 1994). While profit and nonprofit sectors enjoy the benefits of new governmental contracts, the state bears the less quantifiable but no less consequential costs of such transfers because civil servants lose discretion and the state itself also sees its authority being eroded (Milward and Provan 2000; Rhodes 1994). To be sure, the "hollowing out of the state," or the de-centering of the state trend as observed by Hutter (2006), is not unique to developed nations; for example, the power of central governments has been devolved to state and local governments in some developing nations in Asia (e.g., Indonesia in Phelps et al. 2013).

China's turn toward governance came about in the early 1990s for several reasons. First and foremost, the party-state was at the point of searching for ways to reconfigure the role of government vis-à-vis its emphasis on a market-driven economy. Second, policy terms such as "good governance" and "civil society" were introduced to Chinese governing elites for the first time through the policy-focused texts of the World Bank and international non-government organizations when these entities expanded their influence and operations in China (Jeffreys and Sigley 2009). Third, as Chinese social sciences (e.g., political science, sociology, and economics) were reinvigorated by the party-state after a long hiatus since the 1960s, Chinese academics also started to become familiar with governance and other approaches to government. Interest in understanding governance was further accelerated by more returning students and scholars from the West and by Chinese social scientists eager to develop connections with the international academic community (Bray 2009).

Chinese public administration experts attempted to insert emergency management into the broader concerns of governance in the practice of governing, especially during the field formation period of the organizational field. They argued that emergency management should be incorporated as a component of "good governance" (*shan zhi* 善治).[9] Good governance, in the Chinese context, refers to the use of laws and regulation, administration, and the market, among other avenues to engender harmonious governance of society. The goal of a "harmonious society" was also a recurrent theme in banner terms.[10] Given its emphasis on preempting, preparing for, and responding to disasters and crises, emergency management could be framed as a means to maintain and develop a harmonious Chinese society.

Interestingly, while qualities such as accountability, transparency in exercising the power of government, the rule of law, and having a competent and credible judiciary were held up as criterion for "good governance," even within Asia (Shimomura 2003), they were rarely highlighted or discussed in the context of Chinese discussion on linking emergency management to governance. More importantly, even though the Chinese have embraced the idea of governance, it remains to be seen whether the governance approach can improve development in a more general sense (Shimomura 2003) or within the disaster domain (Tierney 2012).

Even though Chinese governing elites were beginning to be concerned with the risks of modernization and to accept the merits of understanding government using a governance lens, since the late 1990s, the utility and relevance of perceiving risks through a governance approach was still not obvious to them, much less sought after. In the next section, I discuss the rise of the concept of "risk governance," specifically the version of the concept propagated by the International Risk Governance Council (IRGC). The IRGC integrated risk governance framework was also the framework that featured prominently among Chinese academic experts in natural disaster management and public administration since its advent in the mid-2000s, not too long after the 2003 SARS crisis.

IRGC's "risk governance" framework

The "risk governance" framework was initially proposed by the International Risk Governance Council (IRGC) in Europe (Renn 2008; Renn and Walker 2008). It is a process-oriented framework that spans the entire risk process, including risk identification, assessment, management, and communication.[11] In other words, it is designed to be a comprehensive framework that comprises all components of the risk process under the term "risk governance." It also attempts to be all-inclusive by considering main stakeholders in a pluralistic society, from governmental bodies and economic players to scientists and non-profit organizations in civil society (Renn 2008). Risk governance is therefore most applicable in situations where there is no single authority to anchor decisions on risk (Aven and Renn 2012). It also builds on a nested model of risk perception, for example, from information-processing heuristics (closest to risk perceptions) and sociopolitical institutions to broader cultural backgrounds (Renn 2008). Interestingly, while the governance approach contends that political culture, especially how governments make decisions regarding risk, shape policy implementation, the framework seems to have exorcised the politics of dealing with and talking about risks (Jasanoff 1990; Jasanoff 2010). As a result, it casts "risk governance" as a rational and administrative process that is largely unproblematic.

The IRGC "risk governance" framework recognizes that the risk process is influenced by broader social forces and incorporates these forces in its analytic process. It is also a prescriptive framework that is entrenched in an interventionist view, reflecting the applied emphasis that has dominated the domain of risk research. This applied emphasis could be why the framework has appealed to the Chinese establishment, which was looking for a means to guide the building of the organizational field of emergency management.

The advocates and pioneers of the IRGC "risk governance" framework have crafted it with "key actors in politics and society and those in transition" in mind, especially when "many of these countries are only now starting to formally think about issues of risk governance and IRGC's providing them with relevant information and knowledge could provide valuable insights and, possibly, help them to avoid some of the pitfalls inherent in dealing with risk" (Renn and Graham 2006:18). In another instance, Renn and Walker (2008) have also clearly indicated that the intended audience for the framework is "senior risk managers and decision makers, as well as risk practitioners" (p. 4), as evidenced by practitioners (e.g., the Head of Group Risk and Compliance from Insurance Australia Group) penned forewords, complementing the utility and timeliness of the framework in the publication.

The conspicuously applied nature of the framework and its genesis coincided with the Chinese interest in ways to better manage emergencies and crises in the wake of the SARS outbreak. In addition, as the Chinese became familiar with and accepting of risk and governance separately, it is not surprising that the combined notion of "risk governance" gained prominence in China within a short period of time. In the next section, I discuss the rise of the IRGC framework in China.

The trajectory of IRGC "risk governance" framework in China

The risk governance framework debuted in China around 2005, about the same time when IRGC published its first white paper on the framework (see for example, Renn and Graham 2006). The IRGC annual conference, which was held in Beijing in late September 2005, received considerable attention from governing elites and academic experts. The timing was impeccable. The recent 2003 SARS crisis, the subsequent preoccupation with threats from domestic emergencies on the part of governing elites, and massive efforts by the emergency management establishment in building a new organizational field meant that a concept that joined risk and governance would be one that the party-state and academic experts could take seriously in the existing sociopolitical environment. The event was well-attended by international and Chinese officials (e.g., Secretary-General of the OECD, the Chinese Minister for Science and Technology), as well as academics (e.g., Ortwin Renn, a prominent advocate for the framework) from around the world. "Risk governance" was promoted as a means to manage the "world risk society" (Beck 1999) – an idea which by the mid-2000s was already familiar to the establishment – and for sustainable development. Within the context of the framework, governments were urged to improve their risk management capability, particularly in the areas of climate change, critical infrastructure, public health, and natural hazards.[12] The concept was also well-received because of its European origins: Europe being a region of the world that is perceived by the Chinese as more "scientific" and advanced in research, "risk governance" confers immediate moral legitimacy when applied to the Chinese context.[13]

Since around 2005, Chinese researchers in the natural disaster realm had been promoting the IRGC "risk governance" framework as a credible source for bringing about a more indigenous framework that would accommodate China's context, meet the needs of the party-state, improve the government's risk management capability, and ensure public security. For example, in his review of the multiple frameworks that China could refer to in building its own framework, Huang highlighted IRGC's framework as a conceptual model that represented a management-centric approach.[14]

The Chinese have mobilized the framework less as an analytic tool, and more as an argument for a comprehensive approach to disaster risk. For example, as Huang explained, there are two ways to engender an integrated approach toward risk management. One would be to consider relationships among different natural hazards, especially their combined and cascading effects on society. Second, the focus could be on one single natural hazard. While Huang favored the former as an integrated risk approach, most Chinese researchers seem more likely to consider both approaches, especially how to come up with ways to mobilize and utilize resources more efficiently toward singular disaster risks, as well as risks that emanate from cascading effects when multiple hazards occur either sequentially or simultaneously.

The natural disaster community's attention to risk governance as a framework seems to have stemmed more from its preoccupation with gaining a more comprehensive understanding of risks and their interrelationships than from concerns about governance. This is evident in the word they use for governance in Chinese, which is *guanli* (管理) rather than *zhili* (治理). Broadly speaking, "governance" tends to connote a more strategic, pluralistic, and inclusive approach and that typically involves multiple parties, within and across organizations; "management," on the other hand, tends to portray a more operational or tactical, restrictive, and authority-based approach, typically within an organization (see for example Tierney 2012). Seen that way, management could be subsumed under the rubric of governance.

However, the natural disaster research community seems to have either conflated management and governance, or perhaps considered the precise English translation as less material; for example, we saw earlier how Huang describes the IRGC framework as a management-centric one. Another piece of evidence that demonstrates the fuzzy definitional boundaries between governance and management in disaster research is a series of annual reports on risk governance supported by the Chinese insurance sector. The Chinese title for all the reports uses the term "*fengxian guanli*" ("risk management"), while its English translation uses "risk governance".[15] When speaking with San, a government official with postdoctoral qualifications, it seemed that Chinese disaster managers on the ground displayed considerable variability in their definitions of governance vis-à-vis management. In San's case, governance was subsumed under management:

> I believe that risk management already incorporates risk governance. . . . Management is a big concept. Governance is a component of management. . . . Management is a box, and everything can be loaded into it. Everything is considered under the realm of management, no?[16]

The cavalier-like attitude of San toward a precise reading of governance resembles social scientist Chi's understanding of *zhi* (治) and *li* (理) – the separate characters that when conjoint gives the Chinese phrase for governance (*zhi-li* 治理) – in that the essence of governance and management is about control and extracting obedience from subjects, and the differences between them are inconsequential. As Chi put it across rather colorfully, using his analogy of the tightening bolts and nuts of "defiant machines":

> Whether you talk about governance (*zhi-li*), or . . . The thing about *zhi* (治), in China, it means to fix you. In Chinese culture when one talks about to render *zhi* onto you, it means to fix you. . . . To fix you means to *zhi* you. For example, this kid, let's say this kid who is not obedient . . . I need to fix him. I need to fix you (meaning the kid). And fixing you twice will make you obedient. In essence it's a kind of power, and through that power, it can make you obey. Therefore, you need to fix, to repair (*xiu li* 修理) whoever. As for *li*, to "*xiu li* you" means to treat you like a machine. Say, you're a machine that doesn't work as I have commanded, so I'll have to tighten some of your screws, and loosen others, and to repair you, so that ultimately you will obediently work according to my wishes. So this entire thing about governance (*zhi li*), most likely, at least for many of those who manage, whether you call

it governance or you call it management, to them, it's all too much the same thing.[17]

Contrast this with academics from the public administration tradition who were also interested in the IRGC risk governance framework: while their Chinese translation of governance also vacillated between management and governance, there existed at least a consensus that governance as a concept is poly-centered and requires the close coordination of multiple parties. This understanding seems to be more in line with the general definition of governance vis-à-vis management and even government.[18] It seems for public administration academics, their interest in integrated risk management, while qualitatively no less than that of natural disaster researchers, was also tempered by their more nuanced understanding of what constituted governance. However, while the IRGC framework remained, Chinese academic experts were also creating their own risk governance framework, as I elaborate in the next section.

Setting the checkpoint earlier: an indigenized risk governance framework

As I pointed out in the previous chapter, the definition of emergency management is not universal across different academic traditions. To elaborate, natural disaster academics take the more literal meaning of *yingji guanli* (应急管理), in which *yingji* means emergency response.[19] In contrast, while being aware of its literal meaning, academics from the public administration tradition (including those investigating industrial accidents) take it to represent the full spectrum of an emergency management cycle, from mitigation and preparedness before the onset of the emergency to response and recovery in its aftermath.[20,21] It seems that the more comprehensive definition of emergency management espoused by the public administration academics was the one that took root. By 2007, Chinese public administration academics had produced a framework that would incorporate components of risks, emergencies, and crises. It is also important to note that the emergence of the framework coincided with the rapid institutionalization and consolidation of the emergency management organizational field between 2003 and 2007. The contemporaneous emergence of a framework and a field lends support to my argument that developments in these two areas were closely intertwined in a process of co-production.

By mobilizing the idea of *guankou qianyi* (关口前移), which literally means to shift the checkpoint earlier, Chinese academic experts argued that in order to manage emergencies more effectively, more attention needed to be devoted to dealing with risks. Furthermore, in articulating how to deal with emergencies as they unfolded in time, the academics proposed to juxtapose crisis management with emergency management. Under the ambit of public safety and security management (*gonggong an-quan guanli* 公共安全管理),[22] the Chinese also constructed a process-based framework that not only covered the entire emergency cycle, using the vocabulary of "professional" emergency management, but equally important, incorporated the various definitions that characterized unexpected events that would putatively threaten societal peace and stability. Figure 4.1 gives the diagrammatic representation of the framework. The reason I give prominence to risk, rather than emergency or crisis, is because the notion of *guankou qianyi* emphasizes the anticipatory work that has to be performed in order to reduce the probability of risks manifesting into unexpected events that could subsequently cascade into crises.[23]

How is it that a "public safety and security" framework exists alongside "risk governance"? I surmise that the choice to frame "risk governance" as concerning public safety and security was strategic, specifically to garner resource and legitimacy from governing elites. This is because the National Program for Long- and Medium-Term Science and Technological Development had subsumed capability and capacity building for emergency management under Public Safety and Security, a newly coined domain that was listed among the 20 domains to be developed at the national level from 2006 to 2020.[24] This maneuver also ensured that the framework would continue to exert influence in the building of the emergency management organization field, especially in the provisional stabilization phase when there was a greater demand for producing and propagating a body of knowledge associated with emergency management.

Notwithstanding the poly-centric nature of governance, the government in the Chinese context would still be the body that would dictate emergency management efforts (*zhengfu zhudao* 政府主导). As one State Council document states, the ideal normative governance arrangement in emergency management would be one that was "led by the government, well-coordinated within government units, with the military and local governments, as well as the participation of the entire society."[25] Despite its emphasis on multi-party participation, in practice the government does not use the term "stakeholder" to address other parties. Academics, too, while favoring and imagining a more participatory mode of governance, could not envision that any alternative governance arrangement could be realized any time soon. As Bai, a political scientist, points out:

> Theoretically speaking, governance should be a process through which a government [not only] shares power with, [but also] returns it to society. At the same time, governance also involves the government, the market, and also charitable components of society. The relationship is that of equal partnership, right? Equal partnership. However, in China, because it's a government-led society, it is quite impossible that it follows the Western model.[26]

Zu, a public policy academic, also highlights the governmental emphasis in Chinese society during emergency response:

> In China, let's talk about a concept, a mental model that people have about emergency response. The first thing most likely many people think about is not what I should be doing. . . . The first thought that crosses [an individual's] mind is, "oh, what should the government be doing?" That's his first

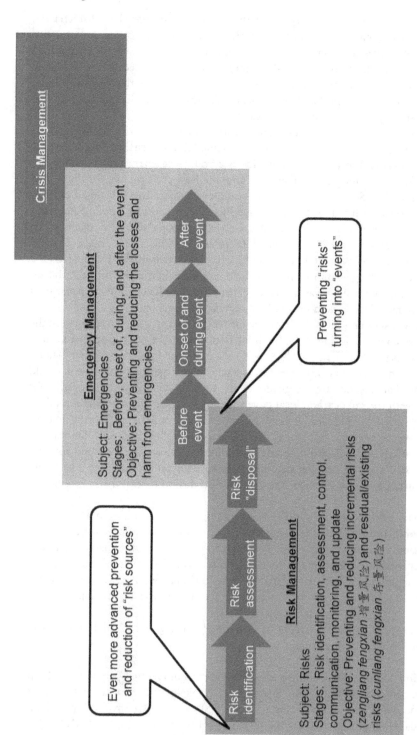

Figure 4.1 Conceptual Risk Governance Framework Comprising Risk, Emergency, and Crisis

Source: Translated and adapted from Shan and Xue (2012, Figure 1–1, p. 30), Xue, Zhou and Zhu (2008, Figure 1, p. 8), and Xue and Zhou (2007, Figure 2, p. 14).

thought. You can say that he's too dependent on the government for emergency management. His first thoughts are not what personal responsibilities I should shoulder for emergency management. Under these conditions, it's very tough to break this tradition. To completely borrow the Western model to here is simply impossible. Absolutely impossible.[27]

Bai's and Zu's comments reveal the central and taken-for-granted position that state intervention occupies in disaster management. The strict application of governance as it is defined in Western research circles, specifically how a government can engage other organized actors as its equals, is inconceivable to my informants to such a degree that they could not offer any cogent explanations (despite my probing) other than reiterating that such an arrangement would be "impossible" in the Chinese cultural milieu. In other words, my informants generally accept that the party-state has the cognitive legitimacy to be involved in disaster management, without requiring further rationalization from the authorities. In neoinstitutional terms, what has been revealed is the cultural-cognitive quality (Scott 2014), or taken-for-grantedness, associated with the role of government in Chinese society.[28]

In addition to the cognitive legitimacy accorded to the party-state, the risk governance framework also relies upon the pragmatic legitimacy afforded by the science of governance, in which "good governance" leads to a harmonious society. That said, the practical merits of the framework, while necessary, are not sufficient; we need to pay attention to who was championing the framework. Specifically, the framework was created and advocated by academic experts, the bona fide producers of specialized knowledge on risk, disasters, and crises (Ainsworth and Hardy 2012). Given the prestige and authority of scholars and scholarship in Chinese society, the framework was a beneficiary of the blend of moral and cognitive legitimacies that were granted by both the governing elites and pioneers of the establishment to the academic experts, albeit in a self-serving way, especially during the intensive field formation period. I consider that moral and cognitive legitimacies are jointly at work owing to the long-held acceptance within Chinese society of intellectuals schooled in Confucian ethics and the classics, who have populated the ranks of bureaucracy since imperial days. The expectation is that intellectuals of ability and character should serve the government to improve the livelihood of subjects.

The indigenized risk governance framework that the emergency management establishment supported in terms of principles also seems to depart significantly from its IRGC reference point. Incompatible components in the "original" IRGC variant seem to simply disappear in the Chinese version, specifically, the "principles of 'good' governance" inherent in the framework that are highlighted in the IRGC white paper on "risk governance," which include "the crucial commitment to participation" and "transparency, effectiveness and efficiency, [and] accountability" (Renn and Graham 2006:12). That said, it is also clear that the proponents of the IRGC framework have intended "risk governance" to be an agnostic platform that could accommodate how China or other countries might practice "risk governance" differently from its original conceptualization.

Admittedly, the Chinese risk governance framework does retain a shade of the "shared power" quality in governance: it acknowledges the involvement of multiple parties, although less as stakeholders or equal partners, and the mix of parties is unique, given the extent of major attention and status accorded to the military. Most nation-states refrain from giving a conspicuous role to the military in domestic emergencies unless a state of emergency has been declared. Furthermore, while the framework includes the public, businesses, and non-profit organizations, and the government is slowly coming to accept a limited government model, it will still continue to be the main body, providing "leadership and guidance" (*zhudao* 主导) in matters concerning emergency management.

Recalling how the academic-official San characterized the idea of management as a box and Chi observed that the nuances between management and governance are immaterial to managers, we begin to discern a particular modus operandi with respect to how Chinese import foreign concepts such as "risk governance." First, the Chinese jettison the ideational content in foreign concepts that they find meaningless or are ambivalent about (e.g., transparency and accountability). By doing so, the residual ideational content in the conceptual artifact will meet the purposes the leadership is advocating (e.g., multi-party involvement). Finally, the Chinese also fill the conceptual vessel with elements that further support their purposes (e.g., building a harmonious society). The result is a concept that is outwardly intelligible to an audience familiar with its Western form, but inwardly it has undergone the purposeful acts of "curation" so that it also appeals to another audience from whom its curators need support.

As a result, the Chinese emergency management establishment bucked the trend of shifting government into governance. It folded governance into government while allowing the concept of governance to remain in name. The Chinese treatment of governance therefore challenges both the decentralization of government patterns observed elsewhere in Asia (Phelps et al. 2013) and the "hollowing out of the state" thesis (Roberts 2010). Instead of a "hollowing out" effect, the indigenized risk governance framework in the Chinese context supports tacitly the notion that the party-state remains as the ultimate legitimate manager of risk, at least within the domain of emergency management.

This example of curation is congruent with what political scientists have observed about how Chinese governing elites adapted foreign ideas as their own for their objectives (Tsai and Dean 2013):

> [R]ather than simply borrowing and imitating concepts from abroad, the [Chinese Communist] Party draws out relevant ideas and incorporates its own influences, often creating new concepts which are akin to their Western counterparts in name alone. . . . [The Chinese Communist Party (CCP)] is able to pick and choose those concepts which are most useful to its own modernizing aims.
>
> (p. 89)

As highlighted earlier, independent of the merits of the risk governance framework, the emergency management establishment needed to present the framework in forms and within contexts that would be familiar to its target audiences – prospective and new members of the new organizational field of emergency management, as well as broader networks of governing elites. Members of the establishment would have to rely upon accounts based on the scripts and schemas that constituted the cultural context in which they and their target audiences were embedded.

In the next chapter, I elaborate on the culturally accepted accounts the establishment used to legitimize the framework and its attendant methodologies and techniques. As my discussion will show, the accounts that the establishment mobilized to support their version of risk governance framework were also used for justifying state intervention in disasters and other emergencies and constructing the emergency management organizational field. In practice, accounts were weaved organically with discussion on the framework and deliberations about the organizational field in the interviews, texts, and conversations.

Notes

1 From Chapter 2, the CICDR was an evolution from the United Nation International Decade for Natural Disaster Reduction (UN IDNDR) initiative to establish national-level committees to implement its disaster reduction strategy. CICDR became SCDR in 2005.
2 Interview with Yang; other sources include, for example, Shi, Peijun. 2005. "Jianzai yu kechixu fazhan moshi – Cong di'erci Shijie Jianzai Dahui kan Zhongguo jianzai zhanlue de tiaozheng (Disaster reduction and sustainable development: Adjustment of disaster reduction strategies of China based on the 2nd World conference on disaster reduction)." *Ziran Zaihai Xuebao (Journal of Natural Disasters)* 14(3):1–7; Shi, Peijun. 2008. "Zhiding guojia zonghe jianzai zhanlue Tigao juzai fengxian fangfan nengli (Establishing national integrated disaster reduction strategy improving catastrophe risk governance capacity)." *Ziran Zaihai Xuebao (Journal of Natural Disasters)* 17(1):1–8.
3 See for example how the genesis of the journal explicitly referred to UN IDNDR. Xie, Li-li. 1992. "Fa kan ci (Message for first issue)." *Ziran Zaihai Xuebao (Journal of Natural Disasters)* 1(1):2–3. Xie was the first chief editor of the journal. Frank Press, Chairman of the U.S. Research Council also sent a congratulatory note to Xie. See same/inaugural issue, p. 4. Press was also credited as being one of the pioneers for the IDNDR initiative in the Chinese translation (see p. 5 of inaugural issue).
4 The white paper was can be found at *China's Actions for Disaster Prevention and Reduction* as published in *Beijing Review*, 20:1–16. Another example of an official document which showed discernible risk-related language on disaster reduction is the 2007 National "11th Five-year" Integrated Disaster Reduction Strategy Plan.
5 See, for example, Beck, Ulrich, Zhenglai Deng and Guolin Shen. 2010. "Fengxian shehui yu Zhongguo (Risk society and China)." *Shehui Xue Yanjiu (Sociological Research)* 5:208–46.
6 Page 11 in Shi, Peijun et al. 2007. "Zonghe zaihai fengxian guanli yanjiu (Research on integrated risk governance)." Pp. 10–22 in Wu, Dingfu, ed. *Zhongguo Fengxian Guanli Baogao (China Risk Governance Report)*. Beijing, China: Zhongguo Caizheng Jingji Chuban She.

7   Page 15 in Zhong, Kaibin and Xing Tong. 2009. "Zaihai shehui kexue: Yizhong xueke zhenghe de keneng – Gainian, kuangjia yu fangfa (Disaster/Hazard social science: An interdisciplinary possibility: Concepts, framework, and methods)." *Zhongguo Yingji Guanli (China Emergency Management)* 1:15–20.
8   Interview with Chi.
9   Xue, Lan. 2007. "Cong geng jichu de cengmian tuidong yingjiguanli (To promote emergency management at an even more fundamental level)." *Zhongguo Yingji Guanli (China Emergency Management)* 1:17–19.
10 More on banner terms in Chapter 5.
11 See for example, Figure 1 (p. 7) in Aven and Renn (2012), originally from Renn and Graham (2006, Figure 5, p. 65).
12 See Hu, Yang. 2005. "Guoji fengxian guanli lishihui (IRGC) 2005 nian Beijing nianhui zongxu (Summary of the international risk governance council 2005 annual conference in Beijing)." *Ruan Kexue Dongtai (News in Soft Science)* 10:157–60.
13 See for example Shi, Peijun et al. 2007. "Zonghe zaihai fengxian guanli yanjiu (Research on integrated risk governance)." Pp. 10–22 in Wu, Dingfu, ed. *Zhongguo Fengxian Guanli Baogao (China Risk Governance Report)*. Beijing, China: Zhongguo Caizheng Jingji Chuban She, and Zhong, Kaibin. 2007. "Fengxian guanli yanjiu: Lishi yu xianzhuang (Risk management research: Its history and current status)." *Zhongguo Yingji Guanli (China Emergency Management)* 11:20–5. I also gathered this impression of Chinese preference for European and U.S.-based concepts and methodologies from my interviews and observations of conferences and seminars.
14 Huang, Chongfu. 2005. "Zonghe Fengxian Guanli De Tixing Jiagou (A trapezoid framework for integrated risk management)." *Journal of Natural Disasters* 14(6):8–14.
15 See for example Wu, Dingfu, ed. 2007. *Zhongguo Fengxian Guanli Baogao (China Risk Governance Report)*. Beijing, China: Zhongguo Caizheng Jingji Chuban She. The English translation is found on the cover of the report. It becomes even more confusing when risk governance has three translations in the book (see pp. 12–13): *fengxian guanzhi* (can be translated as "risk control"), *fengxian jianguan* (can be translated as "risk supervision" or "risk regulation"), and *fengxian zhili* (which is literally "risk governance").
16 Interview with San. The quote is way more colorful in Mandarin, as the phrase "Management is a box, and everything can be loaded into it" almost sounds like a ditty, "*Guanli shi yi ge kuang, shenme dou keyi wang jin zhuang.*"
17 Interview with Chi.
18 See for example Zhong, Kaibin. 2007. "Fengxian guanli yanjiu: Lishi yu xianzhuang (Risk management research: Its history and current status)." *Zhongguo Yingji Guanli (China Emergency Management)* 11:20–5.
19 For example, from interview with Ai.
20 Shan et al. (2012), Wang (2007).
21 To be precise, how the Chinese categorize the various stages does not correspond neatly with the mitigation, preparedness, response, and recovery stages, unlike the professional emergency management "nomenclature" in the United States. The Chinese categorized the phases in the following way. Before the emergency: (1) prevention and preparedness (*yufang and zhunbei* 预防与准备), (2) monitoring and early warning (*jiance yu yujing* 检测与预警). After the onset of emergency, they are (3) emergency response and rescue (*yingjichuzhi yu jiuyuan* 应急处置与救援) and (4) recovery and reconstruction (*huifu yu chongjian* 恢复与重建). See for example Wang (2007).

I am grateful to Tian, a public policy scholar, who pointed out to me that the precise translation for mitigation is not *yufang*, which is prevention, but *jianhuan* (减缓), which means to reduce and minimize.

22 *An-quan* (安全) could mean either safety or security, depending on the context. I choose not to privilege either and include both of them in my analysis.

23 See Xue, Zhou and Zhu (2008).

24 The period 2006–2020 has political significance too. China aimed to quadruple its GDP per capita from US$800 in 2000 to about US$3,000 by 2020.

25 From State Council Document (2006) No. 24, *Guowuyuan guanyu quanmian jiaqiang yingji guanli gongzuo de yijian* (国务院关于全面加强应急管理工作的意见). It was released on May 15, 2006.

26 Interview with Bai.

27 Interview with Zu.

28 I would like to acknowledge Lizardo's (2010) astute methodological advice to be attentive to what informants consider as "senseless," "meaningless," or "unworkable" as a window into what ideas, norms, and practices are taken for granted (i.e., cognitively legitimate), in this case in the Chinese context. I elaborate Lizardo's criterion for observing cultural-cognitive elements in the Appendix.

References

Ainsworth, Susan and Cynthia Hardy. 2012. "Subjects of Inquiry: Statistics, Stories, and the Production of Knowledge." *Organization Studies* 33(12):1693–714. doi: 10.1177/0170840612457616.

Aven, Terje and Ortwin Renn. 2012. "On the Risk Management and Risk Governance of Petroleum Operations in the Barents Sea Area." *Risk Analysis*. doi: 10.1111/j.1539-6924.2011.01777.x.

Beck, Ulrich. 1999. *World Risk Society*. Cambridge, UK: Polity Press.

Birkland, Thomas A. 1998. "Focusing Events, Mobilization, and Agenda Setting." *Journal of Public Policy* 18(1):53–74.

Bray, David. 2009. "Building 'Community': New Strategies of Governance in Urban China." Pp. 88–106 in *China's Governmentalities: Governing Change, Changing Government*, edited by E. Jeffreys. Abingdon, Oxon: Routledge.

Calhoun, Craig. 2006. "The Privatization of Risk." *Public Culture* 18(2):257–63.

Cashore, Benjamin. 2002. "Legitimacy and the Privatization of Environmental Governance How Non-State Market-Driven (Nsmd) Governance Systems Gain Rule-Making Authority." *Governance: An International Journal of Policy, Administration, and Institution* 15(4):503–29.

Hutter, Bridget M. 2006. "Risk, Regulation, and Management." Pp. 202–27 in *Risk in Social Science*, edited by P. Taylor-Gooby and J. O. Zinn. New York, NY: Oxford University Press.

Jasanoff, Sheila. 1990. "American Exceptionalism and the Political Acknowledgment of Risk." *Daedalus* 119(4):61–81.

Jasanoff, Sheila. 2010. "Beyond Calculation: A Democratic Response to Risk." Pp. 14–40 in *Disaster and the Politics of Intervention: The Privatization of Risk*, edited by A. Lakoff. New York, NY: Columbia University Press.

Jeffreys, Elaine and Gary Sigley. 2009. "Governmentality, Governance and China." Pp. 1–23 in *China's Governmentalities: Governing Change, Changing Government*, edited by E. Jeffreys. Abingdon, Oxon: Routledge.

Lizardo, Omar. 2010. "The Problem of the Cultural Determination of Cognition in Institutional Theory." *Culture* 24(2):1, 7, 9, 11.

Luhmann, Niklas. 2005. "The Concept of Risk." Pp. 1–31 in *Risk: A Sociological Theory*. New Brunswick, NJ: Transaction Publishers.

Milward, H. Brinton and Keith G. Provan. 2000. "Governing the Hollow State." *Journal of Public Administration Research* 10(2):359–79.

Nye, Joseph S. and John D. Donahue, eds. 2000. *Governance in a Globalizing World*. Washington, DC: Brookings Institution.

Phelps, Nicholas A., Tim Bunnell, Michelle Ann Miller and John Taylor. 2013. "Urban Inter-Referencing within and beyond a Decentralized Indonesia." *Asia Research Institute Working Paper Series No. 202*. Retrieved from (www.ari.nus.edu.sg/docs/wps/wps13_202.pdf).

Renn, Ortwin. 2008. "Concepts of Risk: An Interdisciplinary Review, Part 1: Disciplinary Risk Concepts." *GAIA: Ecological Perspectives for Science and Society* 17(1):50–66.

Renn, Ortwin and Peter Graham. 2006. "White Paper on Risk Governance: Towards an Integrative Approach." Retrieved from (https://irgc.org/wp-content/uploads/2018/09/IRGC_WP_No_1_Risk_Governance__reprinted_version_3.pdf).

Renn, Ortwin and Katherine D. Walker, eds. 2008. *Global Risk Governance: Concept and Practice Using the Irgc Framework*. Dordrecht: Springer.

Rhodes, R. A. W. 1994. "The Hollowing out of the State: The Changing Nature of the Public Service in Britain." *Political Quarterly* 65(2):138–51.

Roberts, Patrick S. 2010. "Private Choices, Public Harms: The Evolution of National Disaster Organizations in the United States." Pp. 42–69 in *Disaster and the Politics of Intervention: The Privatization of Risk*, edited by A. Lakoff. New York, NY: Columbia University Press.

Scott, W. Richard. 2014. *Institutions and Organizations: Ideas, Interests, and Identities*. Los Angeles, CA: Sage Publications.

Shan, Chun Chang and Lan Xue, eds. 2012. *Yingji Guanli Gailun: Lilun Yu Shijian (an Introduction to Emergency Management: Theory and Practice)*. Beijing, China: Gaodeng Jiaoyu Chubanshe.

Shan, Chun Chang, Lan Xue, Xiu Lan Zhang and Hui Ding, eds. 2012. *Zhongguo Yingji Guanli Dashi Ji (2003~2007) (Memorabilia of China's Emergency Management)*. Beijing, China: Shehui Wenxian Kexue Chuban She.

Shimomura, Yasutami, ed. 2003. *The Role of Governance in Asia*. Singapore: Utopia Press.

Sylves, Richard T. 2008. *Disaster Policy and Politics: Emergency Management and Homeland Security*. Washington, DC: CQ Press.

Tierney, Kathleen J. 2012. "Disaster Governance: Social, Political, and Economic Dimensions." *Annual Review of Environment and Resources* 37:341–63.

Tsai, Wen-Hsuan and Nicola Dean. 2013. "The Ccp's Learning System: Thought Unification and Regime Adaptation." *The China Journal* 69(1):87–107.

Wang, Hongwei. 2007. *Yingji Guanli Daolun (Introduction to Emergency Management)*. Beijing, China: Zhongguo Renmin Daxue Chuban She.

Xue, Lan and Ling Zhou. 2007. "Fengxian Guanli: 'Guan Kou Zai Qian Yi' De Youli Baozhang (Risk Management: The Powerful Assurance from 'Moving the Checkpoint Even Earlier')." *Zhougguo Yingji Guanli (China Emergency Management)* 11:12–15.

Xue, Lan, Ling Zhou and Qin Zhu. 2008. "Fengxian Zhili: Wanshan Yu Tisheng Guojia Gonggong Anquan Guanli De Jishi (Risk Governance: To Perfect and Improve the Basis of National Public Safety and Security Management)." *Jiangsu Social Sciences (Jiangsu Shehui Kexue)* 6:7–11.

5 Taming rivers, saving sheep, and using science

Legitimizing claims using cultural knowledge and party-state ideologies

For the merits of building an emergency management field and its risk governance framework to gain traction among the governing elites, they needed to be introduced in forms and expressions which made sense to them. In this chapter, I elaborate on the legitimizing claims made through cultural accounts the establishment relied upon to do so. These cultural accounts come in two categories. The first category is historical and broad-based, drawing upon what Wang (2012) and Cohen (2009) called "insider cultural knowledge." Its prominent forms are myths and proverbs drawn from Chinese classics. In contrast, the second category is more current and specific, as the accounts relate to party-state ideologies that had been institutionalized or were promoted by governing elites when the organizational field was still forming. Here, the prominent forms are banner terms, communist folklore, and stock phrases. Discussion on stock phrases in particular helps address how the establishment used legitimizing claims to cast existing practices as inefficient and insufficient, and why some of those practices nevertheless remained.

The two types of culturally accepted accounts – insider cultural knowledge and party-state ideologies – provided the "ready to wear" scripts and schemas (Scott 1991) available to the emergency management establishment, which used them to tailor its claims about emergency management as justified interventions and the framework as a justified ideational orientation. The establishment, as a social collectivity, can thus be seen as an interpretive system (Daft and Weick 1984) that purposefully taps into wider worlds of words and meanings to organize actions (Mohr and Friedland 2008; Oliver 1991; Scott 2014). With respect to insider cultural knowledge, the use of Chinese literature and history, and particularly the classics with their dense webs of meanings, spun with myths and highly condensed and contextualized proverbs, is an effective heuristic for accessing the most deeply rooted and taken-for-granted conceptions of social reality. Specifically, the use of cultural knowledge by the establishment bestows legitimacy based on cultural-cognitive elements of the institutional order (Scott 2008). When the establishment grafted the classics onto party-state ideologies, it was also using cultural knowledge to "short-circuit" the process of achieving legitimacy (Zucker 1988).

By the end of this chapter, I will show how the establishment blended practices – new and old – and ideologies into its risk governance framework. These acts legitimized risk governance by evoking timeless qualities that espoused Chinese sagely wisdom or representing timely support of party-state ideologies that prevailed among the governing elites. The discussion also highlights the primacy of cognitive legitimacy over pragmatic and moral legitimacy (Deephouse et al. 2017; Suchman 1995), a nuance not obvious in the literature. Last, I highlight the notion of "curation" as a means to understand how the establishment had been crafting the risk governance framework and mobilizing carefully selected culturally accepted accounts to legitimize the organizational field and its framework.

In the following sections, I first discuss insider cultural knowledge because it represents the broader and more pervasive type of account, and then elaborate on party-state ideologies which inevitably rely upon some degree of cultural knowledge.

Insider cultural knowledge

"Insider cultural knowledge" refers to narratives anchored in Chinese literature and history that most Chinese would have been either exposed to in school or become familiar with through mass media and social settings. The use of insider cultural knowledge is based on how the broader cultural environment shapes words and the worlds in which the establishment is embedded. Therefore, the emergency management establishment's use of insider cultural knowledge is as much deliberate as it is intuitive, particularly for those who have "had the experience of growing up in a Chinese cultural milieu" (Wang 2012:13).

Within the Chinese cultural milieu, I focus on the purposive use of myths and proverbs from Chinese classics and history by the establishment to make legitimizing claims. This maneuver had been successful because even daily life in Chinese society requires a proficient command of the "institutional vocabulary" of its literature and heritage (Suddaby and Greenwood 2005). It would have been even more salient to the governing elites, given that a sizeable portion is college-educated.[1] Therefore, it is not surprising that the emergency management establishment assiduously mobilized Chinese classics in its claims-making efforts. In terms of myths, I highlight Yu the Great, a cultural hero who tamed the flood-prone Yellow River, along with the myth of China's continuous conquest of disasters since time immemorial. With respect to proverbs, I highlight three that have been mobilized frequently and prominently by the emergency management establishment.

Myths

Among mythical figures, Yu the Great (*Da Yu* 大禹) was invoked the most by the emergency management establishment, as he was credited with the introduction of flood control to China and revered for his devotion to taming the Yellow River. The myths tell us that during Yu's entire tenure of flood management, he did not once visit his family, despite passing his residence three different times.[2] Implicit in the narrative is the belief that the ones who ultimately gained the mandate to govern the land would be the righteous who tamed natural disasters for society. Therefore, when heroic figures such as Yu the Great were invoked, the establishment was making salient claims to moral legitimacy through emphasizing the continuity of contemporary China with its imperial history back to high antiquity.

A typical narrative of mobilizing Yu in claims-making is an exhortation that China's history is a history of victories in combating natural disasters, beginning with Great Yu's taming of the Yellow River. The narrative then typically fast-forwards to that of communist China and the multiple floods and other disasters (e.g., the great flood of 1998, 2003 SARS) that the party-state has confronted and putatively conquered.[3] Often appended to narratives on Yu and other mythical figures are phrases such as *zi gu yi lai* (自古以来) which means "since ancient times." For example, natural disasters had created havoc on China's economic development "since ancient times" and the nation's history is a chronicle of assaults by disasters which continue to threaten development and livelihoods in "New China."[4] As one can surmise from the two examples, the invocation of mythical figures such as Yu the Great is often blended in practice into the myth of continuous conquest of disasters since ancient times. This maneuver of using both accounts retroactively constructs a continuity of the mandate to manage disasters from the current Chinese party-state, through successive imperial dynasties, back to Yu the Great. Implicitly, therefore, the narrative positions state intervention and the party-state as the lead emergency manager as unproblematic assumptions. These assumptions rest at best upon a weak historical foundation because, even though state intervention in disasters harkens back centuries, for example, river engineering projects (Dodgen 1991) and granary disbursement as disaster relief (Will and Wong 1991) during imperial times, intervention has been punctuated by disruptions and uneven effectiveness across reigns and dynasties. That said, most Chinese people regard state intervention in disaster management in China as a given.[5] Putting this notion of acceptance in cognitive legitimacy terms, explicit claims as to *why* the government *should* be involved in disaster management would make little sense to many Chinese. They would have taken the party-state's involvement not only as natural and normal. It is then reasonable to expect that most legitimizing claims emphasize pragmatic and moral legitimacy because they require more effort to render the framework and emergency management acceptable.

Proverbs

Besides myths, the establishment also used proverbs to anchor its claims. Proverbs (*cheng-yu* 成语) are effective ideational heuristics as such pithy phrases have come to be accepted by the Chinese populace. As condensations of sagely wisdom, they embody cognitive legitimacy. I highlight three proverbs, beginning with one that has the most obvious moralistic tone. The proverb *qu tu xi xin* (曲突徙薪) argues for the removal of sources of risk to mitigate disasters: one reduces fire hazards by bending the chimney and relocating firewood away from the kitchen stove.[6] In the original story, the house owner did not thank or reward the individual who warned him about the poor chimney design or placement of firewood. Instead, he hosted a banquet for neighbors who rushed to help when his house subsequently caught fire. This proverb has a clear moralistic tone because it implies that one has to warn others of risks independent of incentives or praise. When used by the emergency management establishment, it suggests that the party-state has a moral obligation to establish risk mitigation measures to protect its citizens from natural disasters.

Apart from the moral (legitimacy) dimension, *qu tu xi xin* also has a pragmatic component because it emphasizes that removing the root causes of disasters reduces the likelihood of disasters. It appeals to individual self-interest and organized actors to be involved in risk mitigation. The pragmatic legitimacy component was apparent when I first encountered the proverb in the context of emergency management at a meeting with Hua, a management-turned-emergency policy researcher. He recounted how the Zhouqu mudslide, which killed 1,700 people, would have been prevented with sufficient planning. Unfortunately, response plans and planning were often ignored and did not receive due recognition in emergency management.[7] Given its emphasis on taking precautionary measures, the proverb has been tied to the need to invest in early disaster warning systems, in part because officials on the ground tend to emphasize preparedness and response at the expense of mitigation.[8]

The second example is the proverb *wang yang bu lao* (亡羊补牢). It refers to the act of mending a pen after a sheep has escaped. It is an ancient proverb used to highlight remedial actions that, while too late for preventing the mishap in question, are still better than no action at all. For example, Ai, a veteran geologist, lamented the fact that the practice of *wang yang bu lao* seemed to be a consistent theme in how China has been responding to disasters – only after deaths have occurred:[9]

> In China, many strategies and laws were enacted only after people died. Only this, only this, only this way. . . . Mending the pen after a sheep was lost (*wang yang bu lao*), China has this way (of managing natural disasters).

In another example, it was used to compliment the State Council's swift enactment of the public health emergency regulation during the SARS crisis, also arguing that such an urgent administrative measure should have been unnecessary in the first place, had there been proper laws and regulations.[10] My third example is also related to law: while more regulations and laws had been either established, passed, or amended over the past ten years, they were not anticipatory and were in fact reactive (*wang yang bu lao*) in the wake of disasters.[11] The article singled out natural disasters because no fewer than 94 new disaster-related rules and regulations were put in place within seven months of the Wenchuan earthquake, constituting close to 83 percent of all new or updated legal documents prepared since the dawn of twenty-first century.

The third proverb, *ju'an si wei* (居安思危, see Chapter 2), appears widely across research and policy documents. It means one has to be mindful of danger and threats even during times of peace.[12] This exhortation was particularly prevalent during the early stages of establishing the emergency planning framework. For example, a State Council directive reminded all ministries and their subordinate units to be serious about emergency plans and maintain vigilance during non-disaster times (*ju' an si wei*), so as to improve the government's ability to cope with crises.[13] Given its anticipatory tone, the proverb is also often related to risk management. For example, in the preamble to a paper he wrote with Zhou, Shan emphasized that one needs to be *ju'an si wei* and therefore strengthen prevention and preparation for multiple types of risks and crises *before* an event (italics mine).[14]

On many occasions, several proverbs are used in tandem. For example, an article on building an early warning system for public security emergencies not only highlighted the spirit of *ju'an si wei*, but also explicitly argued that putting in place early warning systems and practicing emergency response were akin to following the advice embedded in the *qu ti* (bent chimney) and *wang yang* (run-away sheep) proverbs respectively.[15] The myths and proverbs also made their way into official documents, particularly State Council directives and white papers, as well as those in which language use could be more moralistic and less legally restrictive. The generous use of Chinese classics by governing elites in general and the emergency establishment more specifically also shows how cultural inferences are often fused with party-state ideologies. That said, party-state ideologies do not rely exclusively upon the classics for legitimacy.

Party-state ideologies ad nauseam: legitimacy through repetition

Party-state ideologies are the other set of scripts and schemas the emergency management establishment had access as a means to garner legitimacy for a new organizational field and its attendant conceptual framework. Specifically, I discuss the following three expressions of party-state ideologies: banner terms (*qihao* 旗号), which are grandiose pronouncements prominently endorsed and propagated by the party-state; pithy proverbs and idioms that are grounded in communist legends or folklore; and stock phrases and statements in official-speak that are recycled to the point of banality.

Although it goes beyond the scope of this book to explain in detail the party-state propaganda machine or the plethora of China's ideological slogans and catchphrases, I attempt to provide sufficient background on the emergence and development of the banner terms, communist folklore, and stock phrases that I highlight in this section. This attends to the notion that the evolution of specific institutionalized political vocabularies takes place in particular historical contexts, highlighting the efforts from the emergency management establishment to anchor the field and its framework by tapping into the scripts and schemas in the broader institutional environment.

Banner terms

Banner terms (*qihao* 旗号) are grandiose pronouncements prominently endorsed and propagated by the party-state. Examples such as "Mao Zedong's Thoughts,"

"Deng Xiaoping's Theory," "Jiang Zemin's 'Three Represents,'" serve as conceptual shorthand for the highlighted leaders' intellectual contributions to the CPC ideological canons on party-state governance. To someone not sufficiently acculturated into China's sociopolitical milieu, the conspicuous and assiduous repetition of banner terms in official documents, state-controlled media, and even often on real physical banners – with minimal or almost no rephrasing – appears contrived and confusing, even comical. Their conspicuous reference in official and public discourse has to be symbolic and consequential: the ascent to prominence, persistence, and disappearance of specific stock phrases serves as a bellwether for whose ideas and their advocacy factions are gaining or losing ground in China's political arena.

Banner terms have increased in significance over the past decade because ideology has gained further currency as a formidable source of legitimacy in the post-Jiang era (Holbig and Gilley 2010) – that is, from late 2002, including when the SARS crisis besieged the country. Increased reliance on ideological catchphrases seems to have originated in governing elites' perception of an imminent legitimacy crisis. The elites' concerns might seem counterintuitive given that the party-state has performed well in stimulating economic growth and promoting a national identity (Holbig and Gilley 2010; Wang 2012). However, governing elites regarded both robust economic growth and a confident national identity as temporary and even unstable sources of legitimacy. Thus, a persistent sense of crisis drove them to search for additional sources of legitimacy. In the wake of the 1989 Tiananmen incident, for example, Deng Xiaoping lamented that insufficient energies were being devoted to political and ideological education (see Holbig and Gilley 2010:409). In addition, the fall of the Soviet Union was not only deeply etched into the collective memory of Chinese governing elites, but also amplified their fear of precipitous regime change due to weak ideological control (Sarotte 2012). As a result, revisiting ideology – the substrate of propaganda in communist regimes – to re-imagine what constitutes the normative foundation for governmental authority was a natural choice to strengthen the governing elites' legitimacy project (Holbig and Gilley 2010).

The banner term most consequential to the building of the emergency management organizational field is the "scientific view on development" (*kexue fazhan guan* 科学发展观),[16] most prominently associated with former party chief and President Hu Jintao. In addition to being *the* focusing event for the emergency management establishment, the SARS crisis also served as *a* focusing event from which Hu tested his ideas on the "scientific view."[17] Hu's scientific view encapsulates two main ideas. First, it is people-centered and puts people foremost (*yi ren wei ben* 以人为本). Second, it emphasizes comprehensive, well-coordinated, and sustainable development, focusing on balanced attention to both the economic and social progress of China's society, as well as the growth of rural and urban regions.

Hu's "scientific view" was formally enshrined and inscribed into party ideology when it was included in the CPC's constitution at the 17th CPC National Congress at the end of 2007. Subsequently, the notion of the scientific view on development shared ideological space with other inscribed ideologies: Mao Zedong's Thoughts (pioneer), Deng Xiaoping's Theory (second generation), and Jiang Zemin's "Three Represents" (third generation). Compared to Jiang who had his ideology ratified only when he relinquished his party chief position at the 16th congress, the inscription of the scientific view was broadly interpreted as Hu's political (and ideological) victory, which he had already accomplished in the middle of his term.

Snippets of the scientific view were already evident at the June 2003 expert conference on SARS and subsequently at the SARS work conference in July 2003, as indicated in the conference summary:

> In building a moderately prosperous society (*xiaokang shehui* 小康社会) and accelerating the building of a new phase of modernization, we must always persist (to maintain) a balanced development between the economy and society, a coordinated development of urban and rural areas, and always persist (to maintain) a harmonious co-existence between man and nature, as well as sustainable development . . .[18]
>
> Through combating SARS, we recognize more profoundly than in the past there was insufficient coordination between economic and societal development, and urban development and rural development in China.[19]

To highlight and amplify, the phrases that emphasize balanced and sustainable development between the economy and society, as well as between urban and rural areas, are hallmarks of Hu's "scientific view." These phrases truly started to gain prominence at the Third Plenum of the 16th Central Committee of the CPC at the end of 2003, although they were yet to be unified under the label of "scientific view on development." The "scientific view" received even more attention at the National People's Congress in March 2004. Throughout this period and immediately thereafter, the scientific view was beginning to be invoked and dutifully replicated in key official documents. For example, in the seminal directive on the framework for emergency planning issued by the State Council in April 2003, the scientific view was indicated as one of the guiding ideologies, together with Deng's theory and Jiang's "Three Represents." It continued to be conspicuous over time, as seen in the National Integrated Disaster Prevention and Reduction Strategy (2011–2015) issued by the State Council in late 2011. It was invoked in academic publications as guiding principles[20] and referred to during conferences.[21]

It is also important to note that in the Chinese political context the term "scientific" (*kexue* 科学) often stands for something that is rational, systematic, evidence-based, and therefore efficient and advanced in the Chinese political context. For example "control of (party) cadres in a scientific manner" (*dang guan ganbu de kexue fangfa* 党管干部的科学方法), is CPC jargon for meritocratic personnel selection (Shambaugh 2008:843). Therefore, when the emergency management establishment argued for risk management as a "scientific introduction" into the organizational field, the use of *kexue* was indicative of efforts to achieve moral legitimacy.

Beyond the specific veneer of legitimacy accorded by *kexue*, the growing acceptance and currency of Hu's banner term (with or without "science") by governing elites also meant that the emergency management organizational field needed to leverage it vigorously in its claims-making efforts. Such currency, especially of prominent state-endorsed and intensely publicized ideology, is crucial in gaining continual approval from intended audiences.

Legitimacy claims become particularly salient during political transitions, as was made clear to me during fieldwork, at an emergency management conference in December 2012. The conference was held soon after the 18th CPC National Congress, at which Xi Jinping succeeded Hu Jintao's positions as general secretary of the party and chairman of the powerful central military commission. I attended the conference as an observer. I noticed that participants – academic experts and government officials alike – made conspicuous efforts not only to invoke and repeat prominent catchphrases, including the scientific view, but also to reference party conferences and new political leaders. For example, a veteran scholar-official who played a critical role in the field's genesis made this opening remark:

> . . . I think especially because our meeting is held after our 18th Congress and the Central Economic Work Conference that has just concluded, our work in emergency management has thus further received clearer directions. In the spirit of the 18th Congress, the Central [i.e., party and government] has repeatedly stressed that we are confronted with many predictable and unpredictable risks and challenges, and therefore has repeatedly asked of us to establish a sense of crisis and awareness of risks. This is especially emphasized in the report and the spirit of the 18th Congress.
>
> Second, the Central in meeting its mission of strengthening and being innovative in societal management, has also made several requests on our work in emergency management. And in terms of building more comprehensive mechanisms for public health emergency response and disaster prevention and reduction, among other things, the Central has also made clear its demands. . . . The Central Economic Work Conference has also prepared the deployment of next year's economic and social development plans, and I think there are several [points of which we should take note]. One is the active and steadfast addressing of the issue of urbanization, and that is very important for our future research in emergency management. Another is the special request from the Central that we have to establish "bottom line thinking" and to be able to be proficient in it. This was especially raised by Comrade Xi Jinping. "Bottom line thinking" refers to making our considerations based on the worst scenarios, and then striving toward its best resolutions.[22]

As seen from the opening remarks, the official made deliberate efforts to highlight the point that the conference specifically and the emergency management field in general were not only consequential to the 18th Congress of the CPC, but also received attention from top party organizational entities (i.e., Central

Economic Work Conference) and leadership (i.e., then-new party secretary Xi). Conspicuous efforts to connect risk management, public health emergency response, and disaster reduction to the utterances made at the recent party congress, especially those of the new leader Xi (i.e., his "bottom line thinking"), are also acts of legitimacy building that are not only current, but rely upon moral legitimacy based on individual charisma (i.e., personal legitimacy) of leaders (Suchman 1995).

Communist folklore

On other occasions, the establishment also mobilized communist folklore, usually expressed as proverbs or idioms that reference narratives from the post-1949 era, glorifying communist camaraderie and spirit. The difference between mobilizing communist folklore and drawing upon the classics is that folklore taps directly into political vocabulary which signifies a stronger association with the party-state than with the broader cultural environment. Folklore can be more useful than the classics when the goal is to make an explicit appeal to the governing elites for their acceptance. As an example, expressions like "whether it's a white or black cat, as long as it catches mice it's a good cat" and "feeling the stones while crossing the river," while not strictly part of guiding ideologies enshrined in formal documents (e.g., the party constitution), evoke the pragmatism and spirit of experimentation associated with Deng Xiaoping's ideology during the earlier era of economic reform in the 1980s. Just like the hidden cultural knowledge, most mainland Chinese would be familiar with idioms like "black cat/white cat" and "feeling the stones."

One of the most prominent phrases condensed from communist folklore was reinvigorated in the SARS crisis and became further popularized during the 2008 Wenchuan earthquake.[23] The proverb in its complete form is *yi fang you nan, ba fang zhi yuan* (一方有难, 八方支援), which means aid will arrive from eight directions when one direction is in distress. The proverb was believed to have first appeared as an editorial in *China Youth Daily*, the newspaper of Communist Youth League, which is run by the CPC. The February 1960 article accompanied a story about how 61 poisoned workers in Shanxi province were saved through the coordinated response from the central to local governments.[24] I came across both the complete and truncated forms of either only the first (*yi fang you nan*) or second half of the proverb (*ba fang zhi yuan*) in fieldwork.

Similar to how myths and proverbs from the classics were retrofitted to latter-day thinking and techniques in emergency management, the establishment also re-interpreted communist folklore in its effort to garner moral, pragmatic, and cognitive legitimacy. For example, a flood specialist and member of the expert committee to the SCDR argued that risk distribution is an instantiation of the *yi fang you nan, ba fang zhi yuan* proverb, in an attempt to argue that the thinking behind risk management is not completely a foreign-born idea and is compatible with China's party-state ideology.[25] Therefore, risk management should be embraced, accepted, and practiced in China's emergency management.

Stock phrases

Besides riding on highly visible ideologies, iconic narratives, and catchy communist proverbs, the establishment also propagated phrases that were more prosaic but nevertheless still carried legitimacy, owing to its usage by senior government officials or taken-for-grantedness in official vocabulary. For example, journal articles, newspaper articles, and government reports are replete with phrases with minor adjustments that emphasize the importance of building a solid foundation, such as *hangshi jichu* (夯实基础),[26] or the urgency to perfect or improve emergency management, such as *jidai wan shan* (亟待完善).[27]

However, it would be a mistake to equate the banality of such stock phrases with triviality. Circulated to the point of becoming taken for granted, some of the commonest stock phrases provide the strongest justifications for state intervention. Many official documents and academic writings open with stock phrases that assert that China is a vulnerable nation and therefore requires continuous vigilance from the state. Such introductions often provide the appropriate segue into proverbs that emphasize mitigation and preparedness, and remind readers to take lessons gleaned from past disasters seriously, such as *ju'an si wei* and *wang yang bu lao*.

Such "China as vulnerable" stock phrases come in various iterations. One emphasizes domestic conditions, particularly the frequency, intensity, and spectrum of natural disasters that besiege the nation – past, present, or future. The following example projects perils into the future. The foreword in the English edition of the 2009 White Paper on Disaster Prevention and Reduction asserts:

> China is one of the countries in the world that suffer the most natural disasters. Along with global climate changes and its own economic takeoff and progress in urbanization, China suffers increasing pressure on resources, environment and ecology. The situation in the prevention of and response to natural disasters has become more serious and complicated.[28]

By highlighting China's current and continued vulnerability into the foreseeable time, the establishment was attempting to ensure emergency management's function in the government for the future, arguing that being vigilant to disasters would require continuous effort and attention. Emergency management might become more critical because, as the White Paper predicts, natural disasters would become "more serious and complicated." This continued vulnerability claim taps into pragmatic legitimacy, as it argues that it serves the interests of the governing elites to continue to support emergency management as a governmental function.

Other claims ascribe China's vulnerability to its status as a society in transition, a nation-state still in the throes of the economic reforms that had begun only in the late 1970s, thus still vulnerable to chaos and instability. At a 2004 emergency response planning conference during which the organizational field was still undergoing intensive institutionalization, State Councilor Hua Jianmin pointed out how China has "entered a new developmental stage" with "growing demands from the people" for "material well-being, spiritual culture, health and safety," arguing that emergency management could be a pillar in helping the nation stay the course of peaceful development. Similar to how the scholar-official conspicuously referenced iconic political events and party ideologies to legitimize emergency management, Hua also emphasized the need to implement Hu's "scientific view" in building "sound public emergency management measures" to ensure stability and security during this precarious transitional period of China's development:

> With China's vast territory, economic and social development foundation still being relatively weak and in a crucial period of institutional transition, as well as the wide distribution of a variety of major natural disasters and its high frequency, many serious threats to public health and safety from infectious diseases have not been effectively controlled, and various societal contradictions are still prominent.[29]

The "transitional stage" argument played up China as still being underdeveloped and its need to better manage its "societal contradictions." This in turn allowed the establishment to make the pragmatic claim that emergency management still has a role to play in the government so as to ensure China transitions smoothly into a more mature and developed stage.

The other oft-cited claim is that China has entered a "rapid development phase" (*kuaisu fazhan shiqi* 快速发展时期), "non-stable state" (*feiwending zhuangtai* 非稳定状态), or "critical period of development" (*guanjian shiqi* 关键时期). Going by the experience of developed nations, it stresses the developing nations are subject to frequent and multiple societal risks, requiring strong state intervention.[30] Just as interesting, a specific range of GDP per capita would often be offered as an indicator of China's status of rapid development but a reference was never given. It was simply taken as fact and circulated as justification, as the example shows:

> The dramatic change in China's social structure is rendering the country a risk society. Now our nation's GDP per capita is more than US$1,000, indicating that economic development has entered a critical period, and (it is) likely to cause social disorder, coordination problems in our economy, psychological imbalance, and other issues, creating factors that will affect societal stability and causing more emergencies to arise in the midst of societal change.[31]

The analyses also demonstrate how the Chinese emergency management establishment legitimized interventions that cast pre-existing practices as insufficient and inefficient, while allowing them to remain. Even though claims of China as "vulnerable," in "critical transition," and "rapid development" cast existing practices of managing emergencies as insufficient and inefficient and paint China's current status as delicate, they are in substance not pegged to specific time periods or to objective failures in performance. My data show that such assertions of weakness and inadequacy were being made throughout the ten-year period of field formation. The sense of inadequacy did not seem to diminish significantly from 2003, when emergency management was yet to be an organizational field, to 2012, when the field was deemed to have attained temporary stability. Claims of precarious and rapid transitions and vulnerability continually played out in documents, interviews, and conferences.

In his case analysis of the U.S. Army's transition from a Cold War to a post-Cold War era, Smith (2012) notices that organized field actors practiced blurring and building boundaries across eras marked by dissimilar ideologies, so as to retrofit their arguments regarding what had changed in military doctrine and remained the same. The establishment in the Chinese emergency management organization field seemed to be enacting similar strategies of blurring and building boundaries. The appropriate application of the timeless claims of vulnerability, along with arguments centering on precarious and rapid transition were critical. Specifically, by blurring together the present and the past, the establishment asserted existing practices – independent of the extent to which improvements had been made – as *always* insufficient and inefficient. By establishing boundaries between the future and the present, the establishment constructed the promise of reform and progress, thereby nudging the party-state to enlist emergency management in its continuous service. Done this way, pre-existing practices were allowed to remain, at least in a nominal fashion, as continual work for progress toward a more perfect emergency management regime. As Meyer and Rowan (1977) noted, "People may picture the present as unworkable but the future as filled with promising reforms of both structure and activity" (p. 356).

Conclusion

In this chapter, I identify the culturally accepted accounts that the Chinese emergency management establishment had relied upon to construct the field, build a risk governance framework, and integrate new and old practices and ideologies. The establishment mobilized Chinese insider cultural knowledge – the cultural-cognitive base with which the governing elites are familiar – and party-state ideologies to legitimize the risk governance framework and emergency management organizational field. The emphasis on prevalent party-state ideologies underscores the time-sensitivity and currency of these ideologies as a critical source of socio-political legitimacy (Fiol and Aldrich 1994). Like fresh produce, these ideologies are perishable and can only offer legitimacy within a limited shelf life. The justifications based on Chinese cultural insider knowledge and party-state ideologies were sustained throughout the ten-year period of field formation because these accounts formed an acceptable and intricate web of claims that wove together the benefits of enacting risk governance to reduce the onset of disasters (pragmatic legitimacy) with exhortations of congruent values and heritage (moral legitimacy), and taken-for-granted presuppositions (cognitive legitimacy) (Deephouse et al. 2017; Suchman 1995).

Despite their foreign origins, concepts of risk, governance, and "risk governance" were creatively indigenized through claims of continuity and congruency with age-old practices and ideologies. Specifically, insider cultural knowledge seemed to be the prominent type of accounts that the establishment used to claim continuity and congruency, even familiarity. As the establishment would argue, these foreign concepts and their more concrete practices in risk and governance were latter-day expressions of ancient and sagely wisdom, so there was no reason to reject them based on their origins and relative newness. At the same time, by connecting these techniques of risk and governance to established party-state ideologies (e.g., Mao Zedong's thoughts) and those newly accepted (i.e., Hu's "scientific views"), the establishment also argued that these ideas and techniques were scientific (moral legitimacy) and helpful for the governing elites to maintain a harmonious society (pragmatic legitimacy). Similar to how claims about China's inadequacies, notions of risk, governance, and emergency management could be argued as timeless and co-exist with old practices and ideologies, they could also be argued as timely and consistent with prevailing party-state ideologies.

Reflecting on cognitive legitimacy in the Chinese emergency management context

To recap on Suchman's (1995) legitimacy typology, cognitive legitimacy rests on the comprehensibility and meaningfulness of the ideas and claims to the target audience. Moral legitimacy originates from the notion that following an idea or supporting a claim is the "right thing to do." Pragmatic legitimacy is granted when ideas or claims appeal to the self-interests of the target audience. In practice, legitimizing claims seldom appeal to one specific type of legitimacy; they invoke a blend of all three, with one or two being the dominant ones.

Primarily, though not exclusively, the establishment attempted to mobilize insider cultural knowledge for cognitive legitimacy and party-state ideologies for moral legitimacy. Interestingly, pragmatic legitimacy, while important, seldom seemed to be sufficient in justifying the emergency management field or considering new ideas and techniques concerning risk and governance. Arguments that attended to pragmatic legitimacy often had to be supplemented with arguments that also invoked moral, cognitive, or a combination of the other types of legitimacy. My findings of the relative "weakness" of pragmatic legitimacy seem to corroborate literature that has highlighted it as the least elusive of the three types of legitimacy (Suchman 1995). For example, earlier stages of institutional change involve pragmatic and moral legitimacy whereas the final stage involves institutionalizing new ideas becoming taken-for-granted, that is, attaining cognitive legitimacy (Greenwood, Suddaby and Hinings 2002).

That said, while acknowledging its "incomprehensibility of alternatives" character (Deephouse et al. 2017:30), the literature has not considered cognitive legitimacy as significantly more important than moral or pragmatic legitimacy, even though it has been argued to be highly elusive and therefore challenging to observe empirically, as it is so deeply embedded in the social order (Suchman 1995). My research suggests that cognitive legitimacy should be accorded more prominence in the literature, especially when it is highlighted not as often as moral and pragmatic legitimacy, as evidenced in this chapter. Cognitive legitimacy takes up less space not because it is less consequential. In the Chinese context, a deep cultural and literary knowledge base fundamentally anchors and informs daily discourse (Deephouse et al. 2017). In addition, using myths, proverbs, and other forms of literary narratives based on insider cultural knowledge as a discursive practice is culturally accepted, even expected, in Chinese writing. The forms and format of expressing Chinese insider cultural knowledge and party-state ideology are already de facto rooted in cognitive legitimacy. Cognitive legitimacy is in fact so pervasive in social life and central to social order that moral and pragmatic legitimacy could not be established without it. To paint an absurd scenario, the emergency management establishment did not use Biblical myths and figures (e.g., the great flood, Noah's Ark)[32] not simply because those cultural accounts were less intelligible to the Chinese, but because even the notion of *considering* them would not have been obvious in the first place.

Curation as intelligible design: crafting risk governance framework and cultural accounts

To recap, the Chinese emergency management establishment crafted an indigenous version of risk governance by assiduously attending to what it intended to retain, remove, and add, based on the IRGC risk governance framework to which it had been introduced. With respect to cultural accounts, while it was natural for the Chinese establishment to rely upon insider cultural knowledge and party-state ideologies, it also pays considerable attention to selecting and amplifying specific elements in available cultural accounts that would help render risk governance and emergency management as effective and natural in the Chinese context. Together, the efforts the establishment had invested in massaging the content of the concept and weaving it with the chosen cultural accounts helped forge the ideational centerpiece of emergency management that fit the Chinese institutional context.

However, what I am trying to emphasize is not the ideational content of the risk governance framework or elements of the cultural accounts that formed or were excluded by the establishment in its legitimization. I have discussed the content and accounts with some specificity earlier in this chapter. Rather, my focus is on something that has greater generalizability and theoretical "travel" across institutional contexts: the crafting strategy that the establishment employed to design the risk governance framework and cultural accounts in ways that would be intelligible to the governing elites to whom it was appealing for acceptance. The umbrella term that I choose to describe the strategy is "curation." Just as a museum curator selects, positions, and omits artifacts, and considers the lighting and paths that visitors take to encounter the arrangements, the establishment was strategic in blurring and building boundaries, specifically in presenting an idea or a practice as both timeless and timely.

While I arrived at the concept of curation independently of Mukti Khaire (2014), who uses same concept in her research on the emergence of the high-end fashion industry in India, I agree with her emphasis on the curatorial function in three respects. First, it is performed by the field gatekeepers. They are the organized actors who police the boundaries of who and what constitute the field. In my case, the establishment, especially academic experts, served as the gate keeper and key field constituent. Second, acts of curation go beyond superficial editing to purposefully cultivate a field-level awareness that goes beyond the sum total of its ideational content and field constituents. For example, the establishment employed an ensemble of cultural accounts, from proverbs and myths to party-state ideological banner terms and stock phrases. While some accounts were featured more prominently, none individually was sufficient to constitute the field. Third, the curatorial function is an ongoing and recurring process. This point is illustrated by how the Chinese emergency management continually mobilized claims such as vulnerability and precarious transitions to justify the framework and its governmental function, independent of the achievements the field had gained since 2003.

In my next and final empirical chapter, I elaborate on the relationship between the organizational field and the risk governance framework, showing how academic experts were working with others in the emergency management establishment to constitute both the field and the framework. More importantly, I explain how their tight coupling gave rise in due time to the governmentalization of emergency management. Through that, I show that organizational actors, not disasters, were the surprising subjects of governmentalization.

Notes

1 When we focus on the Central Committee, the leadership body of the CPC, 92 percent of the 17th (2007–2012) committee members had at least a four-year college education. A sizeable portion held graduate degrees, and of those, many had either education or work experience abroad. For details about China's governing elites during that period, see Bo (2010).

2 Yu the Great (presumably around 2200–2100 BC) was memorialized in Sima Qian's *Historical Records*.

3 For example, Shan, Chun Chang. 2010. "Goujian hexie shehui zhong de Zhongguo yingji guanli (Emergency management in service of building a harmonious society)." *Xingzheng Gaige (Administrative Management Reform)* 8:19–23. Another example, 18 years before Shan's article, shows that the practice of such automatic and unbroken lineage of flood management by the authorities since time immemorial has been a longstanding one: Yang, Huating. 1992. "Guanyu woguo jianzai fangzhen he guanli tizhi de taolun (Discussion on the national disaster reduction policy and management system in China)." *Ziran Zaihai Xuebao (Journal of Natural Disasters)* 1(1):19–27.

4 In Chinese parlance, "New China" refers to post-1949/communist China. The phrase "five thousand years" is also a stock phrase commonly used in Chinese writing to emphasize the long, winding history and depth of culture of Chinese (primarily Han) society. Wang, Qian, Tao Tian, Jun Li and Yongfu Chen. 2009. "Ziran zaihai yu Zhongguo yingji guanli zhidu (Natural disasters and China's emergency management system)." *Zhongguo Nongye Da-xue Xue-bao (Shehui Kexue Ban) (China Agricultural University Journal [Social Sciences Edition])* 26(3):161–70.

5 I am grateful to the anonymous Chinese graduate student who pointed this out (repeatedly) to me.

6 It originates from *The Biography of Huo Guang* in the *Book of Han* (*Han Shu • Huo Guang Zhuan* 《汉书•霍光传》). It is a historical record of Western Han dynasty (206 BC – 25 AD) written by Han historian Ban Gu (班固) in the first century AD.

7 Memo on meeting Hua.

8 An example is Yan, Yaojun. 2012. "Wo guo shehui yujing tixi jianshe de jiujie ji qi pojie (The challenges of building China's early warning system and its resolution)." *Zhongguo Xingzheng Xueyuan Xuebao (Journal of Chinese Academy of Governance)* (4):89–93.

9 Second interview with Ai.

10 Xiao, Jinming. 2003. "Fansi SARS weiji: Zhengfu zaizao falu jianshe he daode chongjian (Reflections of the SARS crisis: Reinventing government, building legal system, and reconstituting ethics)." *Zhongguo Xingzheng Guanli (Chinese Public Administration)* 7:17–22.

11 Zhang, Peng, Ning Li, Bihang Fan, Xueqin Liu and Yuting Wen. 2011. "Jin 30 nian Zhongguo zaihai falu fagui wenjian banbu shuliang yu shijian yanbian yanjiu (Research on close to 30 years of disaster laws and regulations in China)." *Zaihai Xue (Journal of Catastrophology)* 3:25–114.

12 This proverb originates from *Zuo Zhuan*.

13 国务院办公厅,国办函〔2004〕33号,关于印发《国务院有关部门和单位制定和修订突发公共事件应急预案框架指南》的函 (General Office of the State Council, GOSC Letter [2004] No. 33, Notice on the *Distribution* of *Guidelines for ministries and units of the State Council on the use of emergency planning framework for creating and amending emergency plans*). The directive was released on April 6, 2004.

14 Shan, Chun Chang and Ling Zhou. 2008. "Cong SARS dao daxuezai: Zhongguo yingji guanli tixi jianshe de fazhan mailuo ji jingyan fansi (From SARS to the Great Snowstorm [of 2008]: The trajectory of development of and experience-based reflections on China's emergency management system)." *Gansu Shehui Kexue (Social Science Journal of Gansu)* 5:40–4.

15 Wang, Er Ping. 2007. "Quntixing shijian yujing yu shehui fengxian yingsu bianshi (Early warning of mass incidents and the identification of societal risk factors)." *Zhongguo Yingji Guanli (China Emergency Management)* 5:25–7. Wang, who is a researcher at the China Academy of Science, also included the original classical Chinese text, where the proverb appeared as a sidebar in his article. See p. 25 in Wang (2007).

16 Like all translation work, there is no single authoritative translation that could encapsulate its full meaning. Its various iterations include (but are not limited to) "scientific outlook on development," "scientific development perspective," and "scientific concept on development."

17 While the ideas are typically associated with Hu Jintao, it is naïve to believe he is the only one promoting and coining these slogans or "banner terms" (*qihao* 旗号). Comparable to my arguments about the leveraging of intellectual power for institutional entrepreneurship, Hu allegedly relied on several academics, especially those in the Central Party School to germinate, elaborate, test, and refine these ideas. See for example, Shambaugh (2008).

18 2003. 温家宝主持召开专家座谈会 (Wen Jiabao chaired expert conference on SARS [on June 16, 2003]). Retrieved December 16, 2013, from www.people.com.cn/GB/paper39/9451/874763.html.

19 2003. 全国防治非典工作会议 胡锦涛总结八方面经验 (At state SARS prevention work conference Hu Jintao summed up the experience [of managing the epidemic]). Retrieved July 23, 2013, from http://news.xinhuanet.com/zhengfu/2003-07/29/content_998285.htm.

20 See for example Shi, Peijun. 2008. "Zhiding guojia zonghe jianzai zhanlue Tigao juzai fengxian fangfan nengli (Establishing national integrated disaster reduction strategy and improving catastrophe risk governance capacity)." *Ziran Zaihai Xuebao (Journal of Natural Disasters)* 17(1):1–8.

21 Based on my notes from attending an international conference on emergency management in late 2012 and the transcript of a closed-door conference on emergency management I attended in late 2012. Participants were academic experts, specifically "establishment intellectuals" (Hamrin and Cheek 1986), and government officials.

22 I have heavily edited the quote for consistency and intelligibility in English.

23 As an informal indicator, I conducted a search on the China Core Newspaper Database in the China Knowledge Integrated Database (CNKI, http://oversea. cnki.net/) for "*yi fang you nan* 一方有难." I found 1,057 articles. Four articles appeared between 2000 (the earliest available year in the database) and 2002, and 2003 chalked up 23 mentions. The remaining 1,053 appeared between 2003 and 2013. The search was conducted on January 5, 2014.

24 "Eight directions" is a Chinese metaphor that refers to all directions.

25 See p. 56 in Cheng, Xiao Tao. 2007. "Zhongguo hongshui fengxian guanli baogao (A report on flood risk management in China)." Pp. 28–66 in Wu, Dingfu, ed. *Zhongguo Fengxian Guanli Baogao (China Risk Governance Report)*. Beijing, China: Zhongguo Caizheng Jingji Chuban She.

26 For an example, see: 国务院办公厅,《国务院办公厅关于加强基层应急管理工作的意见》(General Office of the State Council, *Suggestions on improving emergency management at the grassroots level*). This directive was issued on July 31, 2007.

27 For example, see: 2011. "Woguo yingj iguanli falu jidai wanshan (Our laws in emergency management need improvement)." *Sichuan Fazhi Bao (Sichuan Legal News)*. Retrieved August 23, 2012, from www.aqsc.cn/101813/ 101946/207322.html.

28 See page 1 in *China's Actions for Disaster Prevention and Reduction* as published in *Beijing Review*, 20:1–16. The white paper was released by the Information Office of the State Council.

29 General Office of Dongguan City Government (in Guangdong province), 关于转发华建敏国务委员在部分省（市）及大城市制订完善应急预案工作座谈会上讲话的通知 (A notice on forwarding State Councilor Hua Jianmin's speech at the work conference on developing and improving emergency response plans at selected provinces [municipalities] and cities). The document was issued on July 28, 2004. I have heavily edited the translation for clarity and intelligibility in English. Retrieved July 23, 2013, from www1.dg.gov.cn/publicfiles/business/ htmlfiles/cndg/s1272/200510/ 23505.htm.

30 Tang, Tiehan. 2003. "Bu duan tigao weiji guanli de nengli: You fangzhi 'Fei Dian' yinfa de shenceng sikao (Never stop improving crisis management ability: Deep reflections inspired by preventing and controlling 'SARS')." *Guojia Xingzheng Xueyuan Xuebao (Journal of the Chinese Academy of Governance)* 4:4–7.

31 Shi, Peijun, Chongfu Huang, Tao Ye, Jing Chen, Junhua Zhou and Jing Zheng. 2005. "Jianli Zhongguo zonghe fengxian guanli tixi (Building Chinese integrated risk management system)." *Zhongguo Jianzai (Disaster Reduction in China)* 1:37–9.

32 This example is also thematically equivalent to the Chinese myth of the great flood in high antiquity and its hero, Yu the Great.

References

Bo, Zhiyue. 2010. *China's Elite Politics: Governance and Democratization*. Edited by J. Fewsmith and Y. Zheng. Singapore: World Scientific Publishing.

Cohen, Paul A. 2009. *Speaking to History: The Story of King Goujian in Twentieth-Century China*. Berkeley, CA: University of California Press.

Daft, Richard L. and Karl E. Weick. 1984. "Toward a Model of Organizations as Interpretation Systems." *Academy of Management Review* 9(2):284–95.

Deephouse, David L., Jonathan Bundy, Leigh Plunkett and Mark Suchman. 2017. "Organizational Legitimacy: Six Questions." Pp. 27–54 in *The Sage Handbook of Organizational Institutionalism*, edited by R. Greenwood, C. Oliver, T. B. Lawrence and R. E. Meyer. Thousand Oaks, CA: Sage Publications.

Dodgen, Randall. 1991. "Hydraulic Evolution and Dynastic Decline: The Yellow River Conservancy, 1796–1855." *Late Imperial China* 12(2):36–63.

Fiol, C. Marlene and Howard E. Aldrich. 1994. "Fools Rush In? The Institutional Context of Industry Creation." *Academy of Management Review* 19(4):645–70.

Greenwood, Royston, Roy Suddaby and C. R. Hinings. 2002. "Theorizing Change: The Role of Professional Associations in the Transformation of Institutionalized Fields." *Academy of Management Journal* 45(1):58–80.

Hamrin, Carol Lee and Timothy Cheek, eds. 1986. *China's Establishment Intellectuals*. Armonk, NY: M. E. Sharpe.

Holbig, Heike and Bruce Gilley. 2010. "Reclaiming Legitimacy in China." *Politics & Policy* 38(3):395–422.

Khaire, Mukti. 2014. "Fashioning an Industry: Socio-Cognitive Processes in the Construction of Worth of a New Industry." *Organization Studies* 35(1):41–74.

Meyer, John W. and Brian Rowan. 1977. "Institutionalized Organizations: Formal Structure as Myth and Ceremony." *American Journal of Sociology* 83(2):340–63.

Mohr, John W. and Roger Friedland. 2008. "Theorizing the Institution: Foundation, Duality, and Data." *Theory and Society* 37:421–6.

Oliver, Christine. 1991. "Strategic Responses to Institutional Processes." *Academy of Management Review* 16(1):145–79.

Sarotte, Mary Elise. 2012. "China's Fear of Contagion." *International Security* 37(2):156–82.

Scott, W. Richard. 1991. "Unpacking Institutional Arrangements." Pp. 164–82 in *The New Institutionalism in Organizational Analysis*, edited by W. W. Powell and P. J. DiMaggio. Chicago, IL: University of Chicago Press.

Scott, W. Richard. 2008. "Approaching Adulthood: The Maturing of Institutional Theory." *Theory and Society* 37:427–42.

Scott, W. Richard. 2014. *Institutions and Organizations: Ideas, Interests, and Identities*. Los Angeles, CA: Sage Publications.

Shambaugh, David. 2008. "Training China's Political Elite: The Party School System." *The China Quarterly* 196:827–44.

Smith, Wade P. 2012. "Narratives of Continuity and Change: Changing Logics and Institutional Work in the United States Army." Master's Degree, Sociology, University of Colorado, Boulder, CO.

Suchman, Mark. 1995. "Managing Legitimacy: Strategic and Institutional Approaches." *Academy of Management Review* 20(3):571–610.

Suddaby, Roy and Royston Greenwood. 2005. "Rhetorical Strategies of Legitimacy." *Administrative Science Quarterly* 50:35–67.

Wang, Hongwei. 2007. *Yingji Guanli Daolun (Introduction to Emergency Management)*. Beijing, China: Zhongguo Renmin Daxue Chuban She.

Wang, Zheng. 2012. *Never Forget National Humiliation: Historical Memory in Chinese Politics*. New York, NY: Columbia University Press.

Will, Pierre-Etienne and R. Bin Wong. 1991. *Nourish the People: The State Civilian Granary System in China, 1650–1850*. Ann Arbor, MI: Center for Chinese Studies Publications.
Zucker, Lynne G. 1988. "Where Do Institutional Patterns Come From? Organizations as Actors in Social Systems." Pp. 23–49 in *Institutional Patterns and Organizations: Culture and Environment*, edited by L. G. Zucker. Cambridge, MA: Ballinger Publishing Company.

6 Governmentalization of emergency management

The previous two chapters describe the genesis and development of the risk governance framework, as well as the role of cultural accounts the emergency management establishment leveraged to make claims that legitimized the framework and the new organizational field of emergency management, especially claims that reconciled tensions between old and new practices and ideologies. This chapter builds on those insights.

The chapter proceeds as follows. First, I highlight ideas from the risk governance framework that were present in the following prominent administrative and legislative landmarks of the emergency management field: the 2003 Administrative Regulation on Public Health Emergencies; the 2005 State Master Plan for Emergency Response; and finally, the 2007 National Emergency Response Law. In doing so, I show the behind-the-scenes advocacy and influence exerted by academic experts during the policymaking process. Next, I ground these empirical observations in theoretical terms, discussing the implications of seeing the emerging of categories, severity grades, emergency management phases, and several other components across the three landmarks as the formation of a technique. By arguing that the evolution of a technique was implicated in the governmentalization of the emergency management field, Foucauldian governmentality as a tool shows how power can be made more obvious in organizational neoinstitutional studies. Last, I highlight how the establishment created training and research programs related to emergency management nationwide when the emergency response law was still in the works. This development shows that academic experts in the establishment made more than just a one-time effort of inscribing the risk governance framework into laws and regulations; beyond that, they were perpetuating and entrenching it as the ideational basis that would further strengthen the organizational field. This becomes more obvious when we take into account that the emergence of the NIEM, provincial emergency management associations, research centers, and other knowledge production entities – in which academic experts were embedded or frequented – also coincided with the acceptance of emergency management as a government function and state research agenda. I introduce the notion of an "institutional evangelist" as a way to characterize the nondiscursive, material, and structural qualities of the role that academic experts played in institutionalizing the field.

The next section begins with the explanation of "technique." The notion of technique serves as a conceptual needle that threads through the regulations, plans, and laws that constituted the emergency management organizational field to show how ideas in the risk governance framework became embedded in these field components.

The birth of a technique: from administrative regulation to national law

The term "technique" in Foucault's concept of governmentality invokes the notion that a specific method has been used to govern a target population. It refers to a configuration of new and pre-existing practices and field constituents, such as establishing emergency management offices in China. The technique associated with the emergency management field and risk governance framework was forged and become more defined over time. Many components of the technique had already been raised in academic discussions, even though they were not apparent before the 2003 SARS crisis. With unexpected "jolts" such as the SARS outbreak (Meyer 1982), and "field events" such as the creation of a legal basis for governmental emergency management (Edelman 1992), along with the confluence of existing and new ideas, these components coalesced into a technique through the efforts of the establishment, particularly academic experts who had advocated for their inclusion in pre-existing disaster policy domains. During field formation, some of these components first appeared in a regulation, continued to be improved on, and then finally were written into a national law, progressively gaining legitimacy in authoritative texts over a period of several years (Lynnggaard 2007).

In the paragraphs that follow, I discuss the administrative and legislative landmarks that appeared in the field chronologically, highlighting components of the technique that I identified inductively from my data.

2003 administrative regulation on public health emergencies

As early as April 2003, when China was still grasping the extent of the SARS epidemic, there were already murmurs within the State Council about formalizing emergency management as a governmental function.[1] By May 2003, the State Council approved a new administrative regulation on public health emergencies (*tufa gonggong weisheng shijian yingji tiaoli* 突发公共卫生事件应急条例). This regulation was the site in which a technique was first being worked on, specifically the prototyping of a definition for emergency, the organizing principles for the practice of emergency management, the early signs of risk management, and the involvement of academic experts.

Article 2 of the regulation is the centerpiece of the document, as it provided the definition of a public health emergency and the motivation for government intervention: a sudden, unexpected incident that is causing or potentially could cause harm to public health. Such an incident could arise because of (but not limited to) a known or yet to be identified epidemic, an incident of severe food poisoning, or a case of industrial contamination. Given that the document could not realistically cover every root cause, the most important feature of the article is therefore the consequences of such a public health emergency, emphasizing how its occurrence was harming or a potential danger to public health, thereby necessitating state intervention. This definition continued to be curated by the establishment in subsequent regulations and laws.

In retrospect, the regulation already contained some of the principles that would organize the field in the future. It referenced the State Council as the highest authority to provide unified command for crisis response during public health emergencies. It also stated the principle of a tiered approach, whereby each level of government would be responsible for public health emergencies in its region.

The regulation indicated that each level of government needed to conduct emergency response planning that covered the emergency management cycle from pre-emergency to post-emergency phases. To elaborate, it identified the three stages of (1) prevention and preparedness (*yufang and zhunbei* 预防与准备), (2) monitoring and early warning (*jiance yu yujing* 检测与预警), and (3) emergency response (*yingjichuli* 应急处理).[2] Furthermore, the regulation stipulated that emergency response plans for public health emergencies must be created and contain components on the building and training of dedicated emergency management staff. Though not explicitly mentioned in this regulation, risks were alluded to as "hidden dangers" (*yinhuan* 隐患) that needed to be identified, analyzed, and reported. Inserting the identification of "hidden dangers" thus paved the way for formal risk management to be included in future administration and legislative components of the field. Last but not least, the regulation also highlighted the specific role academic experts should assume in emergency management: to assess the impact of public health emergencies.

2005 state master plan for emergency response plans

In January 2005, almost a year after a working group and an expert advisory team was established in the State Council for emergency planning, the State Council approved the State Master Plan for Emergency Response Plans (*Guojia Tufa Gonggong Shijian Zongti Yu'an* 国家突发公共事件总体预案), (thereafter the state master plan). It was the authoritative document that directed all levels of government and administrative departments to create emergency response plans. Its purpose was stated up front in the document: to strengthen the government's ability to protect public safety and security and deal with emergencies so as to promote comprehensive economic and societal development in a coordinated and sustainable manner.[3] What is most salient in the statement of purpose was the deliberate reference to the scientific outlook on development, the political ideology endorsed by the governing elites. As highlighted in Chapter 5, balanced and sustainable development in the Chinese economy and society was a prominent feature of Hu's "scientific view on development."

Similar to how a public health emergency was defined in the 2003 regulation, the definition in the master state plan also gestured toward the negative consequences. Specifically, the document defined an emergency as an unexpected and sudden event that is causing or potentially could cause serious levels of death and injury, property damage and loss, environmental degradation and societal harm, and threats to public safety and security. The definition, apart from retaining the characteristics of unexpectedness and suddenness from that of a public health emergency, also expanded the coverage to emergencies in general, specifically natural disasters, accident-disasters, public health emergencies, and public security emergencies, which are the four official categories of emergencies. It also specified the potential harm emanating in these emergencies: death and injury, property loss and damage, environmental degradation (particularly for accident-disasters, including industrial accidents such as oil spills), and threats to public safety and security (from protests and riots).

No longer couched in opaque language, such as "hidden dangers" in the regulation on public health emergencies, risk assessment was explicitly highlighted as an activity to be carried out by the government. The organizing principles of unified command and a tiered responsibility approach were also present in the master state plan. The involvement of academic experts went up a notch; no longer just confined to post-event impact assessment, experts were expected to be involved in emergency management as policy advisors. The document stipulated that a database of experts on various specialized emergency situations should be created.

The four categories of emergency severity made their debut in the state master plan and were subsequently elevated into law. The emergency categories did not emerge *de novo*. They were suggested during the planning for national science and technology development which began in 2003.[4] Emergency management was an area to be developed under the domain of public safety and security. The categories and how they became prominent seemed to be also based on political calculation. Gui, an engineering expert who participated in the planning, pointed out how accident-disasters, a category that included industrial accidents and automobile accidents, gained priority over natural disasters:

> I remembered there was a debate . . . [The work safety experts] said, "Didn't [natural] disasters produce a Tangshan earthquake (estimated 250,000 to 650,000 dead) only every few decades? For us, the number of deaths in accident-disasters for the past ten years was equivalent to a [Boeing] 707 dropping from the sky every day, three hundred deaths, and up to when we were planning (the science and technological development), it was the same as a [Boeing] 747 dropping from the sky, four hundred persons, four hundred deaths in a day."[5] They had included traffic accidents into the count for work safety. And then the accidents from coal mining and non-coal mining were huge too . . .[6]

Gui's quote on accident-disasters overshadowing natural disasters hints at the competition, even conflict, between academic experts who were committed to and vested in the study of different emergency categories. Such tensions are often challenging to discern in open source documents, being hidden from public view. In addition, these tensions intimate the benchmarking complexities in comparing emergencies. Different categories of emergencies not only occur with varying frequencies, but also inflict unequal harm and loss on society.

Because of the difficulties and complexities involved, I was expecting that another new component of the technique – grading of emergency severity – would also turn into a point of contention during field formation. Surprisingly, while emergency severity was prominent during field development, there was consensus between academic experts and the rest of the establishment on the grading system. What finally made it into the state master plan and later the Emergency Response Law was the agreement that the criterion of severity of a calamity would depend on the extent to which it exceeded the coping ability of the affected region. Yang, an established natural disaster scholar said:

> It's determined by the scope of the impact from the extreme and sudden event. It's not based on the seismicity of an earthquake or the death toll. Although later on we did discuss if we should base it on the (traditional, objective measures of) disaster situation to determine the severity grades, but we realized different geographical regions did not have the same capability to manage the same disaster situation, and so [we decided] it would be the scope of impact and not the disaster situation.[7]

As the quote demonstrates, disaster severity was not based on definitive figures related to the physical attributes of the natural disaster (e.g., seismic strength) and losses (e.g., economic cost, death toll). This was a departure from the research trajectory of the natural disaster research community. Researchers over time had produced models to assess severity, typically measuring the impact of extreme events in terms of economic costs and human losses.[8] Instead, the academic experts agreed with government officials to endorse a different idea of what counted as sufficiently severe for the state to intervene in emergencies, and ditched research-based standards. The different idea was to base severity on coping capacities of governments, which was a practice-based concept for government officials.[9]

The next section discusses the 2007 National Emergency Response Law, the legislative document in which we see the technique not only in its entirety, but also fully elaborated.

Enter the "dragon": 2007 national emergency response law

Hailed as the "dragon head" and considered the de facto constitutional document for emergency management, the 2007 National Emergency Response Law was the long-awaited umbrella legislation that filled the legislative gap in the field. The new law provided the overarching legal basis for the establishment to be involved across the entire spectrum of emergency management, from preparatory work before an emergency, to response and containment as the emergency unfolds, to recovery after the emergency has subsided.[10]

For those emergencies that were known to China since imperial times, particularly natural disasters such as floods and earthquakes, the state had accumulated a lot of experience and established practices and organizational arrangements to manage them. However, before November 2007 when the emergency response law came into effect, the government not only had weaker legal power to govern emergencies, but existing laws and administrative regulations were only piecemeal. As noted earlier, they either catered to specific singular events (e.g., earthquakes or floods) or covered only specific phases of emergency management (e.g., the response or recovery stage).

The 2007 law also contained all components of the technique. Among these components, the definition of an emergency seemed to receive the most curatorial effort prior to its inclusion in the emergency response law. The definition now not only neatly weaved in the four categories of emergencies, but also stated explicitly that their negative consequences necessitated state intervention:

> An emergency as mentioned in this Law shall refer to a natural disaster, accident-disaster, public health emergency or public security emergency, which takes place suddenly and unexpectedly, has caused or might cause serious societal damage and needs the adoption of emergency response measures.[11]

Unlike how it was presented in the master state plan, this definition customized the law's scope to fuse with the emergency categories to the extent that it did not need to describe the negative consequences anymore. This was because the impact had turned implicit in the categories it encompassed. The establishment seemed to have been learning from the successive enactments of the public health regulation and the master state plan to perfect the definition of emergency. The resultant effect was that the definition was now not only more condensed, but also announced when an emergency was consequential enough to warrant governmental intervention. The definition now contained its causes, effects, and solutions.

As highlighted in Chapter 2, the new law covered not one but four broad classes of sudden and extreme events and provided a universal four-level severity grading system.[12] These two components were already present in the state master plan and remained more or less unchanged. The organizing principles for emergency management evolved into five principles, however: unified command (*tongyi lingdao* 统一领导), a comprehensive and integrated approach (*zonghe xietiao* 综合协调), responses to be pegged to the emergency category (*fenlei guanli* 分类管理), tiered responsibilities (*fenji fuze* 分级负责), and finally, that emergency operations should be driven by local governments (*shudi guanli* 属地管理).[13] Academics had argued for these principles for various reasons. For example, academics had argued that moving the "center of gravity" of operations to lower levels of government would develop the field more comprehensively.[14] San, the academic-official also points out that the establishment had drawn from the American emergency management principles regarding a tiered responsibility approach and locally led emergency response:

> As you know about the American system, its emergency management moves from the national level down to the state level, and it's a tiered management approach based on strict legal (jurisdictional) definitions, no? This is unlike China where our leaders prefer to descend upon local levels at every opportunity. The Americans escalate emergency management level by level. So we wanted to introduce this idea to our leaders, that is, to operate by law. . . . And as you've also seen in our emergency response plans, this is called locally driven management. We condensed our learning from FEMA in these four characters (i.e., *shu-di guan-li*).[15]

San's explanation was a misreading of the U.S. emergency management. The U.S. model in fact starts with the local, not the national level. However, from what he subsequently said about "locally driven management," it is clear that the establishment was enthusiastic about introducing the state-led and tiered approaches in the U.S. context to create a more a bottom-up and graduated process in Chinese emergency management operations. The shift from a top-down and command structure to a more distributed governance structure was discernible and reflected what academic experts had been advocating in their deliberations on a risk governance framework.[16] This mimics the U.S. system, as reflected in the National Response Plan and Framework, especially the latter.

The stages of emergency management were another component elaborated. Previously missing activities specific to preparedness and prevention were explicitly mentioned in the emergency response law. The new law also covered all phases of emergency management, subscribing to an "all-hazards" and comprehensive model that academic experts had advocated for some time. Risk governance as a guiding concept also could not have been more obvious: besides highlighting risk management and establishing a national catastrophe insurance system, it touched on multiple stakeholders, including academic experts, the military, businesses, and citizens.

Above all, the new law was particularly detailed about the roles, responsibilities, and conduct of officials involved in emergency management. I present two examples below to show how methodical and meticulous the stipulations were for the government officials. The examples come from two articles that appeared in chapters on prevention and preparedness and monitoring and early warning. The chapters elaborated on risk management and disaster early warning, among other activities, and seemed to focus on how *emergencies* should be tamed. They were also components of the technique that had been refined since the 2003 regulation. However, on closer inspection, the articles were paying more attention to specifying what *government officials* should do as dictated under law.

Article 20 in the prevention and preparedness chapter – a chapter that focuses almost exclusively on government officials, except for one clause on schools – stipulates that the provincial government shall conduct the following prevention and preparedness activities:

Investigate, register and assess the risks of, organize the inspection and monitoring of, and order the relevant entities to take safety preventative and control measures for the danger sources and danger areas tending to cause severe and serious emergency incidents within its administrative region.[17] The danger sources and danger areas registered by the local people's government at or above the county level according to this Law shall be timely made available to the public according to the provisions of the state.[18]

The point that I highlight here is the degree of detail that the emergency response law devotes to matters of risk identification, assessment, and communication. These three risk components also appeared in the indigenized risk governance framework discussed in Chapter 4.

The second example, Article 44 from the monitoring and early warning chapter – which is completely devoted to directing officials on emergency management planning, conducting risk identification and assessment, emergency information dissemination, and activating response plans – stipulates the actions that local government officials need to take when they declare emergencies of grade 3 and 4 (i.e., the two least severe grades):

> After issuing a level 3 or level 4 warning and declaring the entry into a period of warning, a local people's government at or above the county level shall take the following measures according to the characteristics of and the damage likely to be caused by an emergency incident that is about to occur:
>
> 1 Activating the emergency response plan;
> 2 Ordering the relevant departments, specialized institutions, monitoring points and personnel with particular responsibility to timely collect and report the relevant information, announcing channels for the public to report emergency incident information, and strengthening the monitoring, forecast and warning of the occurrence and development of an emergency incident;
> 3 Organizing the relevant departments and institutions, specialized technicians and relevant experts and scholars to analyze and assess emergency incident information at any time, forecast the degree of possibility of occurrence, extent of effects and scale of intensity of an emergency incident as well as the level of an emergency incident likely to occur;
> 4 Issuing the forecast information and analysis and assessment results on an emergency incident concerning the general public in fixed time, and managing the coverage of relevant information; and
> 5 Issuing timely a warning that damage is likely to be caused by an emergency incident to the society according to the relevant provisions, publicizing the general knowledge on the avoidance and mitigation of damage, and announcing the consulting telephone numbers.

Similar to the attention to minutiae in the earlier example, article 44 dictates the actions that government officials are legally committed to perform according to the severity of the emergencies and the level of government at which they are situated. The focus on government officials was not exclusive to the examples of the two chapters above. In fact, of the 70 articles in the law, 58 focus directly on the roles, responsibilities, and conduct of the State Council and local governments from the provincial to the county level. In contrast, *only seven articles* dealt directly with individuals, businesses, and other non-governmental organizations. This stark imbalance between the attention given to government officials and non-state actors in the law is interesting, and I will show its significance when I elaborate on the governmentalization of Chinese emergency management.

A particular set of thinking, processes, and organizational arrangements had come together when the Emergency Response Law was enacted. The law represented a specific form of technique engendered by the establishment to govern emergencies, especially with the view of treating emergencies as risks that could be measured and managed by government officials. Table 6.1 juxtaposes the three legislative products of the emergency management field. It demonstrates a progressive articulation and emergence of prominent components that comprised the technique, including the principles of operation, the treatment of risk and its methods, inserting planning and academics into the process, various categories of emergencies to be subject to governance, and clear definitions of the stages of emergency.

The intent to govern disasters following the technique persisted after the emergency response law was enacted; after all, the technique had been honed over successive legislative experiments and it is not surprising that it would influence new and amended administrative and legal documents on emergency management. For example, the NPC passed the revision of one of the legal cornerstones in earthquake disaster management a year after the emergency response law came into effect. The revised 1997 Law on Protecting Against and Mitigating Earthquake (*Fangzhen Jianzai Fa* 防震减灾法) underwent significant expansion in 2008, with two new chapters and 45 new articles added to its original seven chapters and 48 articles. Continuing the focus on government officials, the added chapters elaborated on the earthquake planning responsibilities of departments under the State Council and local governments, as well as the supervision and audit of earthquake prevention and reduction activities, especially finances during the recovery phase. The revised law also articulated the involvement of experts in research and consultancy. Subsequently, the forest fire emergency response plan, first published in January 2006, was revised in December 2012. It conspicuously referenced the National Emergency Response Law, also using that legislation as its template. For example, the revised plan highlighted some organizing principles, and its grading of severity shifted from three grades in 2006 to four grades, and mirrored the language of the grading system in the emergency response law.

How the various components were coalescing into a technique shows that the organizational field of emergency management was forming in specific ways that were envisioned by the establishment and followed closely the risk governance framework produced by the academic experts. The academic experts managed to develop and embed their ideas gradually, first in regulations and plans produced by the State Council, then in legislative documents that enjoyed far more legal power than the administrative documents. Specifically, recognizable components such as emergency categories, risk assessment, severity grades, and emergency management phases were gradually introduced, became better defined as they moved from the Administrative Regulation on Public Health Emergencies, to the State Master Plan for Emergency Response, and finally enacted in the all-encompassing National Emergency Response Law. Thus, the technique was critical in the process of institutionalizing the organizational field. Next, I connect the technique to Foucault's notion of governmentality in the following section.

Applying the governmentality lens to China's emergency management

Foucauldian governmentality: a recap

Foucauldian governmentality refers to an array of institutions, forms of knowledge, and techniques that enable the exercise of power over some target population (Foucault 1991). When Foucault asserts that an entity has been governmentalized, he means that it has assumed a particular form and style of managing its subjects.

As highlighted in Chapter 1, governmentality can be applied in two ways: as an analytic of government and as a problematic of government. As an analytic of government, governmentality attempts to reveal our taken-for-granted ways of doing things, revealing how we think about and question them. In particular, this application relates to a particular regime of practices that "seeks to identify the emergence of that regime, examine the multiple sources of the elements that constitute it, and follow the diverse processes and relations by which these elements are assembled into relatively stable forms of organization and institutional practice" (Dean 2010:31).

Governmentality as a problematic of government examines how an issue when constructed as a problem offers an occasion for intervention and the application of specific solutions (Rose and Miller 1992). For example, considering the rise of corporate social responsibility in the European Union, we see how governmentality shows that social problems that were once strictly issues that the state had to contend with were later recast as opportunities for businesses to work in tandem with the state to identify areas of economic growth and profit (Vallentin and Murillo 2009).

Understanding risk governance in Foucauldian governmentality terms

The rise of risk governance as a policy is consistent with Foucault's historical account of governmentality. The availability of administrative apparatuses to the state to control the population is coterminous with the rise of statistics. Probabilities and costs can be calculated, and hence risks can be revealed and putatively controlled. The control brought about by a keen calculative rationality – evident in the application of statistics in actuarial science, management and accounting, epidemiology, and criminology – also closely relates to the notion of insurability in Beck's concept of the risk society (Beck 1999). Several governmentality scholars point out that risk bears qualities that allow ease of control. As pointed out by Ewald (1991) in his effort to situate insurance as a "technology of risk," risk is in essence a "hollow" concept, emptied of social content. Said another way, risk is nothing, as there is no risk inherent in reality. As a result, anything can be claimed as a risk through strategic maneuvers, so that "a specific mode of treatment of certain events" is tagged as "capable of happening to a group of individuals . . . to a population" (Ewald 1991:199). The flexibility and malleability of this "hollow" quality of risk allows it to draw strength from what is attached. Risk provides an occasion to order reality, rendering it into calculable form, such as through a disaster probability and magnitude. It is a system of representation (Ciborra 2006) that enables events to be "governed in particular ways, with particular techniques and for particular goals" (Dean 2010:206). Castel (1991) provides a case of how this is done. In his explanation of psychiatry in the United States and France, risk as a concept based in probabilistic thinking when applied to patients affects not only the medical practice of mental healthcare, but also the bureaucratic administration in such institutions. Just as important, risk has displaced the concept of dangerousness that is based more on experience and diagnosis. As a result, the threat of a mentally ill person committing violent and unpredictable acts becomes disconnected from psychiatrists' direct observation. It is now condensed to a statistic that represents "a combination of abstract factors which render more or less probable the occurrence of undesirable modes of behavior" (Castel 1991:287).

In sum, the governance of risk ironically is less about what constitutes risk *per se*, but more about how risk is deployed through regimes of practices. It seems obvious then, that the calculative rationality embedded in modern society and its institutions means that statistics and the probabilistic method, with their application in insurance, management, and other domains, will continue to be instrumental in risk governance.

Governmentalizing China's emergency management: would the real subjects please stand up

When we refract the case of China's emergency management through the prism of Foucauldian governmentality, the fact that the nascent organizational field was shaped by the academic experts' risk governance framework becomes obvious. The ensemble of components such as risk, risk management, and the cycle of emergency management became more defined and complete as it evolved from the regulation, to the state master plan, and finally, to the law itself. The emergency management organizational field had amplified and intensified the acts and impulses of "calculated supervision, administration and optimization" and "forces of society" (Jeffreys and Sigley 2009:3), with its emphasis on regulation, audit, and surveillance, as well as bringing in the private, for-profit sector and civil society. The technique was organizing emergency management in very specific, discernible ways – the forms of knowledge enshrined in categories and grading systems, building connections to and among institutionalized organizations, such as the NIEM and the State Council – revealing imprints of the establishment's design of risk governance. The organizational field of emergency management was therefore governmentalized.

If we were to follow an analytic of government and pay close attention to how the technique was forming and how it shaped the organizational field, the target population seemed to be the government officials who were responsible for emergency management. The technique did not focus on the private sector or the civil society, even though both were also highlighted as important constituents which should be subject to governance. In retrospect, the target was also not the emergencies that were assiduously categorized and elucidated, even though in the process the SARS virus, which was initially unnamed and therefore unintelligible, was eventually rendered "governable" under public health emergencies.

The idea that government officials are the target population or subject for governance becomes clearer when we scrutinize the Emergency Response Law, the legislative landmark of the organizational field. As pointed out before, only seven of the 70 articles in the law pertained to the conduct of individuals, businesses, and other non-governmental organizations. The overwhelming majority of the articles elaborated on the roles, responsibilities, and conduct of the officials in the State Council and local governments. Furthermore, examining the new organizational entities created in the emergency management organizational field, such as the EMO-SC, the NIEM, and the quasi-professional associations, it is clear that they were created to direct, coordinate, inform, or train government officials in the policies and practice of emergency management. The true target thus seems to be government officials. The government officials themselves were the subjects whose thinking and behavior were undergoing intensive scrutiny and remaking. They had to familiarize themselves with a plethora of emergency categories, severity grades, and stages of emergency management. They were the ones who needed to undergo training in and to apply risk management methods and produce emergency response plans. These observations suggest that government officials, especially those at the helm of local and central governments, were the ones being rendered more "governable" by the establishment. This is a surprise because one would surmise that the establishment, as part of the state apparatus, would be concentrating its efforts on reining in non-state actors, such as businesses (Hutter 2006; Hutter and Jones 2007) or citizens (Ewald 1991; Foucault 1991), rather than officials.

This interesting insight presents a modification to the study of governmentality. Risk management techniques were putatively used to subdue and govern emergencies, such as natural disasters and epidemics. They were meant to render these events calculable and therefore subject to governance. Even in Foucault's (1991) classic text of governmentality, techniques and regimes of control (e.g., health statistics) are applied to a target population (e.g., households). Instead, in the Chinese emergency management case, the target population was in fact government officials themselves, whereas the techniques and regimes of control such as risk management methods and organizing principles were applied to emergencies.

This realization creates an issue because it contradicts what was being claimed as problematic. Specifically, when we apply a problematic of government to the Chinese emergency management case, the establishment was attempting to problematize emergencies, not government officials. Emergencies were defined as categories of events that disrupt or threaten to disrupt societal stability with death, injury, and economic loss. As a result, they were a danger to continued economic growth and societal status quo, necessitating state intervention. This understanding of emergency as dangerous converges and aligns with Stallings's (1995) analysis of the putative threat the U.S. earthquake establishment was constructing: earthquakes were cast as problems that could be solved by policy and scientific experts familiar with the natural hazard. Similarly, Dombrowsky's (1995) astute observation of law definers as enacting their involvement into the definition of disasters they have created reflects this self-referential quality that a problematic of government elucidates.

This seeming contradiction between the analytic and problematic of government as applied to Chinese emergency management can be reconciled via a two-step process. In the first step, emergencies had to be problematized by the establishment in ways that only the party-state could be the prominent and legitimate provider of the solution. As seen in Chapter 5, the establishment, with the help of academic experts, mobilized insider cultural knowledge and party-state ideologies manipulated to justify emergency management as a state function and a new organizational field.

Once it is clear emergencies were the problem that required the party-state to solve, the state could proceed with the second step, which was to reshape itself to better manage emergencies. As seen in Chapter 4 and this chapter, the establishment forged a technique in which government officials had to govern emergencies in specific ways. This in turn compelled government officials to modify their thinking and practices. Simply put, the first step in the two-step process of governmentalization sets the stage by making the population to be governed as the main actor to solve the issue that was problematized. Once that step was accomplished and legitimized, the second step enacts the ways that would putatively make the main actor better at solving the problem. These maneuvers create the opportunities for governmentalization to unfold.

As mentioned in Chapter 1, governmentalization in Foucauldian studies can be equated to institutionalization in neoinstitutional theory. This is because both processes highlight how particular rationalities are embedded in specific sections of society, to the extent that certain beliefs, goals, and behaviors have become natural and therefore taken for granted. However, governmentality departs from the neoinstitutionalist account in one critical aspect: it reveals how organized actors mobilize ideas such as categories and grading systems along with cultural accounts to ensure that the organizational field is aligned to their goals. Importantly, through governmentalization, what is considered natural in the field is what powerful organized actors have intended to be seen as natural.

In the Chinese emergency management case, the governmentality lens further reveals how the establishment created the organizational field of emergency management to corral officials in ways advocated by academic experts. Beginning in the 1990s the establishment leveraged on the party-state intent to maintain its regime when it launched its efforts to remake the government. As you may recall the existential concerns of the governing elites for the loss of its ideological grip in Chapter 2 and the rise of governance and concerns with risks and disaster risk reduction in Chapter 4, these developments gave the establishment, especially its "establishment intellectuals" (Hamrin and Cheek 1986), the ideational resources to create and curate the technique to its finished version in Emergency Response Law. The purpose of forming an organizational field of emergency management was thus to render government officials in that field to be more governable and useful to the party-state. As Jeffreys and Sigley (2009) note:

> The crucial point to note is that within all this discussion on the changing function of government in China the continued importance and necessity of the CCP (Chinese Communist Party) is not in question. The CCP is *the* "ruling party" and the one and only possible party that can wear this mantle, and hence its cohort of 70 million cadres must be continuously strengthened, disciplined and trained. That task entails . . . disciplining errant and potential errant members through auditing process . . . and training officials as professionals to better meet the new challenges of governing China in the twenty-first century . . .
>
> (p. 13)

In order to maintain and continue the communist regime, the party-state needed to subject its own elites to governance. That includes imposing discipline on "errant and potential errant members," and, most relevant to emergency management, subjecting officials to training. This means that sustaining an organizational field that also meets the broader goals of the governing elites had to go beyond simply one-time efforts that inscribed the technique into the field's regulations and laws. In the next and concluding section, I discuss how analyzing the governmentalizing and institutionalizing of the field requires us to appreciate the role played by organizational entities such as quasi-professional associations, research centers, training institutes, and emergency management educational programs. These entities were the sites for producing and perpetuating new and established knowledge on emergency management. I also highlight another role of academic experts: in addition to being creators of the risk governance framework, which formed the ideational centerpiece of the organizational field, academic experts also played the role of "institutional evangelists" by training and advising government officials in emergency management, as well as collecting feedback that further helped curate risk governance to maintain the field.

Institutional evangelists: perpetuating the field

While the governmentality lens allows us to see how the field was institutionalized in a way that made what the establishment intended to appear natural and

normal, additional questions center on how the field was sustained and perpetuated, especially after the initial intensive institutionalization phase.

Returning to discussions on the field formation process, I highlight the role
of the academic experts as "institutional evangelists" who circulated through the
various organizations such as the State Council, the NIEM, research centers,
and quasi-professional associations with ties to local governments. Because of
the research they conducted, the advice and training they provided, and more
importantly because of their status as "establishment intellectuals" (Hamrin and
Cheek 1986), academic experts enjoyed unique access to governing elites, which
in turn further perpetuated their ability to conduct research and offer advice.
In the paragraphs that follow, I elaborate on the activities that academic experts
performed to develop and sustain the organizational field. I also show how they
nourished their research careers and expanded their spheres of influence by per-
forming these activities.

Emergency management made its way into the state research agenda when
the field was designated to be a domain for development in various state plans,
including the 11th Five-year Plan and the long- to medium-term program on science and technological development. The National Natural Science Foundation
created a dedicated program in 2009 to fund emergency management-related
projects under "non-routine emergency management research."[19] The program
set aside 80 million RMB yuan (US$11 million) for six years. The core research
objectives were to understand how events unfolded and evolved, and how information flowed in emergencies, the theoretical foundation for policymaking in
emergency management, and individual and group psychological responses in
public emergencies.[20] The research focus for each year also varied. For example,
the call for proposals in 2013 asked for better understanding of risks in emergencies using the concept of vulnerability, focusing on principles of business continuity and resilience models.[21]

There was a natural increase in research projects in emergency management
when it became more salient within the state research agenda. As Figure 6.1 illustrates, the total number of research projects on emergency management in both
the physical/natural and social sciences spiked and has grown, albeit unevenly,
since 2006.[22] The term *yingji* (应急) – which I have translated as emergency
response and emergency management, depending on the context – did not even
appear in project titles until 2004, which was a year after the SARS crisis. The
bulk of projects seemed to come from the period of 2008–2011, after the emergency response law had been enacted and in the aftermath of disasters such as
the South China snowstorms, the 2008 Wenchuan earthquake, and the Zhouqu
mudslide. While it is impossible to tell from the graph the extent to which the
projects drew their funding from the dedicated program for emergency management, the numbers capture the general level of interest and attention academic
communities accord to emergency management. Academic experts in disaster
management and public crises were the beneficiaries of this spike in funding.

Academic experts also benefited from new university research centers being
established nationwide to study emergency management. For example, the

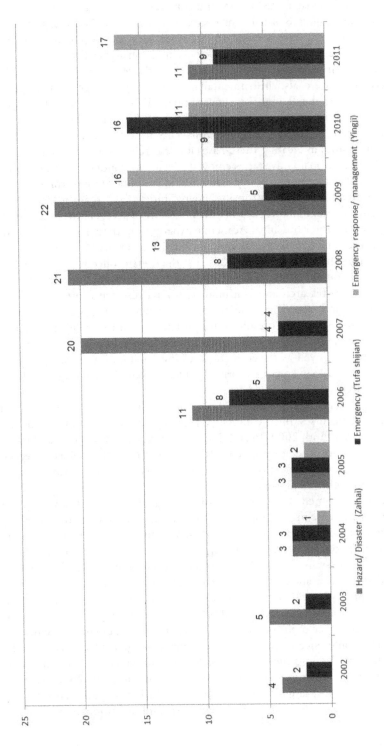

Figure 6.1 Emergency Management Research Projects Commissioned at the National Level (2002–2011)

Academy of Disaster Reduction and Emergency Management (ADREM), founded in Beijing Normal University, was created in 2006 as part of the medium- to long-term science and technological development plan in the public safety and security domain. For example, Shanghai Jiaotong University established an emergency management research center.[23] Additionally, local governments were also instrumental in supporting emergency management research bases; the Beijing city government, for example, helped found the Center for Crisis Management Research in the School of Public Policy and Management (SPPM) at Tsinghua University in 2004. The selection of specific universities in creating these bases for research was not random. Tsinghua and Beijing Normal Universities enjoyed a legacy of conducting either disaster-related or broader public policy research and advising top government leaders in these areas. This is not surprising, taking into account that these universities are located in Beijing, thus enjoying the proximity of access to the administrative and political center of China. Academic experts from these two academic institutions were invited to several key fora discussing emergency response, especially during the 2003 SARS crisis, such as the fourth collective study session of the central committee in April 2003 and the special expert conference in June 2003. Besides research and consultancy, several research centers also offered professional and academic training on emergency management, such as the ADREM and SPPM. As a result of this professional and academic training, several of their graduates also filled other similar organizations involved in research and training, as well as government, creating an alumni web of relationships that connected ex-mentors to former students, schools of thought and ideas, and resources and strategic advice.

Existing academic departments also jumped into the fray to offer emergency management courses. Jinan University of Guangdong started to offer undergraduate courses in April 2009. In addition to research and consultancy and training middle to senior level government officials, the NIEM also trained emergency management instructors at other academies of governance in provinces, municipalities, and other administrative units.

The establishment founded professional organizations in the wake of legislative achievements, responding to the legal requirement of increasingly involving academic experts in emergency management. As noted earlier, the International Emergency Management Society (TIEMS) established its Chinese chapter in July 2009. The national committee for TIEMS China included several academic experts in emergency management, such as members of the EMO-SC expert committee. In July 2010, the first Chinese emergency management association was established in Guangdong by the emergency management office of the provincial government. Its inauguration ceremony was held at a conference on Chinese emergency management legislation, which naturally involved academic experts. Shaanxi province established the second emergency management association in China in April 2012. Similar to the Guangdong emergency management association, the Shaanxi association was to be a forum for both academic experts and practitioners of emergency management to collaborate and improve the quality of emergency management in the province.

At the same time, specific objects of knowledge were created and institutionalized. Some historical or focusing events of the field have been institutionalized, and the historical narratives of the field have become stock knowledge and accepted as truth. For example, across various texts, especially textbooks, the year 2004 would be understood as the year in which the framework for emergency response planning and emergency response plans was being prepared in earnest, and crystallized in the following stock phrase *"Zhongguo yingji yu'an de bianzhi zhi nian"* (中国应急预案的编制之年).[24] The term *yi'an san zhi* ("one 'case' three mechanisms") that the establishment used to describe the field-building strategy was also institutionalized and presented as canon.[25]

The main organized actors who circulated through these organizations, texts, and contexts – research bases, training institutes, professional associations, laws and regulations, and scholarly journals – were the academic experts. Being institutional evangelists, they conducted research about the field, trained and advised government officials, and championed emergency management in the mass media, being the de facto spokespersons who offered extensive interviews on the subject matter. For example, Lan Xue, a prominent U.S.-trained public policy scholar who was already championing crisis management before the 2003 SARS outbreak, lectured at the fourth collective study session in April 2003, attended the special expert work conference in June 2003, and was also a conspicuous contributor to academic discussion of emergency management. In fact, Xue was actively consulted on the eve of the SARS crisis.[26] Together with other academics, such as Zhong, his former doctoral student who became a NIEM-CAG faculty member, they retroactively applied a generational view of the emergency management field, describing what happened before the 2003 SARS crisis as first generation (or version 1.0), what happened after SARS as the second generation (or version 2.0), and thereafter, the emergence of a third-generational stage (or version 3.0).[27] Previously, no one had articulated that emergency management as a "modern" governmental entity existed in China, let alone segmenting the development into intelligible generations or versions. The ideational basis and construction of a historical emergency management system relied on the knowledge-production capabilities of academic experts such as Xue and Zhong.

Just like a new high-end fashion industry was created in India (Khaire 2014), academic experts served as the institutional curators, carefully selecting what went into the collective memory and knowledge base of the emergency management field, and in turn helped determine what would be left outside its boundaries. The knowledge objects created by the academic experts seemed to have not only provided the cognizance of field boundaries and definitions – orienting the establishment to what emergency management should and should not be as it went about building the field – but also contributed to a deeper collective awareness of field membership. That collective awareness was also built on the networks enabled by the academic experts, in their training of and the advice offered to government officials. As Mu further elaborated on the relationship and dynamic between academic experts and government officials:

> The situation in China now is that officials respect academic qualifications, and those with higher qualifications tend to be promoted. Because he's [i.e., an official] highly educated, he's predisposed positively toward those who are also learned. He'd trust scholars, especially when many scholars are his mentors. So there is this teacher-student relationship. Because of this relationship, it allows new ideas to be absorbed by the [well-educated] official in an easier way. It's through such a process . . . As for the Chinese government, it is also moving toward an expert-based [inaudible]. This is to say it has expert advisors and also access to expert think tanks. For example, the emergency management [office] in this city [government] has an expert pool. The [redacted] district [government] in this city also has an expert pool. So how do they interact? It's through the government purchasing consultancy services from the experts. The Chinese government is already doing this. Said in another way, it is the government paying for topics [i.e., projects]. For example, the government wants to know how to conduct a drill according to an emergency response plan, how should it do that? It will pay, say [several tens of thousands] RMB yuan, to an expert to design that. . . . This is how a government organization can get a support team.[28]

Implicit in Mu's explanation is the recognition that academic experts entered into a symbiotic relationship with the officials as they received material resources, recognition, and thus became legitimate in the eyes of the government. In the process, they would acquire an understanding of the ideational and practical requirements of the government and accordingly tailor their research. Given that there are fewer experts and research and training bases than there are officials, more officials would be connected to a smaller nexus of experts and their organizations.

Here, I bring in the notion of networked hegemony (George 2012) to characterize the web of relationships among academic experts and government that helped to create the emergency management field. The networked modifier suggests a distributed yet collective effort that could not be simplistically characterized as hierarchical (top-down) or peer-to-peer (horizontal) (Powell 1990). Just as important, the academics themselves served as the critical network nodes, filling structural holes (Burt 2004) and boundary-spanning (Levina and Vaast 2005), making connections across ideas, organizational access, and resources. For example, Chun Chang Shan, the scholar-expert I have cited heavily, fits this profile. He served on multiple committees, actively gave talks and lectures, and was also extensively interviewed by the media. In one interview, he recounted his formal association with 10 organizations, including expert committees, professional associations, and universities.[29]

Table 6.1 Comparing the Development of the Technique Across Time

Components of Technique	Administrative Regulation on Public Health Emergency (2003)	State Master Plan on Emergency Response (2005)	National Emergency Response Law (2007)
Definition of emergency	A sudden and unexpected incident that is causing or potentially causes harm to public health. An incident could be due to, but not limited to, an epidemic, known or yet to be identified, a case of severe food poisoning, or industrial contamination.	A sudden and unexpected event that is causing or potentially causes serious levels of death and injury, property damage and loss, environmental degradation and societal harm, and endangerment to public safety and security.	A natural disaster, accident-disaster, public health emergency, or public security emergency, which takes place suddenly and unexpectedly, is causing or potentially causes serious societal damage, and needs the adoption of emergency response measures.
Principles of Organization	1) Unified command (*tongyi lingdao* 统一领导) 2) Tiered responsibilities (*fenji fuze* 分级负责)	1) People-centered (*yi ren wei ben*), reduce danger, harm and loss 2) Be mindful of danger (*ju'an si wei*), focus on prevention 3) Unified command, tiered responsibilities 4) Act according to law, strengthen management 5) Rapid and coordinated response 6) Relying on technology, improving emergency management quality*	1) Unified command 2) Comprehensive and integrated approach (*zonghe xietiao* 综合协调) 3) Responses to be pegged to the emergency category (*fenlei guanli* 分类管理) 4) Tiered responsibilities 5) Operations driven by local governments (*shudi guanli* 属地管理)
Emergency Categories	N.A.**	Yes, all four categories	Yes, same four categories
Risk Management	Alluded to as "hidden dangers" (*yinhuan* 隐患) that needed to be identified, analyzed, and reported, but not explicitly as risks.***	Yes, conducting risk assessment under Prevention and Preparedness stage	Yes, conducting risk assessment under Prevention and Preparedness stage Various levels of governments shall take out personal accidental injury insurance for emergency responders and provide them with protective gear. The state shall develop the insurance industry and a catastrophe insurance system.

(Continued)

Table 6.1 (Continued)

Components of Technique	Administrative Regulation on Public Health Emergency (2003)	State Master Plan on Emergency Response (2005)	National Emergency Response Law (2007)
Prevention & Preparedness	Yes	No, but it specifies emergency response plans need to be drilled and exercised.	Yes
Monitoring & Early Warning	Yes	Yes	Yes
Emergency Response & Rescue	Yes, but not in exact same terms.	Yes	Yes
Recovery & Reconstruction	No	Yes	Yes
Role of Academic Experts	Should be consulted *after the onset of emergency* to assess and advise on emergency response.	Specifies the creation of an expert database, the involvement of experts as policy advisors *prior* to onset of emergencies, and to involve them in response if necessary.	Specifies experts should be involved *prior* to the onset of emergencies, particularly in assessing the risk of emergencies (expressed as the possibility and consequence of the events in the law) and its likely severity grade *after its onset.*

* See Article 1.5 of the State Master Plan.
** As the regulation only pertained to public health, it would not highlight other types of emergencies.
*** See articles 15 and 24 of the Administrative Regulation on Public Health Emergency.

Conclusion

In this chapter, I showed how the emergence and evolution of an ensemble of components that could be traced back to the risk governance framework advocated by academic experts was inscribed into the organizational field of emergency management. The components constituted the technique that was most obvious in legislative and administrative landmarks, such as the regulations and laws that were approved and enacted, especially during the intensive institutionalized period of field formation. Following that, I used the concept of technique as a basis to point out how the governmentalization of the field took place. Finally, I introduced the concept of institutional evangelists to show how the framework that was inscribed into the field relied upon the continuous curatorial efforts and circulation of academic experts through various organizational entities in the field. The insights elaborated in this chapter could not be rendered obvious without the thick description and deep analyses performed in Chapters 4 and 5 which elaborated on the organizational field and risk governance framework.

Notes

1 State Council executive meeting chaired by Premier Wen held on April 14, 2003. See p. 6 in Xue, Zhang and Zhong (2003).
2 The third stage was phrased differently from what would be later formalized as emergency response and rescue (*yingjichuzhi yu jiuyuan* 应急处置与救援). At that point in time (May 2003), the fourth stage, recovery and reconstruction (*huifu yu chongjian* 恢复与重建), was not in the document.
3 See Article 1.1 in State Master Plan.
4 Refer to the record dated April 13, 2004, p. 120 in Shan et al. (2012).
5 The numbers cited, while fantastical, unfortunately seem to gel with the statistics in the Chinese emergency management literature. See for example Shan (2011), Figures 1–1 and 1–2, p. 8. To illustrate, the death toll for accident-disasters was 136,755 in 2004. This worked out to be about 375 individuals every day. In contrast, for the same year, the death toll from natural disasters was 2,250.
6 Interview with Gui.
7 Interview with Yang.
8 See for example the 10 grades of severity in Xu, Feiqiong. 1997. "Zaiji jiqi shiyi (Disaster grades and their interpretation)." *Zaihai Xue (Journal of Catastrophology)* 12(1):16–18 and Feng's four-grade system based on Zhongjin Ma's established three-grade system in Feng, Lihua. 2000. "Zaihai dengji yanjiu jinzhan (Development of research on disaster grades)." *Zaihai Xue (Journal of Catastrophology)* 15(3):72–6.
9 Interview with Yang.
10 See for example, Zhong, Kaibin. 2009. "Huigu yu qianzhan: Zhongguo yingji tixi jianshe (Constructing China's emergency management system: A review and its prospects)." *Zhengzhi Xue Yanjiu (CASS Journal of Political Science)* 1:78–88; Shan, Chun Chang and Lan Xue, eds. 2012. *Yingji Guanli Gailun: Lilun Yu Shijian (An Introduction to Emergency Management: Theory and Practice)*. Beijing, China: Gaodeng Jiaoyu Chubanshe; It has also been given other accolades, such as the "silver bullet" for managing the crises of tomorrow (*shangfang baojian* 尚方宝剑; literally imperial sword and a symbol of carte blanche power bestowed by an emperor on officials, granting them complete discretion when discharging their duties, especially to execute criminals immediately). See People's Daily Online.

Jujiao Tufa Shijian Yingdui Fa (Focusing on the National Emergency Response Law). Retrieved from http://politics.people.com.cn/GB/8198/106624/index.html.

11 See Article 3 in the National Emergency Response Law. I have amended the English translation of the law from www.lawinfochina.com.

12 In the law, public security emergencies were implicitly (and curiously) excluded from being subject to the four-level severity grading system (see Article 3). Because I focus on natural disasters, I will not be discussing this observation in this study.

13 See Article 4 in the National Emergency Response Law.

14 Xue, Lan and Kaibin Zhong. 2005. "Tufa gonggong shijian fenlei, fenji yu fenqi: Yingji tizhi de guanli jichu. (Classification of types, levels, and stages of emergencies: The managerial foundation for government emergency response system)." *Zhongguo Xingzheng Guanli (Chinese Public Administration)* 2:102–7.

15 Interview with San.

16 See for example Wang, Hongwei and Keyong Dong. 2011. "Yingji shehui dongyuan moshi de zhuanbian: cong 'minglingxing' dao 'zhilixing' (The paradigm shift in the social mobilization of emergency response: From 'command and control' to 'governance' model)." *Guojia Xingzheng Xueyuan Xuekan (Journal of Academy of Governance)* 5:22–6.

17 "Severe and serious emergency incidents" refer to the two most serious emergencies which are Grade 1 and 2 emergencies.

18 I lightly edited the English translation of Articles 20 and 44 made available at www.lawinfochina.com/.

19 See www.nsfc.gov.cn/nsfc/cen/yjjhnew/menu_11_5.htm. Refer to the side panel for the "non-routine emergency management research" (*fei-chang-gui tufa shijian yingji guanli yanjiu* 非常规突发事件应急管理研究).

20 See for example the 2009 call for proposals: www.nsfc.gov.cn/nsfc/cen/yjjhnew/2009/20090220_03.htm.

21 See the 2013 call for proposals for more details: www.nsfc.gov.cn/nsfc/cen/yjjhnew/2013/20130312_04.htm.

22 In assembling Figure 6–1, I searched for the following phrases – *yingji*, *tufa shijian*, and *zaihai* – in project titles using the databases of the National Natural Science Foundation of China (for physical and natural sciences) and the National Social Science Fund of China (NSSF). I omitted 2012 because the NNSF database did not return results from 2012 onward, although the NSSF did. It was not clear whether no projects had been commissioned (which was highly unlikely) or that they were not yet in the system. In addition, to maintain a ten-year comparison, I started from the year 2002 instead of 2003. There could be cases of duplicate counting, as a project could contain all three phrases. That said, a quick eyeballing of the titles seemed to suggest that overlapping, while present, did not modify the trend significantly.

23 See Gao, Xiaoping and Yihong Liu. 2009. "Woguo yingji guanli yanjiu shuping (shang) (Review on national emergency management (Part 1))." *Zhongguo Xingzheng Guanli (Chinese Public Administration)* 9:29–33. It is less clear when the emergency management research center in Shanghai Jiaotong University is established, but based on an Internet search, it seems to be 2008.

24 See for example Shan (2011), Shan and Xue (2012), and Chen (2010).

25 See for example Shan and Xue (2012).

26 See pp. 5–7 in Xue, Zhang and Zhong (2003).

27 See Xue and Zhong (2010) and Xue, Lan. 2010. "Zhongguo yingji guanli xitong de yanbian (The evolution of Chinese emergency management system)." *Xingzheng Guanli Gaige (Public Management Reforms)* 8:22–4.

28 Interview with Mu.

29 Interview with Shan reported in *Labor Protection* magazine, dated January 17, 2007. Retrieved November 13, 2013, from www.esafety.cn/laodongbaohu/1089.html.

References

Beck, Ulrich. 1999. *World Risk Society*. Cambridge, UK: Polity Press.

Burt, Ronald S. 2004. "Structural Holes and Good Ideas." *American Journal of Sociology* 110(2):349–99.

Castel, Robert. 1991. "From Dangerousness to Risk." Pp. 281–98 in *The Foucault Effect: Studies in Governmentality*, edited by G. Burchell, C. Gordon and P. Miller. Chicago, IL: University of Chicago Press.

Chen, Zheng Ming. 2010. "Zhongguo yingji guanli de xingqi (The Ascendance of Emergency Management in China)." *Dongnan Xueshu (Southeast Academic Research)* 1:41–7.

Ciborra, Claudio. 2006. "Imbrication of Representations: Risk and Digital Technologies." *Journal of Management Studies* 43(6):1339–56.

Dean, Mitchell. 2010. *Governmentality: Power and Rule in Modern Society*. Thousand Oaks, CA: Sage Publications.

Dombrowsky, Wolf R. 1995. "Again and Again: Is a Disaster What We Call a 'Disaster'? Some Conceptual Notes on Conceptualizing the Object of Disaster Sociology." *International Journal of Mass Emergencies and Disasters* 13(3):241–54.

Edelman, Lauren. 1992. "Legal Ambiguity and Symbolic Structures: Organizational Mediation of Civil Rights Law." *American Journal of Sociology* 97(6):1531–76.

Ewald, François. 1991. "Insurance and Risk." Pp. 197–210 in *The Foucault Effect: Studies in Governmentality*, edited by G. Burchell, C. Gordon and P. Miller. Chicago, IL: University of Chicago Press.

Foucault, Michel. 1991. "Governmentality." Pp. 87–104 in *The Foucault Effect: Studies in Governmentality*, edited by G. Burchell, C. Gordon and P. Miller. Hemel Hempstead: Harvester Wheatsheaf.

George, Cherian. 2012. *Freedom from the Press: Journalism and State Power in Singapore*. Singapore: NUS Press.

Hamrin, Carol Lee and Timothy Cheek, eds. 1986. *China's Establishment Intellectuals*. Armonk, NY: M. E. Sharpe.

Hutter, Bridget M. 2006. "Risk, Regulation, and Management." Pp. 202–27 in *Risk in Social Science*, edited by P. Taylor-Gooby and J. O. Zinn. New York, NY: Oxford University Press.

Hutter, Bridget M. and Clive J. Jones. 2007. "From Government to Governance: External Influences on Business Risk Management." *Regulation & Governance* 1(1):27–45.

Jeffreys, Elaine and Gary Sigley. 2009. "Governmentality, Governance and China." Pp. 1–23 in *China's Governmentalities: Governing Change, Changing Government*, edited by E. Jeffreys. Abingdon, Oxon: Routledge.

Khaire, Mukti. 2014. "Fashioning an Industry: Socio-Cognitive Processes in the Construction of Worth of a New Industry." *Organization Studies* 35(1):41–74.

Levina, N. and E. Vaast. 2005. "The Emergence of Boundary Spanning Competence in Practice: Implications for Implementation and Use of Information Systems." *MIS Quarterly* 29(2):335–63.

Lynnggaard, Kennet. 2007. "The Institutional Construction of a Policy Field: A Discursive Institutional Perspective on Change within the Common Agricultural Policy." *Journal of the European Public Policy* 14(2):293–312.

Meyer, Alan D. 1982. "Adapting to Environmental Jolts." *Administrative Science Quarterly* 27(4):515–37.

Powell, Walter W. 1990. "Neither Market nor Hierarchy: Network Forms of Organization." Pp. 295–336 in *Research in Organizational Behavior*, Vol. 12. Greenwich, CT: JAI Press, Inc.

Rose, Nikolas and Peter Miller. 1992. "Political Power Beyond the State: Problematics of Government." *British Journal of Sociology* 43(2):173–205.

Shan, Chun Chang. 2011. *Yingji Guanli: Zhongguo Tese De Yunxing Moshi Yu Shijian (Emergency Management: The Operation Model and Practice with Chinese Characteristics)*. Beijing, China: Beijing Normal University Publishing Group.

Shan, Chun Chang and Lan Xue, eds. 2012. *Yingji Guanli Gailun: Lilun Yu Shijian (An Introduction to Emergency Management: Theory and Practice)*. Beijing, China: Gaodeng Jiaoyu Chubanshe.

Shan, Chun Chang, Lan Xue, Xiu Lan Zhang and Hui Ding, eds. 2012. *Zhongguo Yingji Guanli Dashi Ji (2003~2007) (Memorabilia of China's Emergency Management)*. Beijing, China: Shehui Wenxian Kexue Chuban She.

Stallings, Robert A. 1995. *Promoting Risk: Constructing the Earthquake Threat*. New York, NY: Aldine de Gruyter.

Vallentin, Steen and David Murillo. 2009. "C.S.R. as Governmentality." *CSR & Business in Society Working Paper 04-2009*. Retrieved November 3, 2013, from (http://openarchive.cbs.dk/bitstream/handle/10398/7908/wp%20cbscsr%202009-4.pdf).

Xue, Lan, Qiang Zhang and Kaibin Zhong. 2003. *Weiji Guanli: Zhuangxingqi Zhongguo Mianlin De Tiaozhan (Crisis Management in China: The Challenge of [China's] Transition)*. Beijing, China: Qinghua Daxue Chuban She.

Xue, Lan and Kaibin Zhong. 2010. "Turning Danger (危) to Opportunities (机): Reconstructing China's National System for Emergency Management after 2003." Pp. 190–210 in *Learning from Catastrophes: Strategies for Reactions and Response*, edited by H. Kunreuther and M. Useem. Upper Saddle River, NJ: Pearson Education/Prentice Hall.

7 "Field" work
Building a new emergency management in China

In this chapter, I begin with an overview of what I have achieved by using the conceptual tools highlighted in Chapter 1. I discuss the value of using these concepts and some of the surprising insights that I have gained from the analyses. Next, I discuss the significance of curation and the role of institutional evangelists, specifically the academic experts. Because "curation" and "institutional evangelists" are terms that I derived inductively from this case analysis, I discuss them in greater detail, sketching the modest contributions I add to theory. Last, I highlight the limitations of my study and offer suggestions for future research.

I was interested in understanding the ideational basis of "field" work, that is, which and how ideas were mobilized and by whom during the genesis and early development of an organizational field. The rise of China's emergency management in the wake of the 2003 SARS crisis offered a unique case to understand these processes. As emphasized in the prologue, because the attention of the Chinese governing elites to emergency management was persistent, intensive, and pervasive, it was a natural case of a fledgling field with clear beginnings.

My investigation focused on the culturally accepted accounts that the Chinese establishment used to build a framework that integrated new and old practices and ideologies. It also led me to the strategies that the establishment adopted to juxtapose new interventions and existing practices together, even though the latter had already been cast as inefficient and insufficient. In essence, my analysis elaborates on the legitimacy project on which the establishment embarked to justify the organizational field it was building and the risk governance framework to which the field was intimately connected. The legitimacy project was largely an internal one during the field's early formation stage because the establishment had to build quickly a collective awareness to bind new members of the field together. This understanding of this legitimacy project as a largely inward-looking one provided me another motivation to examine the internal dynamics of China's emergency management because thus far institutional literature on legitimacy has been preoccupied with the external audience, such as the public (Deephouse et al. 2017). My study begins to correct this neglect by turning our attention inward to understand how organizational fields foster the "common enterprise" outlook and commitment by gaining acceptance from internal audiences (DiMaggio and Powell 1983; Goodstein, Blair-Loy and Wharton 2009; Suchman 1995).

The conceptual tools that I assembled to examine the internal legitimacy project were borrowed from three main theoretical bases: institutional literature, sociological studies on disasters, and Foucauldian studies of governmentality. Because I approach the rise of China's emergency management as a legitimacy project, institutional theory forms the basis of my arguments' conceptual architecture (Zald and Lounsbury 2010). Specifically, legitimacy and organizational field formed the core concepts in my theoretical toolkit. The notion of an issue-based organizational field (Hoffman 1999; Wooten and Hoffman 2017) helped me see that the practice of emergency management in China required advocates to push it into the national agenda as a separate governmental function from pre-existing and established domains, such as earthquake management, industrial safety, and epidemic control. Given that emergency management had been defined by these domains, efforts to establish it as a distinctive organizational field could become highly contested. An issue-based organizational field concept was useful because it drew my attention to identifying the stakeholders involved in a much more dynamic manner, accommodating their exits or returns depending on how the field developed (Hoffman 1999; Wooten and Hoffman 2017). That said, upon closer analysis, China's emergency management field was not actually a contested field like other emerging fields (e.g., HIV/AIDS treatment advocacy in Maguire, Hardy and Lawrence 2004). Nonetheless, China's emergency management can still be characterized as a "patchy" field (Quirke 2013), in which its institutional environment was interpenetrated by existing policy domains, such as insurance, disaster management, and industrial safety, and increasingly by issues such as food and drug safety (see, for example, Yang 2008) which were also candidates for being corralled into its domain. Its "patchiness" notwithstanding, China's emergency management managed to develop sufficiently independent and recognizable features, including its ensemble of legislative (e.g., emergency response law), administrative (e.g., state master plan), and organizational entities (e.g., the State Council, NIEM, emergency management offices), which stood apart from other more established fields and domains in which it was embedded.

Legitimacy is one of the key constructs in institutional theory. It describes the shine of acceptance and cultural fit that organized actors seek from their institutional environment. Institutional theorists believe the claims that organized actors make in their attempts at legitimacy have to be read closely against the sociocultural contexts from which they are produced. Therefore, using the idea of legitimacy and legitimacy projects helped me frame the claims that the establishment was making as not just simply rational (read: self-interest) arguments, but also appeals to morality and cultural assumptions, in ways that infuse the field with "value beyond the technical requirements of the task at hand" (Selznick 1996:271). To that end, Suchman's (1995) three-fold legitimacy typology proved to be highly useful. By applying his typology to China's emergency management, I came to the insight that cognitive legitimacy cannot be of equal standing with pragmatic and moral legitimacy in theoretical and epistemological terms. Returning to the notion of insider cultural knowledge, cognitive legitimacy formed the very basis on which myths, cultural heroes, proverbs, and even party-state ideologies were chosen and presented. Therefore, its foundational status, though implicit in the literature, needs to be further theorized. Based on my data, I argue that cognitive legitimacy penetrates both pragmatic and moral legitimacy. Without the deeply held assumptions that are rooted in cognitive legitimacy, what can be claimed to be useful (pragmatic) or ethical (moral) could not have been established in the first place.

Sociological studies on disasters contributed two key concepts to my theoretical toolkit: establishment and claims-making. These concepts were critical to my analysis and theorizing. They allowed me to identify the network of core organized actors engaged in the legitimacy project, namely academic experts, the State Council, and the NIEM, as well as the research centers and training institutes that populated the emergency management field. Acts of claims-making dovetailed nicely with notions of legitimacy in institutional theory as they identify and describe the mobilization of accounts used to justify fields and frameworks.

Last but not least, the governmentality lens from Foucauldian studies provided me with the requisite language to read the inscriptions of power during the phase of early field formation. As pointed out in Chapters 1 and 6, while notions of institutionalization give a benign gloss to how things become naturalized and normalized, applying the lens of governmentality amplifies the observation that ideas, policies, and practices that become natural and normal in an organizational field are precisely those that have been seeded by establishment. Recall how the definitions of an emergency as they evolved from the version in the regulation on public health emergencies to their final iteration in the emergency response law became more succinct and packed with notions of intervention designed by the establishment. More interestingly, applying the governmentality lens reveals that the true target population subjected to governance was not categories of emergencies, the public, or private firms, but government officials themselves. This revelation becomes more convincing when we understand it within the context of an internal legitimacy project in institutional terms, as well as in the context of sociological studies of disasters. The establishment not only mobilized legitimizing claims to justify its field formation efforts, but also developed a technique to corral government officials in emergency management under its purview. This further underscores power inequalities between the establishment and other constituent members of the field.

In addition, contrary to the "hollowing of the state" trend seen elsewhere in the global system, the case of China's emergency management suggests that the party-state has installed itself as the ultimate and legitimate manager of risks from emergencies by putting in place specific structures and processes. The "hollowing-out" thesis rings hollow also because enacting the transfer of government functions and resources to non-state sectors in the Chinese case was, after all, a privilege bestowed by the Chinese party-state. Seen this way, the transfer should be read as a technique of government (Lemke 2001). These insights would not have been possible in analyses using a pure institutional lens.

The curatorial function in institutional context

To recap, curation refers to the strategy that the establishment and especially academic experts used to craft the risk governance framework and legitimizing claims during field formation. The notion of curation emphasizes careful positioning, piecing together, and taking away ideas or cultural accounts. In China's emergency management case, the establishment perspective was deliberately curated in an effort to blur and build boundaries (Smith 2012), specifically by presenting ideas and practices as timeless or timely.

The notion of careful calibration of scripts and schemas is not unique to or absent from institutional theory focusing on ideas. As I have highlighted here, notions of building and mobilizing "institutional vocabularies" in order to articulate specific qualities, such as professionalism (Suddaby and Greenwood 2005:43), are also present in China's emergency management case. Specifically, the establishment instinctively tapped into vocabularies associated with insider cultural knowledge (Cohen 2009) and party-state ideologies to create and justify its risk governance framework.

In retrospect, using the concept of insider cultural knowledge reaped two serendipitous benefits. First, it highlights the cognitive dimension associated with this body of institutional vocabulary. Insider cultural knowledge is not something that is deliberately concealed from non-Chinese; it escapes easy transmission because it has become so taken for granted by Chinese socialized in that particular cultural milieu. In addition, as Cohen makes a special effort to point out, insider cultural knowledge as a form of knowledge is nothing exotic or even unique to the Chinese. To underscore its theoretical "travel" across time and space, Cohen (2009) highlights how the myth of Cinderella would not require explanation to Americans and the invocation of Michael the Archangel and Catherine of Alexandria by Joan of Arc would have been unproblematic to the French of her time.

Employing the concept of curation also provides the occasion to better understand the dynamics of internal legitimacy projects. In China's case, insider cultural knowledge and party-state ideologies are institutional vocabularies that reside in broader institutional domains from which the emergency management field was created. Understood this way, an internal legitimacy project, such as the one embarked upon by the emergency management establishment, would have to first draw on such broader cultural accounts that are already "ready to wear" in the existing institutional environment, while at the same time curating and circulating accounts special and specific to the organizational field. Curation includes attempts at theorization (Greenwood, Suddaby and Hinings 2002; Strang and Meyer 1993; Zilber 2008), in which purposeful (re)assembly of cultural accounts, ideas, and practices specifies the relationships and claims among them, especially by "culturally legitimated theorists" (e.g., academic experts) who occupy prestigious and influential positions within their institutional environments (Strang and Meyer 1993). Therefore, my study contributes to a deeper understanding of internal legitimacy projects by elaborating how such processes are performed.

Within institutional theory, the concept that comes closest to the notion of curation in my study is the notion of "editing" (Sahlin-Andersson 1996). Editing focuses on the continual reformulation of past models in light of current conditions and future visions. For example, when prototypes of research or science parks in Europe were circulated in the public sector across national boundaries, parts that were not congruent with local settings were snipped and those that highlighted similarities across success cases were emphasized (Sahlin-Andersson 1996). Editing has a strong power dimension. As Sahlin-Andersson (1996) argues, editing is characterized by social control, because only a select few enjoy the access and means to censor and amplify. In the science park case, the "editors" included planners and consultants.

However, acts of curation constitute more than editing. They are not constrained to only removing ideas that do not fit particular contexts. They assume a more nuanced quality toward ideas that might not be central but are still germane to the gatekeepers who perform the curation (Khaire 2014). As in the practice of curation in museums, a selection of artifacts takes center stage, whereas others are positioned in ways that complement or contrast with them. Therefore, the notion of curation contributes to institutional theory by adding a nuance that emphasizes careful calibrating and articulating of ideas in addition to "brute" editing. The notion of curation also offers an opportunity to connect with research on institutional work (Lawrence, Suddaby and Leca 2011). Specifically, acts of curation can provide a finer-grained picture of how individuals and organized actors create, maintain, and disrupt institutional arrangements.

The role of institutional evangelists

Institutional evangelists are individuals who assume the role of advocating for and propagating the ideas and knowledge that define and entrench an organizational field. As itinerant agents of institutionalization, they circulate through various organizations and introduce the texts and contexts to constituents of the organizational field. In China's emergency management case, academic experts served as the institutional evangelists offering advice, training, and other services that helped entrench the field.

The notion of institutional evangelists is important because it emphasizes that the process of institutionalization or governmentalization goes beyond that of the discursive dimension. While claims, accounts, and curation are central to and critical during the intensive development phase of a field, what perpetuates and sustains the field are individuals who do the physical work of spreading the word and building the networks, connecting various organizational entities in a field. The role of institutional evangelists therefore stresses the structural and nondiscursive aspects of institutionalization.

Within institutional theory, emphasizing the role of institutional evangelists furthers the understanding of how organizational fields can sustain the efforts of institutional entrepreneurs (DiMaggio 1988; Hardy and Maguire 2017) in field-changing or field-creating events. This is because the notion of institutional entrepreneurship is typically constrained to a narrow set of pioneering activities that create or transform existing institutional arrangements. The role of institutional evangelist, which can be attached to the same individuals or organized actors who perform entrepreneurship, blurs the boundary between the genesis and the immediate growth period of early field formation and shows how an organizational field forms as a continuum.

Similar to how curation potentially contributes to research on institutional work, the role of institutional evangelist also offers a useful starting point to consider the roles of individuals as opposed to collective actors, which have been the focus in institutional theory. Specifically, the notion of institutional evangelists describes and defines the activities of individuals in the retelling of their "institutional biographies" (Lawrence, Suddaby and Leca 2011), such as that of senior academics (e.g., Xue and Shan in Chapters 4 and 6) and political leaders (former Premier Wen in Chapter 3).

With respect to sociological studies of disasters, introducing the role of institutional evangelists enriches the vocabulary for a more fine-grained understanding of the various roles members of an establishment play in its claims-making efforts to turn a putative threat into a policy domain (Stallings 1995). To elaborate, Stallings (1995) observed that claim-makers of earthquake risks participated in several public arenas, specifically on expert panels and committees, in congressional hearings, and on national news. While the avenues are specific to the U.S. institutional policymaking context, the activities carried out by the claim-makers and members of the earthquake establishment in various capacities – advising, educating, and championing – can be folded into the role of an institutional evangelist.

Theoretical limitations and future research

In this final section, I elaborate on the limitations of my theoretical approach and fieldwork design with the aim of suggesting how future research can address them.[1]

Academic experts as groups and individuals

By and large, I have also treated academic experts as a monolithic whole, even though it is clear that distinctive fragmentations exist along several dimensions, the most obvious one being academic disciplines. For example, disaster management researchers tend to be from the natural sciences, such as geology, or the physical and applied sciences, such as civil structural engineering. In contrast, crisis management and governance researchers tend to be from the applied social sciences, such as public administration. Even though I touched on this discipline dimension when I discussed the diverse definitions of governance and management and consensus around the severity grading system in Chapter 4, more could be done to explore the differences within academic expert groups and how those differences shape the ideational landscape of the organizational field. This could be a topic for future studies. In addition, future research could explore the tensions existing among groups to highlight contested issues and the dynamics of power inequalities in field formation, which would further contribute to discussions on power in institutional theory.

An organizational field also requires continual activism and entrepreneurship from individuals as well as groups. In Chapters 4 and 6, I attempted to address this issue by highlighting prominent academic experts (e.g., Lan Xue and Chun Chang Shan) who were instrumental in shaping the field, especially during the intensive institutionalization period of the emergency management field. From my interviews, it is also obvious that some senior academic experts had staked their careers by investing in and committing to then-novel concepts such as IRGC's "risk governance" framework and an "all-hazards" approach toward disaster management. As a result of their entrepreneurial efforts and positions in the establishment, they contributed significantly to building the field legislatively, administratively, and organizationally. Indeed, many were also rewarded handsomely as institutional evangelists. It might be fruitful to consider the individual biographies of these institutional evangelists as a means to understand field formation from a more microscopic and intimate level. When taking this approach, future research would be reclaiming what Mills (1959) considers the more intimate "personal troubles" vis-à-vis the arms'-length "public issues" that are prevalent in institutional narratives.

Academic experts played the role of institutional evangelists in the building of the emergency management field. They were the ones who circulated through the field to advocate and to propagate the risk governance framework through advising, training, and educating other constituent members of the field. Future research could continue exploring the role of institutional evangelists to understand which organized actor or actors in other organizational fields assume this role and under what institutional contexts. This would further the theoretical travel of the concept of institutional evangelists within the institutional literature.

Emergency management in local governments

My study has focused on what transpired at the national level. However, what was happening at the provincial and other levels of government did not always mirror events in Beijing and therefore also merit deeper investigation. For example, emergency management was sometimes folded into the provincial governor's office. On other occasions, it manifested itself as multi-agency committees chaired by other senior administrators, such as deputy governors. During fieldwork, my informants also highlighted there were constantly new initiatives of emergency management being promulgated at local levels. For example, the Guangdong provincial government introduced several interesting initiatives, such as building a volunteer corps in emergency management.[2] One informant in local government suggested some initiatives at the national level could have been first proposed and piloted by local governments.³ If so, how did these ideas flow up to the national level? Were they transmitted mainly through bureaucratic processes (e.g., submission of proposals) or personnel movement (e.g., promotion of officials) where individuals repurposed their past experiments in their new offices?

Coping with incompleteness in social organization

No acts of organizing lead to completely successful outcomes as envisioned by the organized actors. Social organization and institutionalized fields therefore are replete with instances of incomplete successes and failures. Organizational efforts are often accompanied by resistance, moments of breaks, and the presence of inconsistencies. Strategic actions are also not necessarily complete, stable, or successful; they can result in partial success, tentative completion, or even utter failure.

Agreeing with Malpas and Wickham (1995), researchers have been preoccupied with success and completion, to the extent that they may have neglected that failure and incompleteness are also pervasive and perennial features of social life. The reference to success and completion imitates the view of failure as an aberration and as an expression of temporary breakdown in the social order. The implicit promise is that in due time and with sufficient effort, everything will be restored to a state of success and completeness. That is a normative commitment to an imagined state of perfection, especially when instances of failure and partial success are also part of the universe of social outcomes and actions.

From my research, notions of incomplete success are evident in situations in which academic experts did not manage to embed their ideas into policies; even when they did, they were unable to exert the expected effect in policy outcomes. For example a topic excluded from the legitimacy afforded by administrative legislation, psychological counselling was included in the recovery and reconstruction chapter in various versions of the draft bill but ultimately did not make it into the emergency response law.⁴ That said, psychological well-being as a topic did not fade away but continued to gain prominence in research,⁵ suggesting that while the paths of ideas in academia and legislation in government did intertwine at some junctures, they were also developing independently of each other.

Besides psychological well-being in emergency management, there are several other ideas that gained traction in research, but were less obvious or even absent in policymaking, let alone enactment into law. One reason was that these ideas were either not useful or not of obvious utility to officials. Social scientist Chi, in our discussion on social theories and policies, gave a colorful illustration of this sense of "non-usefulness." Speaking specifically about the emergent and self-organizing behavior of grassroots organizations based on research conducted during the 2008 Wenchuan earthquake, Chi pointed out that public policy academics and sociologists came to different conclusions when observing the wiping out of grassroots leaders immediately after the earthquake. Public policy academics noted the dearth of government officials and party cadres on the ground and suggested the need to rebuild and regain grassroots authority to lead disaster response, relief, and recovery efforts. In contrast, sociologists tended to consider how grassroots organizations could emerge naturally from civil society to fill the sociopolitical vacuum. As Chi recounted:

> The problem is that if you approach the issue from the sociological idea of grassroots organization, you're thinking about the problem in a wrong way. We're thinking about self-organization because we in sociology definitely harbor the ideals of the members of the public organizing themselves spontaneously. The government just doesn't like to hear this. What self-organization? This year you [meaning the public] organize yourselves for disaster recovery and relief; next year you organize for other causes, how am I going to deal with this? The government just doesn't like to listen to this. But if you say strengthening authority at the grassroots level, they love hearing that, right? . . . If you say strengthening the capacity to self-organize, that's so meaningless (to them).[6]

Chi also pointed out how the idea of social capital in sociology was then gaining popularity in disaster relief and recovery research but had not entered the consciousness of officials. Academics broadly agree that social capital refers to the resources immanent in social relations that promote collaboration and cooperation within and between actors (Chua et al. 2012; Nahapiet and Ghoshal 1998; Portes 1998). However, the immediate associations that some officials inferred from social capital hardly implied such relationships or the capacity for collective action. Instead, their lay definition misconstrued social capital as economic resources (i.e., strictly financial capital) that were dormant in civil society (i.e., social). According to Chi, the officials therefore even opined that such disparate financial reserves should be pooled and harnessed toward more useful ends.

Indeed, some ideas can be considered "the flotsam and jetsam" that littered "settled" institutional paths, in the wake of effortful and intensive institutional change (Schneiberg 2007). These scripts, while legitimizing the organizational field, also double as institutional junkyards. Understood this way, ideas remain and are left undefended not because they have become institutionalized and thus taken for granted; it is simply because they serve no purpose (Zucker 1988). These instances of benign neglect might be a candidate for future curatorial work, to be resurrected, recycled, or refashioned during other field formations (Schneiberg 2007; Wooten and Hoffman 2017).

The observation that the state of the organizational field of China's emergency management cannot be simplistically taken as complete and conclusive cannot be overemphasized. There were also shifts that were unanticipated, for example, the move from proposing a state of emergency bill to a more subdued and limited emergency response bill. In addition, while the field appears to be "settled" at this point, it is impossible to say whether this might remain so.

A case in point would be the new Ministry of Emergency Management (MEM) established in 2018. My informants had impressed upon me repeatedly that a FEMA-like structure would not be possible in China. Conceptually, it did not make sense to them. This is because in their view, an emergency management ministry would lack the legitimacy, hence the hierarchical authority, to summon coordination and control from other ministries, which are going to be its organizational peers and counterparts. The EMO at the State Council could do so as it stood above the ministries. And even so, the functions the EMO served were also limited, given it was more about information gathering and coordination. So it was a surprise to many when MEM was announced and took shape. The organizational make-up of the new ministry was pulled from several ministries and government bodies,[7] not unlike how FEMA was established in the United States when it consolidated several disparate organizational units and functions across several departments.

This new entrant to the organizational field deserves closer scrutiny at least on two accounts. First, it seems to indicate a narrower representation of the "common enterprise" of the field, as the new ministry focuses on specific emergencies – such as natural disasters (e.g., earthquakes and floods) and industrial accidents – and functions, such as firefighting and disaster assistance and relief.[8] I would have anticipated an expansion of coverage over the years, given the prominence of financial crises and cybersecurity threats, but they were not brought into the fold of the emergency management organizational field. Second, there were obvious curatorial efforts and the legitimizing claims at boundary work (Khaire 2014; Smith 2012) again. For example, the setting up of the ministry was framed as an attempt to rejuvenate and remake emergency management (*tuo tai huan gu* 脱胎换骨).[9] To highlight one example, what was seen as efficient and effective in building the EMO-SC in 2005 was cast as insufficient in 2018. While the functions of the EMO-SC remain in the new ministry, it was "only an office," with its roles and responsibilities also insufficiently defined.[10] More research is needed to flesh out the institutional context that led to such development, and the accompanying theoretical implications to changes in maturing organizational fields. For example, how and to what extent did the 2015 Tianjin port explosion contribute to the theorization of the need for a change in the field (Wang and Wu 2019)?

In the face of the next jolt (e.g., COVID-19 pandemic), emergency management as an organizational field, as settled as it may seem at this moment, may yet be subjected to other dramatic changes that we have yet to imagine. In my epilogue, I reflect on the state of the emergency management organizational field in China, with my preliminary take on the COVID-19 crisis that is still unfolding in the summer of 2020.

Notes

1 I address methodological limitations in the Appendix.
2 See for example, Zhang, Lei. 2012. "Yingji jiuyuan duiwu jian she Deguo moshi ji jiejian (Building emergency rescue teams, learning from the German model." *Guojia Xingzheng Xueyuan Xuebao (Journal of the Chinese Academy of Governance)* 3:125–9.
3 I thank Tian for this interesting revelation.
4 See p. 428 in Mo, Yu Chuan, ed. 2007. *Zhonghua Renmin Gonghe Guo Tufa Shijian Yingdui Fa Shiyi (Interpretation of People's Republic of China Emergency Response Law)*. Beijing, China: China Legal Publishing House.

5 See for example Zhang, Yan, Jiuchang Wei and Wei Qin. 2011. "Tufa shijian shehui xinli yingxiang moshi yu zhili jizhi yanjiu (Social psychological influence of emergencies model and governance mechanism research)." *Zhongguo Yingji Guanli (China Emergency Management)* 6:34–8.

6 Second interview with Chi.

7 The State Council of People's Republic of China. 2018, March 13. "China to form ministry of emergency management." *www.gov.cn*. Retrieved from http://english. www.gov.cn/state_council/ministries/2018/03/13/content_281476076465 182.htm.

8 See for example, 2019, April 16. "Nihao, wo shi yingjibu! (Hello, I'm ministry of emergency management!)." *Xinhua Net*. Retrieved April 25, 2020, from www. xinhuanet.com/yingjijiuyuan/2019-04/16/c_1210110733.htm.

9 Ibid.

10 Ma, Zhuopeng. 2018, March 13. "Experts decode the newly-formed ministry of emergency management: Focusing equally on disaster reduction, prevention, and rescue and assistance (Zhuanjia jiedu xinzujian yingjiguanlibu: Zhuoyan jianzai、 fangzhi yu jiuyuan bingzhong)." *Peng Pai (The Paper)*. Retrieved April 25, 2020, from www.thepaper.cn/newsDetail_forward_2027723.

References

Chua, Cecil Eng Huang, Wee-Kiat Lim, Christina Soh and Siew Kien Sia. 2012. "Enacting Clan Control in Complex IT Projects: A Social Capital Perspective." *MIS Quarterly* 36(2):577–600.

Cohen, Paul A. 2009. *Speaking to History: The Story of King Goujian in Twentieth-Century China*. Berkeley, CA: University of California Press.

Deephouse, David L., Jonathan Bundy, Leigh Plunkett and Mark Suchman. 2017. "Organizational Legitimacy: Six Questions." Pp. 27–54 in *The Sage Handbook of Organizational Institutionalism*, edited by R. Greenwood, C. Oliver, T. B. Lawrence and R. E. Meyer. Thousand Oaks, CA: Sage Publications.

DiMaggio, Paul J. 1988. "Interest and Agency in Institutional Theory." Pp. 3–21 in *Institutional Patterns and Organizations: Culture and Environment*, edited by L. G. Zucker. Cambridge, MA: Ballinger Publishing Company.

DiMaggio, Paul J. and Walter W. Powell. 1983. "The Iron Cage Revisited: Institutional Isomorphism and Collective Rationality in Organizational Fields." *American Sociological Review* 48(2):147–60.

Goodstein, Jerry, Mary Blair-Loy and Army S. Wharton. 2009. "Organization-Based Legitimacy: Core Ideologies and Moral Action." Pp. 44–62 in *Meaning and Method: The Cultural Approach to Sociology*, edited by I. Reed and J. C. Alexander. Boulder, CO: Paradigm Publishers.

Greenwood, Royston, Roy Suddaby and C. R. Hinings. 2002. "Theorizing Change: The Role of Professional Associations in the Transformation of Institutionalized Fields." *Academy of Management Journal* 45(1):58–80.

Hardy, Cynthia and Steve Maguire. 2017. "Institutional Entrepreneurship and Change in Fields." Pp. 261–80 in *The Sage Handbook of Organizational Institutionalism*, edited by R. Greenwood, C. Oliver, T. B. Lawrence and R. E. Meyer. Thousand Oaks, CA: Sage Publications.

Hoffman, Andrew J. 1999. "Institutional Evolution and Change: Environmentalism and the U.S. Chemical Industry." *Academy of Management Journal* 42(4):351–71.

Khaire, Mukti. 2014. "Fashioning an Industry: Socio-Cognitive Processes in the Construction of Worth of a New Industry." *Organization Studies* 35(1):41–74.

Lawrence, Thomas B., Roy Suddaby and Bernard Leca. 2011. "Institutional Work: Refocusing Institutional Studies on Organizations." *Journal of Management Inquiry* 20(1):52–8.

Lemke, Thomas. 2001. "'The Birth of Bio-Politics': Michel Foucault's Lecture at the Collège De France on Neo-Liberal Governmentality." *Economy and Society* 30(2): 190–207.

Maguire, Steve, Cynthia Hardy and Thomas B. Lawrence. 2004. "Institutional Entrepreneurship in Emerging Fields: HIV/AIDS Treatment Advocacy in Canada." *Academy of Management Journal* 47(5):657–79.

Malpas, Jeff and Gary Wickham. 1995. "Governance and Failure: On the Limits of Sociology." *Journal of Sociology* 31(3):37–50.

Mills, Charles Wright. 1959. *The Sociological Imagination*. New York, NY: Oxford University Press.

Nahapiet, Janine and Sumantra Ghoshal. 1998. "Social Capital, Intellectual Capital, and the Organizational Advantage." *Academy of Management Review* 23(2):242.

Portes, Alejandro. 1998. "Social Capital: Its Origin and Applications in Modern Sociology." *Annual Review of Sociology* 24:1–24.

Quirke, Linda. 2013. "Rogue Resistance: Sidestepping Isomorphic Pressures in a Patchy Institutional Field." *Organization Studies* 34(11):1675–99.

Sahlin-Andersson, Kerstin. 1996. "Imitating by Editing Success: The Construction of Organization Fields." Pp. 69–92 in *Translating Organizational Change*, edited by B. Czarniawska and G. Sevón. Berlin; New York, NY: Walter de Gruyter.

Schneiberg, Marc. 2007. "What's on the Path? Path Dependence, Organizational Diversity and the Problem of Institutional Change in the US Economy, 1900–1950." *Socio-Economic Review* 5(1):47–80.

Selznick, Philip. 1996. "Institutionalism: 'Old' and 'New'." *Administrative Science Quarterly* 41(2):270–7.

Smith, Wade P. 2012. "Narratives of Continuity and Change: Changing Logics and Institutional Work in the United States Army." Master's Degree, Sociology, University of Colorado, Boulder, CO.

Stallings, Robert A. 1995. *Promoting Risk: Constructing the Earthquake Threat*. New York, NY: Aldine de Gruyter.

Strang, David and John W. Meyer. 1993. "Institutional Conditions for Diffusion." *Theory and Society* 22(4):487–511.

Suchman, Mark. 1995. "Managing Legitimacy: Strategic and Institutional Approaches." *Academy of Management Review* 20(3):571–610.

Suddaby, Roy and Royston Greenwood. 2005. "Rhetorical Strategies of Legitimacy." *Administrative Science Quarterly* 50:35–67.

Wang, Bing and Chao Wu. 2019. "China: Establishing the Ministry of Emergency Management (M.E.M.) of the People's Republic of China (P.R.C.) to Effectively Prevent and Control Accidents and Disasters." *Safety Science* 111:324.

Wooten, Melissa and Andrew J. Hoffman. 2017. "Organizational Fields: Past, Present and Future." Pp. 55–74 in *The Sage Handbook of Organizational Institutionalism*, edited by R. Greenwood, C. Oliver, T. B. Lawrence and R. E. Meyer. Thousand Oaks, CA: Sage Publications.

Yang, Dali. 2008. "Regulatory Learning and Its Discontents in China: Promise and Tragedy at the State Food and Drug Administration." Pp. 139–62 in *Regulation in Asia: Pushing Back on Globalization*, edited by J. Gillespie and R. Peerenboom. New York, NY: Routledge.

Zald, Mayer N. and Michael Lounsbury. 2010. "The Wizards of Oz: Towards an Institutional Approach to Elites, Expertise and Command Posts." *Organization Studies* 31(7):963–96.

Zilber, Tammar B. 2008. "The Work of Meanings in Institutional Processes and Thinking." Pp. 151–69 in *The Sage Handbook of Organizational Institutionalism*, edited by R. Greenwood, C. Oliver, K. Sahlin and R. Suddaby. Thousand Oaks, CA: Sage Publications.

Zucker, Lynne G. 1988. "Where Do Institutional Patterns Come From? Organizations as Actors in Social Systems." Pp. 23–49 in *Institutional Patterns and Organizations: Culture and Environment*, edited by L. G. Zucker. Cambridge, MA: Ballinger Publishing Company.

Epilogue: going forward

"But [the new post-SARS crisis management] mechanism works better in emergency situations that we are familiar with, such as typhoons," Professor [Lan] Xue said. "A limitation is that we still don't know how to recognise an unfamiliar emergency situation."[1]

The 2003 SARS crisis offered a "teachable moment" (Stallings 1986) because the situation involved those in power imposing familiar but inappropriate categories onto foreign diseases, which was exacerbated by institutionalized secrecy and rivalry. The Chinese party-state took heart, and moved swiftly and decisively. It is impossible to ignore how much attention and resources were committed to build such an emergency management field so quickly. That said, in light of the more settled state of the field in the last few years, the verdict is still out on whether the emergency management establishment and its field constituents have become truly more adept at governing the unintelligible or more adroit at managing familiar emergencies. To be fair, China is neither unique nor alone in its mixed bag of success and failure in mitigating risks before they mutate into emergencies and metastasize into crises.

This becomes apparent in the early days of the COVID-19 pandemic when China took close to a month before the central government mounted a nation-wide response to contain the contagion. There were news reports of Wuhan medical professionals being silenced when highlighting the risk of an outbreak in late December 2019, as well as the continuation of mass gatherings and signature annual political events in January 2020 when the virus could have been spreading beyond Hubei province.[2] Similar to 2003, *chun yun* was allowed to proceed as the country segued into the Lunar New Year festive mood in January. At the very least, mistakes and misjudgment were committed during the early response to the novel coronavirus crisis.

While established protocols in emergency management were followed, such as raising the emergency severity to Grade I (Severe) which called for interventions from the central government, there were also moments when China deviated in various degrees from standard response. It may be premature to judge their efficacy and significance, especially when one approaches them from an institutional, longer term perspective. Just to highlight a few: the lockdowns and the setting up of a temporary leadership body orchestrating the crisis response from Beijing. The lockdowns imposed across China as a measure was drastic and unprecedented in recent times, albeit attempted before in history. Rather than seeing it as radical innovation, the massive scaling up of isolation measures stipulated in the public health emergency regulation and plans can also be read as an improvisation, a moment of institutional bricolage (de Jong 2013; Weick 1993), as well as stitching together fragments of ideas from "ready to wear" scripts and schemas (Scott 1991; Seo and Creed 2002). During the 2003 SARS crisis, the State Council, led by former Premier Wen, established the SARS Prevention and Control Headquarters. This practice – which preceded the SARS event and was also observed in responses to natural disasters – came to be inscribed in the 2007 Emergency Response Law. Fast forward to the COVID-19 outbreak, while Premier Li led the response, the leadership body highlighted was not the State Council, but a freshly-created one under the CPC Central Committee. Called the Leading Group on Novel Coronavirus Prevention and Control,[3] this seemed to be a deviation from the protocols in the emergency response law (see Chapter 2). It might be more accurate to read the response efforts as essentially a party-led initiative. The purported delegation of power for prompt and self-directed response as set out in the revised laws and regulations, either in spirit or text, should also be examined more closely, such as when then-mayor Zhou Xianwang alluded to the need to seek approval from the central government to act and release information.[4] The multiple delays and deviations can be read in several ways, such as improvisations, bricolage, or shifts in power (and responsibilities). They also point to longstanding issues of institutional secrecy and rivalry – underlying issues that also plagued the 2003 SARS crisis response – which had persisted over the years.

In studying the impact of the COVID-19 pandemic on the emergency management field, we also need to account for the differences in the broader environment that gave rise to its rapid and pervasive contagion. Apart from the deadly nature of the SARS-CoV-2 virus, the world in 2020 is also markedly different from that in 2003. It is much more interconnected through more frequent and denser trade, informational, and cultural exchange. We need to situate the growth and stabilization of the emergency management field in the midst of rapid and remarkable innovation, and the adoption of cutting-edge technology in the country from which the establishment and other field constituents benefited immensely. To highlight, there was the rise of digital mobile technology and China's indigenous tech giants, Baidu, Alibaba, and Tencent (also known as BAT). The Chinese tech sector also made formidable forays into emerging domains such as artificial intelligence or AI (e.g., SenseTime) and civilian drones (e.g., Da Jiang Innovations or DJI). Genome sequencing and biotechnology also took off, with the likes of companies like BGI, a capability that may contribute to the ongoing vaccine race to address the COVID-19 pandemic. In fact, drawing back to theory, Foucaldian's notion of calculative risk and governmentality seem to have become more conspicuous with technology (e.g., AI) enabling more intimate monitoring and tracking of people and near-real-time updates of cases.

Similar to the 2003 SARS crisis, the reading of the COVID-19 pandemic as a focusing event could only become more apparent given fermentation over time. A key question would be to what extent it would radically reconfigure China's emergency management field. My reading is such a possibility would be limited. I give two reasons. First, the domestic political context surrounding the crisis is different. The SARS epidemic gripped the nation in the midst of a pivotal leadership transition over 2002 and 2003. The ambiguity surrounding that power transfer meant that the outbreak could immediately threaten the legitimacy of the new Hu-Wen administration during that sensitive period. The threat was exacerbated when drastic actions were delayed until when the capital, the seat of power, saw its first cases in early April 2003. Conversely, the Xi-Li administration is already in their second term of leadership and has inherited an established emergency management field.

Second, given the ongoing and intensifying trade wars between China and the U.S. and China's relations with other global actors, such as nation-states and international organizations (e.g., WHO), the interpretation of the COVID-19 pandemic according to China's governing elites is unlikely to be confined within the concerns of administrative inefficiencies and weak crisis management capacity, as it largely was in the wake of the SARS outbreak. Issues related to diplomacy, international trade dynamics, scientific and technological transfer and knowledge sharing, just to name a few, have instead come to the fore. This is to say, the pandemic could still be a focusing event (Birkland 2007), a jolt (Meyer 1982), or a critical juncture (Collier and Collier 1991) for other issues central to other organizational fields, existing ones or to be created anew, but perhaps less so for emergency management. That being said, given how the broader environment is a complex of several fields (Quirke 2013), emergency management might experience indirect effects owing to the development and demise of others.

At this point of writing, China has become sufficiently confident with its tentative success to hold its annual political meetings in late May 2020, which have been postponed from its usual March appearance. Known as the "two meetings" (*lianghui* 两会), the events are a landmark in China's governance calendar. Therefore, it is not surprising the party-state had spared no effort to contain the virus when there was an inkling of a second wave in Wuhan. As observed from the two meetings, the pressing issue is to enable and sustain economic recovery, particularly on reducing poverty and keeping unemployment low.[5] Given the fluidity of so many conditions, at this point in 2020, it remains too early to decipher the extent to which the COVID-19 pandemic might trigger shifts in China's emergency management field.

I close the epilogue with a passage from the esteemed Sinologist Simon Leys. He wrote about Lu Xun, a Chinese literary giant who came to prominence at the beginning of the twentieth century and endured a love-hate relationship with the Communists:

> More than half a century ago, the writer Lu Xun (1881–1936), whose prophetic genius never ceases to amaze, describe the conundrum of China-watching:

Once upon a time, there was a country whose rulers completely succeeded in crushing the people; and yet they still believed that the people were their most dangerous enemy. The rulers issued huge collections of statutes, but none of these volumes could actually be used, because in order to interpret them, one had to refer to a set of instructions that had never been made public. These instructions contained many original definitions. Thus, for instance, "liberation" means in fact "capital execution"; "government official" meant "friend, relative or servant of an influential politician," and so on. The rulers also issued codes of laws that were marvelously modern, complex, and complete: however, at the beginning of the first volume, there was one blank page; this blank page could be deciphered only by those who knew the instructions – which did not exist. The first three invisible articles of these non-existent instructions read as follows: "Art. 1: Some cases must be treated with special leniency. Art. 2: Some cases must be treated with special severity. Art. 3: This does not apply in all cases."

Without an ability to decipher non-existent inscriptions written in invisible ink on blank pages, no one should ever dream of analyzing the nature and reality of Chinese communism.

(Leys 2011:392–3)

My research has helped me interpret the recent conduct of China's governing elites with respect to disaster and risk management, at a time when the COVID-19 pandemic continues to unfold as we enter the summer of 2020. That said, efforts to truly understand China, let alone predict and preempt the behavior of its governing elites, are what Leys has characterized as "interpreting non-existent inscriptions written in invisible ink on a blank page."

Notes

1 Kwok, Kristine. 2008. "A high price for progress: Five years since a deadly virus hit, our five-part series looks back and asks what lessons have been learned. Part 4: The mainland crisis." *South China Morning Post*, p. 14.
2 See for example, Zheng, Sarah. 2020, January 23. "Wuhan mayor under pressure to resign over response to coronavirus outbreak." *South China Morning Post*. Retrieved from www.scmp.com/news/china/politics/article/3047230/wuhan-mayor-under-pressure-resign-over-response-coronavirus.
3 See for example, *Xinhua Net*. 2020, January 26. "Li Keqiang chairs leading group on novel coronavirus prevention and control meeting (*Li Keqiang zhuchi zhaokai Zhongyang Yingdui Xinguanzhuang Bingdu Ganran Feiyan Gongzuo Lingdao Xiaozu huiyi*)." Retrieved from www.xinhuanet.com/politics/2020-01/26/c_1125504004.htm/.
4 Zhou, Cissy and William Zheng. February 11, 2020. "Coronavirus: Heads roll in Hubei as Beijing's patience runs out." *South China Morning Post*. Retrieved from www.scmp.com/news/china/politics/article/3049937/coronavirus-hubei-province-health-officials-removed-over.
5 Hofman, Bert. 2020, May 29. "Commentary: Embattled China knows its national priority is the economy." *Channel News Asia*. Retrieved from www.channelnewsasia.

com/news/commentary/china-hong-kong-national-security-law-us-tensions-growth-economy-12778316.

References

Birkland, Thomas A. 2007. *Lessons of Disaster: Policy Change After Catastrophic Events.* Washington, DC: Georgetown University Press.

Collier, Ruth Berins and David Collier. 1991. *Shaping the Political Arena: Critical Junctures, the Labor Movement, and Regime Dynamics in Latin America.* Princeton, NJ: Princeton University Press.

de Jong, Martin. 2013. "China's Art of Institutional Bricolage: Selectiveness and Gradualism in the Policy Transfer Style of a Nation." *Policy and Society* 32(2):89–101.

Leys, Simon. 2011. "The Art of Interpreting Non-Existent Inscriptions Written in Invisible Ink on a Blank Page." Pp. 389–402 in *The Hall of Uselessness: Collected Essays*, edited by Simon Leys. New York: New York Review of Books.

Meyer, Alan D. 1982. "Adapting to Environmental Jolts." *Administrative Science Quarterly* 27(4):515–37.

Quirke, Linda. 2013. "Rogue Resistance: Sidestepping Isomorphic Pressures in a Patchy Institutional Field." *Organization Studies* 34(11):1675–99.

Scott, W. Richard. 1991. "Unpacking Institutional Arrangements." Pp. 164–82 in *The New Institutionalism in Organizational Analysis*, edited by W. W. Powell and P. J. DiMaggio. Chicago, IL: University of Chicago Press.

Seo, Myeong-Gu and W. E. Douglas Creed. 2002. "Institutional Contradictions, Praxis, and Institutional Change: A Dialectical Perspective." *Academy of Management Review* 27(2):222–47.

Stallings, Robert A. 1986. "Reaching the Ethnic Minorities: Earthquake Public Education in the Aftermath of Foreign Disasters." *Spectra* 2(4):695–702.

Weick, K. E. 1993. "The Collapse of Sensemaking in Organizations: The Mann Gulch Disaster." *Administrative Science Quarterly* 38(4):628–52.

Appendix
Research methods

> This study uses documents, surveys, interviews, and participant observation. The author visited China on two occasions (2011 and 2012) and interviewed Chinese officials and scholars in the emergency management field. . . . Interviews in particular have provided valuable material for this study and I was surprised at the frankness with which interviewees described the situation. Minor problems were encountered in the collection of data, but I judge they have not influenced the main findings of the project.
>
> Imagined method writing based on fictitious example
> in Heimer and Thøgersen (2006:1)

I could have written methods in a way described above, as a carbon copy of stylized methods chapters. Such a sterile description about fieldwork and data collection papers over the dynamics, detours, and dead ends that researchers have to negotiate in the field. I choose to write it differently. Before I describe my multi-method research approach, I give an account of how my research strategy evolved and changed in response to conditions on the ground.

This methods appendix then proceeds as follows. First, I describe my data collection strategy. Next, I discuss how I coded and interpreted the data. My detailed accounts of my fieldwork, coding, and analysis provide a basis to assess my research on quality criteria, such as veracity, authenticity, and perspicacity (Gold-Biddle and Locke 1993; Stewart 1998). I conclude by discussing the limitations of my methods and suggestions for improvement in future research.

Evolution of fieldwork site and data collection strategy

This was my dissertational research project. My initial plan was to conduct fieldwork at the National Institute of Emergency Management (NIEM) at the Chinese Academy of Governance (CAG), which has historically been a training ground for high- to mid-level civil servants, senior administrators, and government policy researchers. The official mission of the NIEM is to train emergency management officials at the national level, conduct research on emergency management policy, and engage in international exchanges and cooperation. This mission is in line with the broader mission of the CAG, an entity designated as a think tank offering policy advice to the party and the government.[1] Given CAG's high status as a ministerial-level unit under the direct control of the State Council (which has merged with the Central Party School since March 2018), it is both symbolic and strategic that it housed the newly formed emergency management institute.

Because training institutes typically serve as initial and recurring points of passage for new entrants and existing members, respectively, throughout their careers, they serve as a means for ideas, policies, and practices to be legitimized through both formal instruction and informal interactions. Therefore, I considered the NIEM to be an ideal site to observe how the concept of emergency management and the blend of new and legacy structures, processes, products, and intended outcomes became infused with "value beyond the technical requirements of the task at hand" (Selznick 1996:271). My initial research strategy was contingent upon access to the NIEM which I was assured would be "*mei wen ti*" ("no problem").

The original plan was to use four interrelated approaches: document collection and analysis; in-depth interviews; participant observation; and survey questionnaires administered to NIEM staff and students. Documents of interest fell into two categories. First, laws, regulations, policies, and research publications would provide the institutional context in which China's emergency management system evolved over time. Second, the course materials and NIEM communication products (e.g., syllabi, course descriptions, and newsletters) would reveal the Chinese emergency management leadership's approach to the management of extreme events, such as foreign natural disasters that were considered salient to the Chinese (e.g., 2005 Hurricane Katrina, 2010 Haiti earthquake), and their rationale for any new framework adopted by NIEM.

I planned to interview the students, faculty, and senior management officials at NIEM. For students, I planned to capture their initial and evolving reactions to newer conceptualizations of risk governance, as well as the extent to which initiatives were being implemented at their own levels of government. For faculty, I intended to focus on their experience in emergency management and their views on new governmental initiatives. For senior management, I planned to examine their accounts of the genesis of the emergency management field and experience in realizing the outcomes for NIEM.

For participant observation, I was counting on attending courses, chronicling interactions during class (e.g., questions to and responses from instructors) and student and faculty informal interactions during breaks, meals, and other occasions. Finally, I planned to administer the survey questionnaire before and after selected courses. My primary focus was to collect information on student perspectives on the government's philosophy, goals, objectives, and strategies for risk governance, both prior to and after the emergency management courses.

As everyone says about war, the best laid plans don't survive when the bullets start flying. The plan for NIEM as the fieldwork site had to be abandoned almost immediately upon my arrival in Beijing in late July 2012. With hindsight, the writing was on the wall. Given that 2012 was the year to usher in the once-in-a-decade political leadership transition for China, it became obvious that my presence at the NIEM could be challenging. The leadership transfer was to be kicked off at the 18th national congress within the CPC in late 2012. The Hu Jintao-Wen Jiabao leadership was carefully orchestrated to give way to the obvious but then still-to-be-confirmed Xi Jinping-Li Keqiang cohort. I surmised that the underlying administrative and political ambiguity of any high-profile transition was not conducive for a non-indigenous individual like me to be embedded at the pinnacle of administrative training. I was advised that I was better off studying newspapers online and microblogs on Weibo. Nonetheless, I continued to conduct fieldwork in Beijing during the latter half of 2012.

Improvised fieldwork and data collection strategy

Choosing to enter the field in the second half of 2012 then turned out to be a blessing in disguise. Being in the national capital over those five months provided me a rare opportunity to witness and be immersed in the mood of the political leadership transition which culminated in Team Xi-Li taking over the regime from the Hu-Wen leadership. The experience helped me better appreciate the sociopolitical context in which China's emergency management field had been developing, especially at the turn of the last transition between late 2002 and early 2003 when the SARS crisis gripped China before the rest of the world. More importantly, by attending conferences, seminars, and meetings *in situ*, interacting with local academic experts, and reviewing documents only available in China, I gained intimate first-hand knowledge of how the ideational landscape of the emergency management establishment was taking shape and in turn shaping the nascent field.

My research assumed a stronger ideational flavor for two reasons. First, it was practical. Due to constraints and concessions in the field as I have highlighted earlier, it was easier for me to access academic experts, the academic literature, and open source data on China's emergency management than to meet officials and review internal documents. Second was a methodological epiphany when I fussed about access. I realized the academic literature on emergency management could be treated as data for my study to probe the genesis and development of the emergency management field. Understood this way, the theories, frameworks, methods, and approaches in disaster- and risk-related disciplines – mainly materials from natural disaster and public administration studies – could be seen as the intellectual resources from which China's emergency management establishment built the organizational field and the risk governance framework. This conceptual maneuver to focus on the ideational aspects of the emergency management field prompted me to leverage my gatekeepers who were in academia themselves, because of their access to archives and informants.

My fieldwork and data collection strategy were document review, in-depth interviews, and participant observation. I focused mainly on laws, regulations, policies, and research publications, spoke with academic experts in the emergency management organizational field, and observed conferences, seminars, and meetings on emergency management. Among the three methods, my efforts in the field were primarily driven by document collection, especially hardcopy archives inaccessible outside of China, supplemented by interviews and observation of conferences and seminars.

Using these three methods in concert encourages triangulation to reveal both consensus and contradictions across events, issues, and themes (Small 2011; Yin 2017). Triangulation also addresses significantly the issue of the naïve treatment of texts as authentic reflections of actors "meaning what they say." Institutional theory highlights that publicly available discourses are generated through anticipation of reward or retaliation, and are products of political considerations and symbolic posturing (Schneiberg and Clemens 2006). Furthermore, triangulation adds "richness, rigor and breadth and depth" to my inquiry (Denzin and Lincoln 2008:7). In reviewing documents and observing key actors in various settings, I also achieved two goals. One was to mitigate the retrospective or recollection bias in interviews when my informants recounted field development in emergency management (Scott 1990b; Webb et al. 1981). Second, by bringing in document review and participant observation, I also responded to the call in sociological disaster research to consider using less obtrusive methods in addition to the current "toolkit" of surveys and interviews (Phillips 2002). Furthermore, the multi-method approach has also been useful in institutional research. For example, Purdy and Gray (2009) used interviews, surveys, and archival data gathered through reports and academic discourses, and attending annual meetings on conflict resolution to study the emergence of U.S. state offices of dispute resolution in that emerging organizational field.

Document review

As the products of the organizational winepress of claims-making and definitional processes (Kitsuse and Cicourel 1963; Schneider and Kitsuse 1984), archival documents provide revelatory information. They are the "unintended testimony to past actions" (Scott 1990b:5), revealing the interests and judgments of the emergency management establishment. The documents that I reviewed were mainly from publicly available sources (e.g., scholarly journal databases, commercially available publications). Most materials were in Chinese. They include but are not limited to the following types of documents:

Official documents

These include formal proclamations related to emergency management released by the Chinese government at the national level to the public, including laws, administrative regulations, State Council directives, emergency response plans, and governmental white papers. In order to better relate the field and its documentation to the political context in which they were produced, I also collected the five-year plans covering the years 2001 to 2015.[2]

Non-governmental publications

I focused on books related to emergency management and approached them according to whether they were published before, during, or after focusing events (Birkland 1997) in the field (e.g., 2003 SARS epidemic, 2007 National Emergency Response Law). I also included publications that chronicle main events (e.g., Shan et al. 2012, which recorded field development from 2003 to 2007). Due to the sheer volume of literature available, I also selectively considered legal books that offered interpretations and the background for the disaster-related laws passed and amended. There are also special reports, such as the UNESCO's case study report on the Wenchuan Earthquake, and annual reports on risk and emergency management.

Academic and official trade journals

Academic texts carry the imprints of the broader ideational and institutional commitments that academic experts inherit and enact. I began first with three journals: (i) *Journal of Catastrophology* (*Zaihai Xue* 《灾害学》), (ii) *Journal of Natural Disasters* (*Ziran Zaihai Xuebao* 《自然灾害学报》), and (iii) *China Emergency Management* (*Zhongguo Yingji Guanli* 《中国应急管理》). The first two journals are the main academic journals on natural disaster management. I surveyed the journals from their inaugural issues to end of 2012, but paid closer attention to the ten years in which the organizational field of emergency management was taking shape (i.e., 2003–2012). *China Emergency Management* is important for several reasons. It was not only inaugurated after the establishment of the Emergency Management Office at the State Council and just before the passing of the 2007 National Emergency Response Law, it was also created and supported by the State Council, a prominent organized actor in the field. Table A.1 gives the inception year and publishing frequencies of the journals.

The journals also sensitized me to the appropriate professional and cultural jargon with which members of China's emergency management field are familiar: for example, the term of art, *yi'an san zhi* (一案三制, "one 'case' and three mechanisms"), which describes the national strategy for developing the organizational field. I saw displaying "selective competence" of such jargon (Lofland

Table A.1 Inception Year of Journals

Journal	Inception Year	Frequency
Journal of Catastrophology (*Zaihai Xue* 《灾害学》)	1986	Quarterly
Journal of Natural Disasters (*Ziran Zaihai Xuebao* 《自然灾害学报》)	1992	Quarterly
China Emergency Management (*Zhongguo Yingji Guanli* 《中国应急管理》)	2007	Monthly

Note: Journal of Catastrophology was renamed from *Journal of Disaster Science* since its second issue of 1987. Its Chinese title remained the same.

and Lofland 1995) during my interactions with my informants and in social settings, such as conferences and seminars, as a means to enhance my credibility as a junior and non-indigenous researcher gaining mastery in China's emergency management.

The journals also serve another function. As chroniclers of field-level events, they regularly publicize events with ideational consequences for the field, such as specialized conferences on legislation on states of emergency. They also summarize meetings and report verbatim prominent political speeches. These records further call attention to the elements of "thought work" (*sixiang gongzuo* 思想工作), in addition to "organization work" (*zuzhi gongzuo* 组织工作) and "political and legal work" (*zhengfa gongzuo* 政法工作) in China's party-state affairs (Tsai and Kao 2013:395).

For the books and journals, I paid more attention to how their introductions were constructed, especially the arguments in those sections about how specific ideas are relevant in China's context. This is in line with the theorization and accounts focus (Orbuch 1997; Scott and Lyman 1968; Strang and Meyer 1993) which I use to understand how the governing elites framed the problems to be solved by them. I also noted the countries and models used and how the authors deliberated about applying those ideas to China. While reading these documents, I was also mindful of their invisible "hierarchy" in which their relationships demonstrate various degrees and scope of institutionalization, especially what and how ideas are elevated by authoritative texts. By "authoritative texts," I mean legal and administrative documents, such as laws, regulations, and directives, which hold the highest degree of institutionalization because they have "usually gone through protracted formal and informal processes of selection and authorization among a wide range of agents and are – if infringed – often linked to various kinds of formal as well as informal sanctions" (Lynnggaard 2007:298).

I also used snowball and purposive sampling to expand my coverage of documents, with an eye for materials that offer theoretical variation over statistical representation (Yin 2017). These additional materials are in general often or prominently cited in either the three journals (*Journal of Catastrophology*, *Journal of Natural Disasters*, and *China Emergency Management*) or the nongovernmental publications. My informants also made recommendations to me about materials that I should cover. Specific to journal articles, apart from snowball and purposive sampling, my informants also provided recommendations. I added about 140 articles to the set of academic papers for review. They came mainly from social science journals: sociology, political science, economics, management, and public administration, as well as niche periodicals in law and the practice of disaster reduction. A sampling of the publication titles include but are not limited to *China Soft Science* (*Zhongguo Ruan Kexue* 《中国软科学》), *Journal of the Chinese Academy of Governance* (*Guojia Xingzheng Xueyuan Xuebao* 《国家行政学院学报》), *Legal Forum* (*Faxue Luntan* 《法学论坛》), and *Disaster Reduction in China* (*Zhongguo Jianzai* 《中国减灾》).

Feedback from my gatekeepers and informants also prompted me to include official documents that I had inadvertently overlooked or was not even aware of, such as directives of the State Council. They considered these materials to be prominent markers of development in the field. Without such explicit guidance from them, the significance of these documents would have been opaque to me, a novice to China's emergency management.

Most of my data collection for texts and publications was performed from 2011 to 2013. I tried my best to update them for the book. Not surprising, several web links are now defunct. For those sources I cannot update with new links, I have indicated the date of retrieving the information online.

In-depth interviews

Sampling methods

I used two sampling techniques to identify and select academic experts as prospective informants. First, I used purposive sampling, relying upon publicly available name lists of expert committees, such as the expert committee to the State Commission on Disaster Reduction, which advises the State Council on natural disasters. When possible, I made my request for interviews through my gatekeepers. In addition, publications, especially journals, also provided another means to identify prominent contributors to the ideational resources of the emergency management organizational field. I emailed authors whom I identified in journals to request interviews. On several occasions, I also followed Gold's (1989) "guerilla interviewing" approach which refers to "unchaperoned, spontaneous but structured participant observation and interviews as opportunities present themselves" (p. 180). These usually took place at conferences where I "waylaid" prospective informants – whom I identified based on their expert committee membership or prominently cited papers – with requests for interviews.

Second, I used snowball sampling to ask informants at the end of our conversation for suggestions, and when possible, introduction to other experts for interviews. I attempted to capitalize on their shared membership with prospective informants in several domains: either they sat on the same expert committees, worked in the same organizations, shared research interests, or were alumni of past organizations and work units. I tried to leverage the "invisible college" to which my informants belong by familiarizing myself with their biographies before interviews (Crane 1977).

Profile of informants

Of the 30 academic experts whom I had planned to meet, I managed to interview 21, achieving an acceptance rate of 70 percent. Three declined my request to meet, citing schedule conflicts as the reason. The remaining six did not respond to the request from me or my gatekeepers. Of the 21 informants, I conducted 23 interviews; I interviewed two individuals twice. On average, each interview took about 76 minutes. Table A.2 presents the informant profiles with their pseudonyms. As Table A.2 shows, I divide my informants into three groups: public

Table A.2 Interviews and Their Details

Discipline	Pseudonym	Number of Informants	Number of Interviews
Social Sciences (e.g., sociology, economics, political science, public administration)	Guan, Quan, Tian, Xuan, Zhuang, Zu, Bai, Chi, Hua, Jia, Wen, Zhu	12	13
Engineering, Physical, and Environmental Sciences (e.g., civil and structural engineering, geology)	Ai, Da, Gui, Jun, Liang, Mu, San, Yang, Yin	9	10
Total		21	23

policy and public administration; social science; physical and environmental sciences. I conducted interviews alternating among the three groups to ensure that my emergent understandings held across different contexts, and also to seek out purposefully reorienting or disconfirming observations from other groups (Stewart 1998). Practical urgency overrode all other priorities: I met informants immediately who were available only for a very narrow window of opportunity.

Nineteen individuals gave me permission to audio record our conversation in its entirety for transcription. Two informants declined my request for audio recording. I made an effort to take more notes during these interviews, but at the same time was mindful not to allow my note-taking to impede my informants' willingness to speak freely. To be specific, when my informants demonstrated tentativeness or discomfort with information they had just offered me, I deferred my writing, holding the notes in my head (Emerson, Fretz and Shaw 1995). I scribbled the contentious portions when they moved on to other issues. For the two interviews without audio recording, I typed my notes within two hours of completing the interviews.

My informants' expertise covered public policy, social, physical, and environmental sciences. Not all respondents worked in universities; nine held senior research or administrative positions in government research bodies. Almost everyone either currently sat or used to sit on expert advisory committees attached to emergency management bodies at the central or other levels of government, giving them first-hand experience in witnessing or exerting expert intellectual influence on governmental actions in emergency management. For matters of confidentiality, I will not go into their specific affiliations. All informants experienced extensive dealings with government officials. Some were CPC members on the record. Some were also former officials or academics who held dual appointments (*guazhi* 挂职) at their academic institutions and emergency management bodies at various levels of government.

The interviews were conducted at several venues – mostly in the offices of my informants, but also public spaces such as cafés and restaurants, and quasi-public spaces. By quasi-public spaces, I refer to venues where access is rendered provisional by membership, for example lobbies of hotels where these areas were temporarily cordoned off for conference use.

During interviews, I adopted the stance of the "known" investigator in the field (Lofland and Lofland 1995). The informants were aware that I was a doctoral candidate seeking to understand their contribution to emergency management. I also deployed a "portfolio" of roles and identities that was contingent on the context of the interviews. In contrast to "selective competence," the other pre-sentational tactic I used was "acceptable incompetence," so as to draw out elabo-ration from the informants (Lofland and Lofland 1995). Using the deferential "teacher-pupil routine" (Kjellgren 2006) or what Wildavsky calls the "teach-me approach" (Wildavsky 1989:69 in O'Brien 2006:35), served me well – especially with senior academic experts. The technique typically encouraged them to be more engaging, fleshing out their arguments, such as relating real-life examples to illustrate their abstract ideas.

I treated my semi-structured interview guide as a dynamic document that would naturally undergo iterative revisions to better organize data collection and extract data (Rubin and Rubin 1995), especially when data saturation had been reached for specific topics during interviews. For example, it was established very early in my interviews that informants viewed the 2003 SARS epidemic as the key focusing event (Birkland 1998) that defined the organizational field of emer-gency management. The iterative and spontaneous revisions came about because I was also continually improving how I conducted my interviews in Mandarin, refining phrases and expressions that suited the institutional vocabulary (Suddaby and Greenwood 2005) of my informants. Several such improvements were also made on the fly when I promptly switched to their jargon in lieu of my original expressions.

I took sparse notes during our guided conversation. Besides serving as a memory device during the interview (Lofland and Lofland 1995), my notes also formed the basis for more reflective memos that captured overall impressions, key ideas, analytical and methodological points from the interview, as well as queries to follow up on in future interviews.

I was also mindful of situations in which my questions and expressions did not make sense to my interviewees. Those moments of meaning lost were data points to be mined for a better understanding of the cultural-cognitive aspects of the institutional order (Scott 2014; Suchman 1995). Typically, those reflections were captured when I reviewed my notes and wrote my memos after the inter-views. Otherwise, those insights came to me when I was vetting the interview transcripts. I either noted my reflections as footnotes in the interview transcripts or added them to the interview memos that I created immediately after the inter-views but before transcribing the recordings.

Informants also provided me with suggestions on documents that I should consider adding to my document review. The interviews further supplemented my document review with how academic experts were influencing the practice of emergency management and its related laws, regulations, and policies in China.

I noted how and the extent to which their production of knowledge was assimilated into the emergency management establishment's thinking.

As for the informants I could not reach for interviews, I relied on their publicly available interviews. This option was available for some, including those whom I had already interviewed, as they were prominent scholars and highly sought-after government advisors in this area of expertise. For purposes of confidentiality, I will not identify the specific individuals. In all, I added five interviews from reports available in the public domain to the 23 interviews I had conducted.

Participant observation

Conferences, seminars, and meetings gave me the then-most current thinking and approaches to emergency management of the establishment. Often, presentations offered glimpses into ongoing policy revisions (e.g., updating existing laws) and preoccupations (e.g., scenario planning as a new approach to emergency response planning). In Beijing, I attended and observed four conferences, four seminars, and two informal meetings with academics. I also complemented the Beijing observation sites with a panel I organized on the development of China's emergency management at a U.S.-based disaster conference. See Table A.3 for the profile of conferences, seminars, and meetings I observed during fieldwork.

I attended these events either by formally registering as a participant or being invited by the organizers. I took notes on public behavior, that is, the content and interactions during the events. Capturing participants' observations about the practices and policies that relate to emergency management in these settings provided insights beyond what were available in documents and even interviews. During observation, I took notes whenever I could. When it was impossible to do so, I took "head notes," mentally tagging significant events, gestures, and other observations (Emerson, Fretz and Shaw 1995). Following recommended ethnographic practices to mitigate memory loss (Lofland and Lofland 1995), I either typed or elaborated on my written field notes in the same day of my observations, often within the first two hours after leaving the field sites. Besides noting what transpired in the field, I also chronicled tentative themes, identified technical and literature queries, and methodological concerns that I needed to address or anticipate in subsequent fieldwork.

Learning from my ethnographic study on IT administrators (Lim 2011), I deliberately deferred my impulse to pen down immediately animated interactions on interesting topics until conference participants moved on to more mundane ones. This strategic delay between observation and note-taking reduced the likelihood of eliciting negative responses from the conference participants, particularly when they were disclosing sensitive information, such as comments on policies or political figures. I also engaged participants in casual conversations, while remaining mindful that my "interventions" might disrupt their "authentic" ongoing discussions.

Table A.3 Conferences, Seminars, and Meetings Attended

Type	Theme	Duration	Remarks
Conference	Disaster risk management	Three days	International audience; technical/engineering-focus conference; focus on risk governance.
Conference	Disaster risk management	Two days	International audience; emphasis was on the physical sciences and engineering.
Conference	Emergency management	Two days	International audience; mainly officials.
Conference	Emergency management	Half-day	Domestic audience; comprised mainly senior scholars and officials.
Seminar	Emergency management	Four hours	Organized by a research center in a university.
Seminar	Risk management	Four hours	Organized by a university environmental science department.
Conference panel	Emergency management	1.5 hours	I was co-organizer for this panel at an international conference.
Informal meeting	Emergency management	One hour	Discussion between a public policy academic and a Chinese graduate student; topic concerned career paths of officials in emergency management.
Informal meeting	Emergency management	Two hours	Discussion among four academics on collaborative research on emergency management and organizing a workshop.

Identity work

My fieldwork strategy relied upon my multiple identities: a native Singaporean of Chinese descent; a former civilian public affairs official in the Singapore defense ministry who had work exposure to crises and natural disasters; a graduate student from an American university; my affiliation with the Natural Hazards Center. These multiple identities allowed me to enter the field as an individual who lies between a "Martian" and a "Convert" (Davis 1973). I was a peripheral member in various settings (Adler and Adler 1987): someone who is an outsider but possesses some "insider cultural knowledge" (Cohen 2009). My identities and experience helped and hindered my fieldwork.

These attributes helped in the following ways. Because I look Chinese and am proficient in Mandarin and written Chinese, I was able to cultivate rapport quickly with my gatekeepers, informants, and conference participants. In addition, when my accent piqued their interest, I attributed it to my Southern Chinese ancestry (Fujian), which usually satiated their curiosity.

The above characteristics also helped me blend into Chinese society. In part because of these characteristics, unlike most Western-based researchers who had assistants in the field while in China (see for example Yeh 2006), I worked without one, regardless of whether I was at the archives, interviewing my informants, or attending an event. That said, I would not have achieved this level of access and collected the types and quality of data without my network of gatekeepers, who helped negotiate and even offered "safe passage" for my access.

My identity as a native Singaporean also generated interest and goodwill with my gatekeepers and informants, partly due to the Chinese state's fascination with my home country especially during the early days of its fervent economic reforms in the 1980s and 1990s (Lee 2001). In addition to being a city-island-state with an ethnic Chinese majority (more than 70 percent), Singapore has managed to achieve high standards of living in the span of four decades under a dominant single-party arrangement while maintaining social stability and economic growth. Needless to say, Chinese officials have flocked to Singapore for study trips and public management executive programs that the Singapore universities have created exclusively for them.

Finally, my identity as a graduate student from the Natural Hazards Center had helped open doors on some occasions when I contacted prospective informants without my gatekeepers as intermediaries. As I soon found out in China, the Natural Hazards Center was well known within the specialized circle of natural disaster research.

My identity also created ambiguity in the field that I tried to leverage to my advantage. I recount one such incident, when I was at an international conference on emergency management. I was the only international participant of Chinese descent at the meeting. During the first lunch of the conference, I followed the international contingent to be seated at a separate dining area from the domestic/Chinese participants, but I was stopped by an attendant who insisted that I should use the dining hall reserved for the latter. She was utterly confused when

I told her in Mandarin that I am ethnically Chinese but not a Chinese national. Finally she relented, leaving it to me to choose as I deemed fit. In that situation, my identity, which initially could have hindered my access, subsequently allowed me to transit between and interact freely with both mainland Chinese and international participants.

Coding and analysis

I used inductive and deductive methods simultaneously for my coding and analysis. Similar to how Hoffman and Ocasio (2001) studied the influence of media coverage on the responses from the U.S. chemical industry to environmental issues, I began my analysis using the conceptual toolkit I constructed from the literature. I also relied on my data to form my working hypotheses and theoretical model.[3] This is especially clear when I used governmentality as an approach to understanding emergency management as an organizational field and a way of organizing the practice of emergency management. Governmentality guided me *where* and *what* to look for (e.g., practices, rules, regulations, methods) but it could not tell me *how* manifestations of the governmentalization in China's emergency management context were going to look precisely. The design and definition of its arrangements had to emerge from data.

I first captured my initial impressions of the materials, as one can get quickly de-sensitized to the data (Emerson, Fretz and Shaw 1995). I was also aware that my multiple identities influenced how I would read, code, and analyze the materials. By "materials," I refer to the three bodies of text that I had collected and generated during fieldwork: documents, notes based on participation observation and reflection, and the interview transcripts and notes. At the beginning, I analyzed these three bodies of text separately, while noting their tentative points of consensus and contradictions.

For journals, in order to negotiate the sheer volume of texts, I established a routine to identify articles that had direct relevance to national emergency management and risk governance. I did this by reviewing article titles and abstracts (if available) for topics that highlighted the following: different phases of emergency management (such as preparedness and response) and risk management (e.g., identification and assessment); and discussions on governance with respect to emergency and risk management. In addition, because of my emphasis on how ideas from afar could have prompted rethinking by the Chinese, I identified non-Chinese case studies for further reading and coding. Based on the routine described above, I removed articles that focused on single extreme events at lower levels of administration (e.g., cities or counties) and analyses on imperial and republican China (i.e., prior to the year 1949). Based on my exploratory study conducted in Beijing during the summer of 2011, I was aware that I had to take special notice of extreme events generally accepted as focusing events by the Chinese, such as the 1976 Tangshan earthquake, 1998 Yangtze River flood, 2003 SARS outbreak, and 2008 Wenchuan earthquake.

I read documents, especially those from the government (e.g., notices and directives) and books (particularly historical background sections) with an eye to reconstructing the genesis and trajectory of development of the emergency management field. Given my emphasis on recounting the field's development, I heavily adapted the analysis strategy from my work on the social construction of risks in complex IT projects (Lim, Sia and Yeow 2011). I used a process approach to analyze how the field was socially constructed. I paid attention to "the sequences of interactions and activities that unfold over the duration of the entity being studied in context" (Van de Ven 2007:197). I also followed Langley's (1999) advice of using a narrative strategy for my analysis. Narrative strategy essentially involves the construction of a detailed story from the data. Accordingly, I crafted an in-depth and chronological narrative of the entire field formation. It became the base document to summarize the vast amount of information from my archival and interview data.

It was through this process-oriented analysis that I realized my efforts needed to be focused on the first five years of field formation. I observed that by 2009 the main organizational bodies for knowledge dissemination and the prominent ideas around what constituted emergency and risk management were enshrined in law. In order to see such developments more clearly, I created visuals to help me organize the narrative, such as Figure 3.1 in Chapter 3.

I bracketed "codable moments" (Boyatzis 1998) when reading the materials. The moments refer to fragments of text in my field notes, documents, and interview transcripts that related to efforts to endow the field with legitimacy. For example, I would take note of materials that could become the ingredients for "proto-institutions," which are "candidates for institutionalization, if only enough members of the field adopt them" (Zietsma and McKnight 2009). These can be references to new practices, rules, and technologies (Lawrence, Hardy and Phillips 2002). These "codable quotes" provided the foundation for subsequent first and second cycle coding (Saldaña 2009). For example, this process helped me identify the term of art *yi'an san zhi* as a potential proto-institution when I noticed its first appearance in 2004. It was quickly established as the shorthand for the strategy used to develop the field. Soon the term was also appearing in national research databases as a topic of investigation in emergency management, especially by public administration researchers.

During first cycle coding, I used a mix of simultaneous coding (also known as double coding), descriptive coding, *in vivo* coding, process coding ("-ing" coding), and initial coding (also known as open coding) to identify carefully those highlighted instances (Saldaña 2009). I conducted line by line coding in this stage. *In vivo* coding evolved to be instrumental in my coding toolkit, given that Chinese government writing repeats phrases in their entirety or with minimal variety in expressing officially sanctioned ideas. This allowed me to observe the "travel" of prominent ideas condensed into stock phrases across documents. The trajectory of *yi'an san zhi* from government announcements to its appearance in titles of research projects approved by national research organizations, and subsequently in academic journals and textbooks, is one such example.

Based on the first cycle coding, second cycle coding solidified the groundwork necessary for conceptual scaffolding (Ritchie, Spencer and O'Connor 2003), especially to reconstruct the claims that legitimized the field and the risk governance framework. The notion of accounts played an important guide at this stage of my coding and analysis. Legitimizing claims as accounts are tied to institutions because they are "standardized within cultures so that certain accounts are terminologically stabilized and routinely expected when activity falls outside the domain of expectations" (Scott and Lyman 1968:46). Such accounts justify and problematize, especially in the evaluative sense, why something is wrong and what should be done, and they also offer excuses for mistakes. Therefore, by paying attention to "socially approved" or institutional vocabularies (Lyman and Scott 1970; Scott and Lyman 1968; Suddaby and Greenwood 2005), I could identify and reconstruct those claims, especially the theorization involved (Strang and Meyer 1993) and their connections to legitimacy (Suchman 1995). For example, a government advisor attributed what he perceived as the successful emergency response to 2012 Superstorm Sandy in the U.S. to meticulous scenario planning initiated in the wake of Hurricane Katrina (theorization of cause and effect) and was arguing at multiple forums why the methodology was scientific (moral legitimacy) and China should adopt it. The above example also shows how such accounting becomes especially important in the temporal sequencing of events and attributional statements, and is mobilized to impose order (Orbuch 1997). This chain of influence became clearer as I observed how at one forum, government officials approached the scenario advocate during conference breaks to organize scenario planning sessions at their departments.

In actual practice, the distinction between first and second cycles of coding was never strict and always subject to reiteration. I moved between both stages to refine the codes so that while they remained close to the data, at the same time, they also became more precise and abstract in terms of what I wanted to label, and how I intended to organize the codes. Both cycles revealed the requisite first-order concepts that subsequently crystallized into second-order concepts that provided more "travel" across specific settings and forms of data (Stewart 1998; Van Maanen 1979). Following Warren and Karner (2010), while I describe the analytical process as an exercise that seemed sanitized and removed from my close interaction with my materials, my analysis was constantly informed by my deeper appreciation of the social and cultural context in which they operate. For example, I returned to my materials, especially the academic journals, to start coding for disaster and emergency categories and the ways in which the categories were graded in terms of severity when I realized from my interviews that it was a negotiated process largely based on administrative and political considerations.[4] I was also looking for clues on how academics could have influenced those deliberations.

With respect to the concept of legitimacy, I was further guided by arguments that moderated the cultural-cognitive claims of institutional theory. As pointed out by Lizardo (2010), a strong cultural-cognitive argument is empirically unsustainable and substantively vacuous. This is because if something is truly taken-for-granted, it would be inconceivable that the researcher could reveal that it is in fact institutionalized in the cultural-cognitive manner. The solution, Lizardo suggests, is to loosen the inconceivability criterion to a "meaningless" or "senseless" one. This weaker criterion is empirically more plausible and analytically separable because the researcher can observe how alternative arrangements are rejected. These arrangements are rejected not because they are not sanctioned in the legal/formal sense (regulative element), or because they are immoral (normative element), but because they do not make any sense (weaker cognitive-cultural element). I found Lizardo's suggestion especially useful during my coding and analysis to identify cultural-cognitive elements in my data. Such evidence is typically presented as moments when something seemed to make little sense or when substantial measures had to be used to claim that something, especially foreign ideas or new techniques, in fact made *complete sense* to be included or excluded from emergency management. For example, in Chapter 5, I highlight how emergency response plans are rendered intelligible when they are explained through classic Chinese proverbs, cognitive heuristics with which educated Chinese – especially governing elites – are more than familiar in their cultural milieu.

Methodological limitations

Public versus hidden transcripts

Being mainly open source and published documents, the data I collected largely fall into what James Scott (1990a) considers as "public transcripts," in which they represent open interactions among members of the organizational field, especially academic experts and the rest of the emergency management establishment. While my interviews and conference observations offered some insights into the "hidden transcripts" of organizational life, I recognize the accounts that I provided are at best partial.

As pointed out by policy researcher Zhuang, the actual policymaking processes at the highest level in the Chinese party-state are enclosed in a black box and remain obstinately opaque even to academic experts who appear close, even core, to the regime.[5] That being said, by speaking with academic experts who enjoy access to tightly controlled internal official documents and senior government officials, I hope my findings offer some glimpse into the black box of policymaking and field building. Future research should consider innovative means to reach out to government officials, perhaps retired ones or those who have left government, to extract the hidden transcripts more deeply and completely. Vis-à-vis my study, studies of that nature can be a great opportunity for comparative analyses. Unfortunately, access to internal official documents will remain a challenge, especially for researchers who do not have ties to or the trust of gatekeepers. Future research should also consider expanding the coverage of journals to systematically examine other prominent publications, such as *Zhongguo Jianzai* (《中国减灾》 *Disaster Reduction in China*).

Limits of interviews

Most of my interviews were intensively conducted over a relatively short period in 2012, during which field formation had already entered a stabilized phase. Relying on informants to recount how the organizational field of emergency management was built over the past ten years, it is inevitable that their retrospective accounts were vulnerable to memory slips and other social psychological biases, such as retrospective interpretation. I attempted to mitigate this limitation with active triangulation of interviews with documents and observations. Future studies that track the continual formation of the emergency management field should consider other interview methods, such as extended interviews of informants at regular intervals so as to "capture reality in flight" (Pettigrew 1997:347). In addition, timely interviews with informants immediately after focusing or field events might further capture the initial sentiments and accounts of field formation activities.

Notes

1 The CAG (*Guojia Xingzheng Xueyuan* 国家行政学院) was modeled after the French *Ècole Nationale d'Administration*. Its original English name reflects the legacy: China National School of Administration. Although the CAG is a government body that was established in 1994, the idea for its establishment was suggested as far back as 1988. Interestingly, while CAG's English title has ditched "administration" for "governance" since 2010, its Chinese name retains its French legacy.
2 Five-year plans are a prominent feature of centralized planning, especially in communist states. In my case, they specifically covered the 10th, 11th, and 12th five-year planning periods in China: 2001–2005, 2006–2010, and 2011–2015 respectively.
3 By working hypotheses, I simply mean data verification, and not a purely positivist approach toward research.
4 Specifically, interviews with Yang and Gui prompted that consideration.
5 Interview with Zhuang.

References

Adler, Patricia A. and Peter Adler. 1987. *Membership Roles in Field Research*, Vol. 6. Newbury Park, CA: Sage Publications.
Birkland, Thomas A. 1997. *After Disaster: Agenda Setting, Public Policy, and Focusing Events*. Washington, DC: Georgetown University Press.
Birkland, Thomas A. 1998. "Focusing Events, Mobilization, and Agenda Setting." *Journal of Public Policy* 18(1):53–74.
Boyatzis, Richard E. 1998. *Transforming Qualitative Information: Thematic Analysis and Code Development*. Thousand Oaks, CA: Sage Publications.
Cohen, Paul A. 2009. *Speaking to History: The Story of King Goujian in Twentieth-Century China*. Berkeley, CA: University of California Press.
Crane, Diana. 1977. "Social Structure in a Group of Scientists: A Test of the 'Invisible College' Hypothesis." Pp. 161–78 in *Social Networks: A Developing Paradigm*, edited by Samuel Leinhardt. New York: Academic Press.
Davis, Fred. 1973. "The Martian and the Convert: Ontological Polarities in Social Research." *Urban Life* 2:333–43.

Denzin, Norman K. and Yvonna S. Lincoln. 2008. "The Discipline and Practice of Qualitative Research." Pp. 1–43 in *The Landscape of Qualitative Research*, edited by N. K. Denzin and Y. S. Lincoln. Thousand Oaks, CA: Sage Publications.

Emerson, Robert M., Rachel I. Fretz and Linda L. Shaw. 1995. *Writing Ethnographic Fieldnotes*. Chicago, IL: University of Chicago Press.

Gold, Thomas B. 1989. "Guerilla Interviewing among the Getihu." Pp. 175–92 in *Unofficial China: Popular Culture and Thought in the People's Republic*, edited by P. Link, R. Madsen and P. G. Pickowicz. Boulder, CO: Westview Press.

Gold-Biddle, Karen and Karen Locke. 1993. "Appealing Work: An Investigation of How Ethnographic Text Convince." *Organization Science* 4(4):595–616.

Heimer, Maria and Stig Thøgersen, eds. 2006. *Doing Fieldwork in China*. Honolulu, HI: University of Hawai'i Press.

Hoffman, Andrew J. and William Ocasio. 2001. "Not All Events Are Attended Equally: Toward a Middle-Range Theory of Industry Attention to External Events." *Organization Science* 12(4):414–34.

Kitsuse, John I. and Aaron V. Cicourel. 1963. "A Note on the Uses of Official Statistics." *Social Problems* 11(2):131–9.

Kjellgren, Björn. 2006. "The Significance of Benevolence and Wisdom: Reflections on Field Positionality." Pp. 225–46 in *Doing Fieldwork in China*, edited by M. Heimer and S. Thøgersen. Honolulu, HI: University of Hawai'i Press.

Langley, Ann. 1999. "Strategies for Theorizing from Process Data." *Academy of Management Review* 24(4):691–710.

Lawrence, Thomas B., Cynthia Hardy and Nelson Phillips. 2002. "Institutional Effects of Interorganizational Collaboration: The Emergence of Proto-Institutions." *Academy of Management Journal* 45(1):281–90.

Lee, Lai To. 2001. "The Lion and the Dragon: A View on Singapore–China Relations." *Journal of Contemporary China* 10(28):415–25.

Lim, Wee-Kiat. 2011. "Freezing and Restocking Knowledge Through 'Booted-Up' Bodies: Knowledge Management in an IT Vendor." Paper presented at the 71st Annual Meeting of the Academy of Management, San Antonio, Texas, US.

Lim, Wee-Kiat, Siew Kien Sia and Adrian Yeow. 2011. "Managing Risk in a Failing IT Project: A Social Constructionist View." *Journal of the Association for Information Systems* 12(6):414–40.

Lizardo, Omar. 2010. "The Problem of the Cultural Determination of Cognition in Institutional Theory." *Culture* 24(2):1, 7, 9, 11.

Lofland, John and Lyn H. Lofland. 1995. *Analyzing Social Settings: A Guide to Qualitative Observation and Analysis*. Bermont, CA: Wadsworth Publishing Company.

Lyman, Stanford M. and Marvin B. Scott. 1970. *A Sociology of the Absurd*. New York, NY: Appleton-Century Crofts.

Lynnggaard, Kennet. 2007. "The Institutional Construction of a Policy Field: A Discursive Institutional Perspective on Change Within the Common Agricultural Policy." *Journal of the European Public Policy* 14(2):293–312.

O'Brien, Kevin J. 2006. "Discovery, Research (Re)Design, and Theory Building." Pp. 27–41 in *Doing Fieldwork in China*, edited by M. Heimer and S. Thøgersen. Honolulu, HI: University of Hawai'i Press.

Orbuch, Terri L. 1997. "People's Accounts Count: The Sociology of Accounts." *Annual Review of Sociology* 23:455–78.

Pettigrew, Andrew W. 1997. "What Is Processual Analysis?" *Scandinavian Journal of Management* 13(4):337–48.

Phillips, Brenda. 2002. "Qualitative Methods and Disaster Research." Pp. 194–211 in *Methods of Disaster Research*, edited by R. A. Stallings. Philadelphia, PA: Xlibris Corporation.

Purdy, Jill M. and Barbara Gray. 2009. "Conflicting Logics, Mechanisms of Diffusion, and Multilevel Dynamics in Emerging Institutional Fields." *Academy of Management Journal* 52(2):355–80.

Ritchie, Jane, Liz Spencer and William O'Connor. 2003. "Carrying Out Qualitative Analysis." Pp. 219–62 in *Qualitative Research Practice: A Guide for Social Science Students and Researchers*, edited by J. Ritchie and J. Lewis. Thousand Oaks, CA: Sage Publications.

Rubin, Herbert J. and Irene S. Rubin. 1995. "Keeping on Target While Hanging Loose: Design Qualitative Interviews." Pp. 42–64 in *Qualitative Interviewing: The Art of Hearing Data*, edited by H. J. Rubin and I. S. Rubin. Thousand Oaks, CA: Sage Publications.

Saldaña, Johnny. 2009. *The Coding Manual for Qualitative Researchers*. Thousand Oaks, CA: Sage Publications.

Schneiberg, Marc and Elisabeth S. Clemens. 2006. "The Typical Tools for the Job: Research Strategies in Institutional Analysis." *Sociological Theory* 24(3):195–227.

Schneider, Joseph W. and John I. Kitsuse, eds. 1984. *Studies in the Sociology of Social Problems*. Norwood, NJ: Ablex Publishing Corporation.

Scott, James C. 1990a. *Domination and the Art of Resistance: Hidden Transcripts*. New Haven, CT: Yale University Press.

Scott, John. 1990b. *A Matter of Record: Documentary Sources in Social Research*. Cambridge, UK: Polity Press.

Scott, Marvin B. and Stanford M. Lyman. 1968. "Accounts." *American Sociological Review* 33(1):46–62.

Scott, W. Richard. 2014. *Institutions and Organizations: Ideas, Interests, and Identities*. Los Angeles, CA: Sage Publications.

Selznick, Philip. 1996. "Institutionalism: 'Old' and 'New'." *Administrative Science Quarterly* 41(2):270–7.

Shan, Chun Chang, Lan Xue, Xiu Lan Zhang and Hui Ding, eds. 2012. *Zhongguo Yingji Guanli Dashi Ji (2003–2007) (Memorabilia of China's Emergency Management)*. Beijing, China: Shehui Wenxian Kexue Chuban She.

Small, Mario Luis. 2011. "How to Conduct a Mixed Methods Study: Recent Trends in a Rapidly Growing Literature." *Annual Review of Sociology* 37:57–86.

Stewart, Alex. 1998. *The Ethnographer's Method*. Thousand Oaks, CA: Sage Publications.

Strang, David and John W. Meyer. 1993. "Institutional Conditions for Diffusion." *Theory and Society* 22(4):487–511.

Suchman, Mark. 1995. "Managing Legitimacy: Strategic and Institutional Approaches." *Academy of Management Review* 20(3):571–610.

Suddaby, Roy and Royston Greenwood. 2005. "Rhetorical Strategies of Legitimacy." *Administrative Science Quarterly* 50:35–67.

Tsai, Wen-Hsuan and Peng-Hsiang Kao. 2013. "Secret Codes of Political Propaganda: The Unknown System of Writing Teams." *The China Quarterly* 214:394–410. http://dx.doi.org/10.1017/S0305741013000362.

Van de Ven, Andrew H. 2007. *Engaged Scholarship: A Guide for Organizational and Social Research*. Edited by A. H. Van de Ven. New York, NY: Oxford University Press.

Van Maanen, John. 1979. "The Fact of Fiction in Organizational Ethnography." *Administrative Science Quarterly* 24(4):539–50.

Warren, Carol A. B. and Tracy Xavia Karner. 2010. *Discovering Qualitative Methods: Field Research, Interviews, and Analysis.* New York, NY: Oxford University Press.

Webb, Eugene J., Donald T. Campbell, Richard D. Schwartz, Lee Sechrest and Janet Belew Grove. 1981. *Nonreactive Measures in the Social Sciences.* Boston, MA: Houghton Mifflin Company.

Wildavsky, Aaron. 1989. *Craftways: On the Organization of Scholarly Work.* New Brunswick, NJ: Transaction Publishers.

Yeh, Emily T. 2006. "'An Open Lhasa Welcomes You': Disciplining the Researcher in Tibet." Pp. 96–109 in *Doing Fieldwork in China,* edited by M. Heimer and S. Thøgersen. Honolulu, HI: University of Hawai'i Press.

Yin, Robert K. 2017. *Case Study Research and Applications: Design and Methods.* Thousand Oaks, CA: Sage Publications.

Zietsma, Charlene and Brent McKnight. 2009. "Building the Iron Cage: Institutional Creation Work in the Context of Competing Proto-Institutions." Pp. 143–75 in *Institutional Work: Actors and Agency in Institutional Studies of Organizations,* edited by T. B. Lawrence, R. Suddaby and B. Leca. New York, NY: Cambridge University Press.

Index

Note: Page numbers in *italics* indicate a figure and page numbers in **bold** indicate a table on the corresponding page.

sampling methods 143
SARS crisis (2003): administrative
    regulation and 95; banner terms
    and 81; as catalyst for emergency
    management 26–28; legitimacy
    and 35; "one 'case' three mechanisms"
    framework and 28–30; risk society and
    60; as teachable moment 132–133
scientific view/scientific view of
    development 80–82, 85, 87
September 11 attacks 25, 59
Shan, Chun Chang 112, 125
Sichuan 2008 earthquake 1–2
social constructionism 7
social fitness 11
sociological institutional theory 7–12
Stallings, Robert 17
State Master Plan on Emergency
    Response 30, 96–98, **113–114**
state of emergency 29
stock phrases 84–86

technique 13, 94–103
theorizing/theorization 14, 122, 128,
    142, 151
Three Mile Island nuclear plant accident
    16–17
Tianjin Port explosion (2015) 128

TIEMS *see* International Emergency
    Management Society (TIEMS)
trade journals **141**, 141–143
transcripts 152–153
"travel of ideas" 10

unworkable 73n28, 86

Wang, Zheng 1–2
Wenchuan earthquake 41, 108
Wen Jiabao 26, 28, 40, 46, 53
winter storms (2008) 40–41
Wu Bang-guo 56n15

Xi Jinping 46, 82
Xue, Lan 111, 125

Yangtze River flood (1998) 53, 56n20
yi'an san zhi 29, 37n20, 150; *see also* "one
    'case' three mechanisms" framework
yi fang you nan, ba fang zhi yuan 83,
    91n23
yinhuan 96
Yushu earthquake 44
Yu the Great 75–76

Zhang Wenkang 26–27
Zhouqu mudslide 44, 108